BEHIND THE

GREEN DOOR

BRENDON OWEN

PHOTOGRAPHY BY NIGEL ANDREWS

Published by First Stone
An imprint of Corpus Publishing Limited
PO Box 8, Lydney,
Gloucestershire, GL15 6YD

ISBN 1 904439 23 3

Printed by Bell & Bain Ltd., Glasgow
Manufactured in Great Britain

10 9 8 7 6 5 4 3 2 1

CONTENTS

For my sons, James and Tim

The author would like to thank all those involved with *Ciderspace*, which is always a font of knowledge and information. Thanks to Lin for being a good companion on many a long away trip, and to my publisher, John Sellers, for keeping me on the straight and narrow.
Thanks also to all those who work so hard for Yeovil Town Football Club, especially to John Fry, Gary Johnson and Steve Thompson for allowing me the run of Huish Park.

About the author

Brendon Owen, a legal adviser, was born in Somerset in 1950 and later moved to the south-east with his family. After a mis-spent youth watching Southend United, he returned to the county in 1976 and has supported Yeovil ever since. He now lives in the nearby village of Montacute with his wife, Lin. Brendon describes himself as an ordinary football fan, but the extraordinary success of his first book about the game, *Yeovil 'Til I Die!,* has elevated him to cult status among many grass roots supporters.

INTRODUCTION

W hy do we do it? Why are we so preoccupied with 22 men and a ball? We spend a fortune chasing after them all over the country in uncomfortable coaches, or squeezed in the back of a friend's car. And for what? Three points if you're lucky. Our weekends are spoken for, disrupted and sometimes ruined. We can't go and do anything else because there is football on Saturday afternoon. We have to turn down invitations to visit friends and relatives in far-off places. "Sorry, we're at home to so-and-so that day. Perhaps we'll come and see you in June." The whole calendar has to be mapped out according to the fixture list, careful that nothing is pencilled in for a Tuesday night, because we might just be away to City, Town or United. Families and friends are neglected, or worse, ignored and abused, should the wrong thing be said at the wrong time.

Our work suffers following a poor defeat… well, any defeat to be honest. Who, on a Monday morning, can concentrate on mundane things like earning a living when on Saturday points were frittered away and we've slipped down the table? Perhaps by Friday we may be back to some sort of efficiency.

We can be up there on cloud nine and down in the pits of despair all in the space of 90 minutes. Our emotions are in a constant state of turmoil, ranging from joy to manic depression.

But we are a breed apart from other mere mortals. We know the secret of true happiness. That energy rush as the ball hits the net is something a millionaire could not buy. You may have a villa and a yacht, but if you cannot understand the joy of being part of the beautiful game, you have nothing. Football fans know the meaning of life.

There is something fresh and magical about the start of every season, with all of the hurt and pain of previous years washed away. We are like a child with a new toy. All the teams start as equals, but our team is naturally far more equal than all of the others. With no points on the board, that is a fair belief to hold. Time, of course, alters that perspective, but despite reality hitting us between the eyes, often at a very early stage, we cling to our belief. We are eternal optimists.

At Yeovil Town, of course, things are very different. No pain or hurt for us. We had the season to beat all seasons in 2002/3, as we waltzed our way through the Conference to become champions.

Now, here we are at the start of another season – not just any old season, of course, but our first in the Football League. What aspirations can we possibly hold for the coming campaign? The bookies and pundits have piled on the pressure by saying that we will stroll straight through Division Three. Others are not so sure. The more level-headed amongst us say that they will be content with a top-half finish. Relegation is not a word that is being banded around. In truth, I think that most of us are just so, so pleased to be here that we will take it as it comes and enjoy every minute of it.

So come with me, fasten that safety belt, put on your hard hat and let's run and jump, dive and fall, scream and shout, curse and swear our way through this historic event in the life of Yeovil Town Football Club and the fantastic fans who follow them. On to victory!

CHAPTER 1

THROUGH THE HOOPS

Just because Yeovil Town won the Conference in April 2003 doesn't mean that, as a fan, I can relax and take things easy. No slacking for me. Preparations have to be made for the historic venture into the Football League. It's rather like a schoolboy leaving the safety and comfort of a junior school, feeling like a big fish in a small pond, and swapping it for the unknown: the big boys' league. How will we be treated by the old hands, the Hulls and Huddersfields, the Swanseas and, of course, the Gasheads of Bristol? No longer will we have the largest home crowds, or take the biggest away support. We are used to being in the majority on many occasions at Conference grounds, but all that is swept away at a stroke. We need to be respectful of our elders (although not necessarily our betters). Time will tell on that one.

And just like the child moving up to the big school, the uniform has to be bought. It was some way into the summer holidays that the decision was made by the club, with full supporter participation, that the team would enter the new era clad in hoops! "Never heard of such a thing!" cried many on the fans' forum. "That's not our club's kit. We've never done hoops before." Fears that we would be mistaken for Glasgow Celtic fans and duly assaulted on the London Underground by rabid Rangers' supporters were keeping more than a few Yeovil lads awake at night. The proposed boycott of the new strip failed to materialise, and green-and-white hoops began to sprout like grass in the rain. My only dilemma was whether I should buy large or extra large. Last season I sported large, and, to be totally honest, I could have done with a little more room in places. So extra large it is. Now I've swung the other way, but, as my mum said about that first school blazer, I'll grow into it. At 53 that may seem unlikely, but if I continue to follow the John Smith Extra Smooth diet, I may just do it. My wife, Lin, however, has made a stand. "I don't like the hoops and I shall wear my last year's shirt." That's okay. Be in the minority.

A very fine Glovers beach towel was purchased in anticipation of spreading the word in a missionary style (if not position) to unbelievers in foreign climes, but tragedy struck even before the wretched thing was hung over a hotel balcony. One of the two cats that live next door, but spend most of their free time with us, found the towel, still in pristine condition, laid out on our bed and chose to exercise its talons by unpicking the threads of the club logo. I now have the only Yeovil towel with the words 'Eve by Ity' as its motto (Achieve by Unity, it used to be). Lin did a pretty good job of sewing back all the other raggedy bits, but that cat has a lot to answer for.

Another part of the major preparation for the new life is the shelling out of hard-earned cash to buy our season tickets. We've decided to stay with the lucky seats from last year, so block K in the Bartlett Stand will have our company for the coming year. At great expense (some £30,000-£40,000, I believe) we are going to have an automated ticketing system. One swipe from the plastic season ticket and, whoosh, we should be in the ground. I come out in a sweat when I think what might happen if the system fails just as I'm swiping. I could be stuck in an electronic turnstile with no way of getting in or out. I could be stuck there until half-time. Kevin Gall could have a hat-trick by then! Another problem is the mug-shot on the ticket. 'Not transferable' it says in the rules, so the turnstile operators will be looking out for impostors. But with all of us having suffered somewhat in the production process, and our pictures becoming elongated to such an extent that we look like the pointy head people from Planet Zog, are they going to allow any of us in?

I couldn't go on the pre-season tour to Belgium and Germany. Lin and I were soaking up the sun on the Adriatic coast in Croatia. Now there's a peculiar looking football shirt if ever I saw one. Red and white, and half-covered in checks. You could play chess on that one. Hoops? We've never had it so good. Maybe it's just as well I didn't go on the European jolly. Having heard the tales of one lad, who was arrested by two Belgian policewomen and frog-marched to a cash machine, I don't think I would have lasted the course. The football seems to have been a success, though. Higher league opposition tested the lads, who had volunteered to come back early from their summer break to start training. That is the sort of thing that fans like to hear: commitment and dedication. Well, all except one, who seems to have had a little disagreement when substituted early on in a game.

Unfortunately, upon his return, with masses of encouragement from his agent, he said all the wrong things about his relationship with the club and his perception of his own talents. The 'Scottish One' seems to have put his foot well and truly in it. At the very least he seems to have been badly advised, and will now have to seek pastures new. Michael McIndoe was an important part of our championship-winning team last season, and for that I thank him. He is not, however, the sun around which the other players orbit, and Yeovil's solar system will function very well without him.

The pre-season continues with a friendly against Chard, a good win against Brentford and a magnificent draw with Preston North End. I must confess to having had a sharp intake of breath when we played at Dorchester. Adam Stansfield, like a young foal on wobbly legs, was clattered at his least favourite venue and went down. The silence was eerie, everyone remembering that accident in which he broke his leg almost 12 months previously. This time he got to his feet and we later learned that, although it was again his right leg that was clobbered, only a twist occurred. I suggest that if we draw Dorchester away in the F.A. Cup that we leave Adam off the team-sheet.

Until the Wolves game at home, Gary has used some 22 trialists. Fascinating for those of us watching, but it must have been a nightmare for anyone trying to put a report together for *Ciderspace*. I saw Blue Stew sucking hard on his pencil as he tried to fathom out who was who. Out of those who have donned the new strip we have signed two – Jamie Gosling from Bath City, and Hugo Rodrigues from Portugal. I thought Jimmy Aggrey was a big lad, but I reckon Hugo is taller still. Some dispute as to whether he is 6ft 8in or 6ft 10in. I know he nearly hit his head on the door lintel when leaving Dorchester's social club. I'm going to have to watch Lin with this one. She likes them big and strong. That's why she married me, but I think I must have shrunk in the wash!

Tonight it is Wolverhampton Wanderers. Dennis Irwin and Paul Ince at Huish Park. Dave Jones, Wolves' manager, hoped to be able to parade his latest signing, Italian international Barros, but the timing wasn't quite right. For a July day the weather has been bad. Hope it clears before this evening.

Rain, what rain? Once again the sun was shining in our sky. 2-1 to the mighty Yeo, with 'Silver Boots Gally' firing in the winner. Great fun to hear the Premiership's new boys being mocked by the Westland End with "Are you good enough for the Conference?" The level of play at times was breathtaking. More of the same against Brighton brings another 2-1 victory. Bring on the Rochdale. Give me league football, now!

A final note on the 'Scottish Player'. Gary has shipped him out to Doncaster (First Division?) Rovers for a fee rumoured to be £50,000. What a very foolish lad he has been.

Tiverton 0 Yeovil 2 on Monday night, and we are now into the final few days of our lives without League football. The first fans have left for the long haul to Rochdale – by bike. They are doing it for charity, and I should think, by the time they ease their butts off the saddles on Saturday, they will deserve all the support they can get.

Saturday 9 August 2003 has arrived. The meticulous planning has been completed, everything is ready and the years of waiting are almost over. A couple of thousand Glovers' fans are rising early, pulling on their new hooped shirts and climbing into their chosen form of transport for the journey north to the match at Spotland. I, too, have risen early, offered up my prayers for the lads, had my first coffee of the day from the Glovers mug and also pulled on my shirt. The only difference between me and the other Yeovil fans is that I am adding cuff links and a tie to mine. Lin and I are off to the match at Sherborne Castle today – the wedding of our eldest son, James, to his beloved Cathy is at noon on the very day that Yeovil Town take their first historic step in the Football League. It was through what you might call an error in the early planning that such a momentous day was chosen. James, an Arsenal fan, was working from the Premiership fixtures calendar, which, as we all know, starts a week later than the League. He hadn't realised this, and I didn't twig it until it was too late.

As the wedding car purred through the south Somerset countryside, carrying Lin, James, Tim (the best man) and myself, my mobile phone rang. Elinor Oldroyd and Filo Holland from BBC Radio 5 Live were on the line and wanted a short chat to the fan who was left behind. So that's how James and Cathy's wedding became known to listeners from Land's End to John O'Groats. Not a bad start.

The ceremony went off without a hitch, the champagne and photographs down by the lake were very pleasant and then it was off to the reception at a hotel in the town. An hour-and-a-half to kick-off. I had planned to take a small radio and ear piece with me, but, in the excitement of the day, I had forgotten to slip it into my pocket. Still, I had a back-up. A friend, Cath, will be texting me from Spotland with the scores.

The heat of the day is fantastic now. The waistcoats and ties are discarded, and plenty of liquid is being consumed. I hope Gary's boy have been taking plenty of water on board. They could lose pounds this afternoon. Smashing meal, funny speeches and the bride is looking beautiful, but I can't help the odd thought straying north.

Three o'clock. is upon us. I wait anxiously for the first news of a Glovers goal. Half-an-hour goes by, I hear nothing and I am thinking nil-nil. Another guest sidles up to me and says, "One-nil to the boys." While I am thrilled, I wonder why I didn't know that already. I find to my horror that the reception for my mobile is particularly poor in Sherborne. Nothing is coming through. I've lost contact; I'm like an astronaut who is separated from NASA. I rush out through the French doors on to the large lawns, pressing buttons like a demented lunatic when, all of a sudden, there is the message "It's one nil to Yeovil. Bring it on!" Yes, I'm back. Another message arrives. "One-all, I'm afraid." No cartwheels on the grass at this stage, then.

By the time that "Three-one now" flashes up on my little screen I think just about every guest at the wedding is willing the Glovers on to victory. All, that is, except the guest who was born in Rochdale and came to tell me about her father, who had been a season-ticket holder since the year dot. I took great delight in ribbing her for the rest of the evening. I weave my way to the gents (all that liquid refreshment taking its toll), and, as there is no one else in there, I let rip with a "Hey Gary Johnson, ooh Aah." That feels good. I phone Gary Johnson on his mobile to congratulate the lads. He laughs when he hears it's me, as he knows about the wedding situation. I think he must have been in the dressing room or on the team coach, as there was lots of happy background noise. He told me that Gally had bagged two, and Lee Johnson the other. "Great game, and the boys all played well." What more did I need to know? Thanks, Gary.

The national newspapers the next day go wild for the Town. The new kids on the block have certainly captured the headlines this time. The facts are that more than 2,000 fans in a 4,164 crowd went wild with delight when Kevin Gall hit Yeovil's first-ever League goal; and what a peach it was. Then Lee Johnson, with a free kick not dissimilar to the one he produced at Doncaster last season, tore the hearts out of Rochdale. After that the scorching sun made it a misery for the Dale players while the Yeovil lads romped through the second half and Gally got the third. Oh, and Rochdale somehow managed to get a goal somewhere along the line, too.

Lin and I decide to take a few days' break after the excitement of the wedding. Lin wants to go to Bude in Cornwall for a bit of body-boarding in the Atlantic breakers. I, on the other hand, would quite like to visit the wonderful county of Bedfordshire, taking in, perhaps, that historic town of Luton. What's that? Yeovil are going to be up there playing in the Carling Cup on Tuesday evening? Wow, that's a coincidence. We break the deadlock between us by Lin deciding that if the surf is up we will go to Bude; if not, we take the trip east. I love the detail that Ceefax gives, don't you? North Cornwall: sea flat to one foot. I'll pack my hoops, then.

We leave Monday morning and take in a bit of culture on the way, stopping for the night in Woodstock in Oxfordshire (not a hippie nor a band in sight). We take the guided tour of Blenheim Palace, and admire the amazing architecture, before moving on to Kenilworth Road, home of the Hatters. Who can answer this riddle? What's the difference between Blenheim Palace and Luton's ground? Answer: one is an ancient pile in a good state of repair, and the other isn't. Sandwiched between rows of back-to-back terraced housing, this poor old ground has been dragged, kicking and screaming, into the 21st century. Seats have been shoe-horned into every possible nook and cranny. We are required to occupy a section behind one of the goals where, during construction, the phrase 'leg room' played no part. Knees are up around chins as about 800 Yeovil fans gaze across to the far stand, which bears a large advert for a low-cost airline. We could be forgiven for thinking that our stand was situated a couple of miles away at Luton Airport and we were just about to take off for Majorca.

Luton are fast, fit and skilful. So are the Glovers, but just a little slack marking in the box allows the Hatters to go in at half-time with a 1-0 lead. From the start of the second half Yeovil run riot and put Luton under a lot of pressure. So much so, that it results in an own goal which, once we have untangled our legs, is celebrated in good style by the sweat-drenched travelling fans. We are back in this match, big style. Unfortunately, there's more slack marking and we find ourselves 4-1 down by the whistle. I don't feel terribly disappointed because the football we played was great. The reception given to the players at the end indicates to me that most people feel the same. You would have thought we had won the cup. Good luck to Luton. They were good opposition, certainly better than anything we faced in the friendlies.

After spending a hot and sweaty night in Dunstable we complete our grand tour of the country by driving back west to Ross-on-Wye, Herefordshire. Looking out of our B&B over the sparkling, meandering River Wye, we thank our lucky stars we are back in the West Country, only a couple of hours away from Yeovil and the forthcoming clash with Carlisle United. Happy, happy days.

Even though we have only been away for three nights it is good to flop into our own bed again. We have a waterbed (and, yes, it is good for sex) and if you haven't tried one, you haven't had a good night's sleep. So when we go away it is like sleeping on a bed of nails. Having said all that, I slept badly on the Friday night and woke at about 4am with a thundering headache. I think it was brought on by the dream I had of perpetually climbing those nasty metal stairways at the back of the away end at Luton. I was like a man on a treadmill, up and down, up and down. So at this early hour I was up searching for the tablets, and then it dawned on me that it was only 11 hours to the first League game ever to be played at Huish Park. Our collective dream is about to come true.

Saturday 16 August 2003 is the day when all the stay-at-home supporters and those with wedding commitments get the chance to see the boys set out their stall in the Third Division. How are we going to do? The bookies and football pundits are putting serious pressure on us. Everyone who thinks they know anything about football is saying that we are going to go straight up. I think that we must give due respect to the other teams in the division. If we should end up in mid-table we will have done well. That's my official line. Truth is, I am screaming inside that we are going to walk it. Cocky, is what I could be called by other supporters, but I don't care. I'm a Yeovil Town supporter.

It is the first day of the new measures to ease the traffic congestion. A park-and-ride scheme has been arranged. One bus will start in Yeovil, making several stops before arriving at the Council Offices car park where, it is anticipated, some 300 cars will be parked. The assembled crowd will hop on the bus and zoom up to Huish Park. Hang on. One bus? Zoom? I don't think so. How is the bus going to get through the traffic that will still be jamming the road up to Huish Park? We'll see.

Lin and I walk up through the Houndstone estate and, as we do, my heart begins to pump faster and faster. This is just where we left off at the end of last season – a big crowd (6,347), great atmosphere and a universal belief in our team. Yeovil seem intent on carrying on from last year, as well. Four minutes and Kevin Gall makes it 1-0. Eighteen minutes and he sweetly blasts in a second. There is much consternation in the Carlisle camp, especially from the John Travolta look-a-like who doubles up as United's manager. Do they all wear awful suits like that up north? By half time, Gally could have had five or six and Yeovil could have been 7-0 up. Pinch me, someone. The second half is a lot more even. In between some nasty fouling, Carlisle play some nice football, which must give hope to the 200 or 300 fans that are doing the 600-mile round trip to see their lads. Yeovil keep playing the possession game that we know and love, and are duly rewarded in the 79th minute with a peach of a third after good forward running and a knock in from Kirk Jackson.

Lin and I, believing we deserve a drink after all the excitement, dash to the new marquee and celebrate with a couple of beers. I'm quite impressed with the set up. It's like an Arab prince's camp at a desert oasis. Careful, Lin, I might get offered a herd of camels for you. Thanks to a big-screen TV, we are able to cheer and chant "We are top of the League" when the table flashes up. The only concern that I have about the afternoon is that my voice gave out early into the second half. I tried a "Hey, Gary Johnson" and bugger-all came out. Some serious vocal training will have to be undertaken by the time we hit the capital next Saturday.

As we had walked into the ground behind the Copse Road End, among the sea of green and white, we had seen two ducks, mallards I reckoned, waddling along the tarmac. I tried to think what it could mean. I came to the conclusion that it foretold a 0-0 draw. But I hadn't read the omen correctly. I realised later on that it had meant Carlisle 0 goals, 0 points. Yeo ducks! Oh, and Doncaster Rovers are in second place and the park-and-ride bus broke down.

Monday morning, Dorchester Crown Court. It was like being a celebrity; everybody wants to talk Yeovil Town. The security guard at the car park, the probation officer and the gaoler – "Everywhere I go, people want to know, who are the boys in green and white?" It's like floating high in a bubble. I know bubbles burst, but let's enjoy this while we may.

Our elevation to the higher reaches has produced a bonus already. G.J. has obtained on loan from Bolton Wanderers' Jermaine Johnson, their Jamaican international, who needs a little first-team football and a dose of man-management. He has come to the right place. Paul Terry from the Daggers is also expected to sign this week. I've always been impressed at the way he has played against us and in their F.A. Cup appearances on TV. I hope we can get him.

I remember back to this time last year – only one point from the first two games and I was just about to leave the job that I had held for more than 30 years. I was nervous on both counts. Now, here we are sitting pretty, and my self-employed venture has blossomed. If Yeovil and my fortunes continue to be inter-twined, I should be a millionaire in a few years. Premiership Glovers and fat cat Owen. Nice.

It is Friday afternoon and I have just returned from Taunton Crown Court. I got a little bit nervous as the judge wittered on, because I knew I had to get to the shop at Huish Park to buy Lin's new hooped shirt. Yes, she has lasted all of two League games without one. We're off to Leyton Orient tomorrow and she wants the shirt in time. Fortunately, the shop had new stock in this morning, but I was told that some 70 large shirts had already gone today and all small sizes were once again sold out. Lin is a medium, so she is in luck.

Saturday 23 August promises to be a hot slog up the A303 and round the motorways to east London. Forecasts of the busiest Bank Holiday traffic ever are a slight concern as we leave Huish Park with the Independent Supporters' Association at 10am. With our promotion to the League has come promotion in coach quality. We now have seats with leg room, a video, TV and a toilet. How the other half live! There is some uncertainty as we approach the M25 as to whether we should go north or south. I chip in my pennyworth, suggesting north and then down the M11. Sometimes it just doesn't pay to get involved because, all of a sudden, as we leave the M11, I have become the local expert and have been hauled down to the front of the coach, a pile of maps thrust in my hand and an impassioned plea from the driver to direct him to Brisbane Road, Leyton. Fortunately, I recognise the road we are on, realising that we are heading due east towards Southend and the North Sea, and Leyton Orient is fading fast. Like an Indian scout leading the seventh cavalry through dangerous territory, I somehow manage to get the coach back on the right path and eventually direct her into Brisbane Road. Let's hope the lads' coach trip has been less stressful. We hear that one of the other coaches has left Mrs Johnson behind. Yes, THE Mrs Johnson. That doesn't bode well for the afternoon.

At three minutes past three Lee Johnson delivers a beautiful ball that curls right in front of Kevin Gall. Like a Whippet, he is off to the by-line and puts over an accurate cross. Jackson dummies, and it goes to Gavin Williams, who has time and space, with the whole goal gaping before him. Somehow he strikes the ball into the body of the flailing keeper. Yeovil's best chance of the game has come and gone. Seconds later, we are punished when Orient take the lead with a scrappy goal, and it is all uphill. An added problem occurs when Roy O'Brien is forced to leave the field with blood pouring from his nose. The second half produces a couple of chances that, on another day, might have been converted, but the ball is not running kindly and Orient punish us further with a well-struck shot that gives Chris Weale little chance. Wealey had kept us in the game with two magnificent saves that make him my man of the match. 2-0 and no complaints from Glovers' fans as we file out of the ground. In truth, I think many of us are stunned. We haven't lost a League game since Boxing Day last year, and we have grown accustomed to coming away with the points. This wasn't a typical performance from our lads; I felt that we weren't up for it as much as Orient were. They appeared to have a greater hunger for the ball, which gave them better possession and the chance to dictate the play. Still, we have to learn. Most of us know, now, that this league is going to be hard work.

We got up to London a little later than we had expected, so a fair number on the coach are now gagging for a pint, and arrangements are made to drop into a pub in Hemel Hemstead, just five minutes off the motorway. Five minutes if you take the correct exit, that is. Best part of an hour if you don't! To make matters worse, the toilet seems to have broken down. Into what is now a very hot and stuffy coach comes the added delights of the aftermath of too many Orient hot dogs. Promotion certainly has its price.

Sunday morning. A chance to calm down, get it all in perspective, look at the long term, be philosophical – but still mourn those three lost points. Gary Johnson was obviously not too happy with the team's performance and kept the dressing room door locked for an hour while he explained a few things. He said afterwards: "It wasn't crisp, and I just said to the boys that I didn't think we played our game in the first half. In fact, we didn't really play our game until late on in the second half, when it was a bit too late. We've said a few harsh words in there. Even our captain, Terry Skiverton, who wasn't on the field of play, said some home truths along with Steve Thompson and myself. We've hit them straight between the eyes and they've got to come out fighting on Monday." On the injury front, poor Roy O'Brien is sporting a very swollen hooter, which may or may not be broken. You didn't see that elbow then, ref? Or the one the same player caught Hugo with a couple of minutes later? It is not comforting to see that the standard of the officials is no higher than in the Conference.

Our prospective Premier League star, Jermaine Johnson, has been shipped back to Bolton. It seems that he arrived carrying an ankle injury, which became apparent in training and during the reserve game on Wednesday. In G.J.'s words: "He wasn't firing on all cylinders." Perhaps we'll see him later when he is fit. On a more serious note is the news that Tom White received a nasty knock while playing for Tiverton. At least a month out is no way to persuade G.J. that he is fit enough to join the squad again. Some players have no luck whatsoever, and Tom seems to be falling into that category. He was so steady for us a couple of seasons ago, but he has had nothing but ill-fortune since.

Bank Holiday Monday morning, 25 August. I feel more nervous than I have for many a match day. What are we going to do? Bounce back, or fall again? I haven't got a clue as to which way this will go. Northampton, big spenders during the close season, have been tipped to be there or thereabouts at the end of the season, but have only won once – 1-0 against struggling Darlington. They have, however, put Norwich out of the Carling Cup. This will surely be a test of how good we really are, not just how good we think we might be. As they say, it's a funny old game and fortunes are so fickle.

I think this as I trudge back to the car, having downed a consolation pint in the hospitality tent, or should that be the disappointment tent, beaten 2-0 by a team that took two of the three chances that came their way. Yeovil played some attractive football, but could never overcome a well-disciplined defence. They had half chances, but nothing clear-cut. I don't know if Northampton are going to be one of the front runners as the season unfolds, or simply one of the bread-and-butter teams that we will often meet. But we shall have to be a bit more inventive down the wings and in the penalty box. That said, we have no divine right to success. Let's face it, it has taken us 108 years to get this far. We have to learn to walk before we can run. Come on, you Glovers! I suppose I could search back and look to see when we last lost two games on the trot, or when we failed to score in two successive matches. But what's the point? It only hurts, and I'm doing my best not to be knocked off course by this blip. So I'll put the statistics away and go and have a drink instead. If in doubt, turn to alcohol. Did G.J. say that once?

I immerse myself in work. Well, it helps to pass the time until Saturday. No more sitting around at home these days waiting for the phone to ring. Since my redundancy and the first few anxious months of nothingness, the work has been flowing in. I have been involved in a three-day trial at the Crown Court this week – not a lot of time to be thinking about Yeovil Town. Instead, I've been concentrating on how I can sit more comfortably on the back-breaking seats they have in this old courtroom. Obviously, the jury must have had the same problem. Three days of evidence and barristers' speeches have driven them to return their verdict in only 25 minutes. They definitely want to be out of there. Pity they came down against my client. Still, that's life.

Lin didn't enjoy the coach ride to Orient, and doesn't fancy the trip up to Macclesfield. She would rather head in the opposite direction. It's that call of the surf again. It may be the last weekend of the summer and another chance of enjoying the big waves in Cornwall might not come along this year. I have to agree with her and begin to make arrangements for an overnight stay in a B&B. I should be able to pick up Somerset Sound down there and keep in touch with the game. By Friday the weather forecasts are beginning to work against the plan. Much cooler temperatures and a northerly wind make me think that beach and sea may not be a good idea. We check the surf forecasts and Lin is disappointed that, at nearby Newquay, the waves are running at under one foot. Well, you can't bodyboard in that. Yes, that is what we like to do – we are like a couple of big kids when we get down there. We never had the opportunity to learn to surf when we were young, so we do the next best thing. But this time we abandon the trip.

Come Saturday 30 August, we don't do anything. Shall we go here? Shall we do this? One of those days when you just don't get going and, in the end, the day has gone. During the week I bought two new Yeovil Town, Division Three coffee mugs. I thought, "New season, better have a new set." The old ones brought us great luck, but they have probably been worked out now. So the morning starts well – all the correct procedures are undertaken to ensure that the Glovers have a successful day and, despite the weather forecast, the sun is shining and it is turning quite warm.

By three o'clock I am out in the garden, on my hands and knees, scraping out moss and weeds from between the gaps in the patio paving slabs. An extension lead runs from the house, and the radio, suitably tuned into Moss Rose, is bringing me live coverage of the game. Interviews with some of the 400 travelling fans before the kick-off reveal a fair amount of optimism about Yeovil's chances. I feel the same way. Come on, lads, today's the day. Well, it would have been if Macclesfield hadn't had the luck of the Devil. An aimless centre loops off Roy O'Brien and goes straight into the top corner. Shortly afterwards, the radio commentator announces an obvious hand ball, a point that the referee seems to have missed, and then the inevitable consequences of the official's slip, the second goal. Am I going to bat on about the quality of referees all season? I had hoped for something a little better this time round.

Weeds and moss are being gouged out with a vengeance now. How are Yeovil going to come back from this bloody awful start? The commentator keeps saying that we are not getting the run of the ball; it is bouncing just the wrong side of a forward's foot, or it is ricocheting into the path of a Macclesfield player. It certainly isn't going our way. Then comes a glimmer of hope. Adam Lockwood has powered into the box and slammed a full-blooded header into the net. A loud whoop goes up from the garden in Montacute. "Macclesfield are there for the taking," says the football pundit. Get it on, Yeo! I've got a nasty suspicion that the pundit on Radio Macclesfield was saying something similar about Yeovil. Minutes later the Silkmen are 3-1 in front and, to rub it in, two minutes from time they score again. Okay, I shouldn't have sworn quite so loudly, being out in the garden and all, but sometimes that is all there is left to do.

CHAPTER 2

THE COACH PARTY

I am feeling sorrow – sorrow for those lads who brought us so much joy just a few short months ago. They are the same players, giving the same 100 per cent, but nothing is going right for them. We, the supporters, are suffering too. Many of the younger ones have grown up over the last few seasons accustomed to perpetual winning. Us older, more seasoned, onlookers have, of course, seen it all before. In fact, most of us have seen more defeats than victories, so our experience should stand us in good stead if the worst comes to the worst. It won't, of course. We shall soon get it sorted and be back with smiles on our faces. All we need is a little bit of luck.

The *Ciderspace* forum is full of conflicting views, some wanting root and branch changes in the squad, others calling for a steady hand on the tiller (or words to that effect). Before the season began Gary Johnson said that he was going to stick with the boys who had done us proud. He would give them 10 League games to see if they could make the grade before considering any major movements. Some of the fans are counting down from 10, like the launch of a space rocket. They are demanding moves to strengthen the back, tighten up the midfield or spend, spend, spend on a mega-forward. I am being patient. I have faith in G.J. One thing that surprises me, though, is how much we miss the 'Scottish Player'. I know he was good, but I didn't think we were going to miss him this much. We seem to have lost the ability to play wide across the park. We have become narrow, and that makes it a lot easier for the other side to prevent us playing the way we would wish. We have, of course, lost our other winger, Nick Crittenden, for a few games, thanks to a thigh strain. These things are bound to unbalance a squad and, perhaps, it is no great surprise that we find ourselves on the end of three consecutive defeats. Again, I say that if we can only get a bit of luck then heads will rise and we will fire on all cylinders.

Talking of luck, I think mine is following a similar path. It is Monday morning, I'm all dolled up in my sharp suit, and I'm through the doors at the Crown Court ready to meet my client. "What's the name of your case?" the usher asks. "Not on my list," she says. It transpires that the court, in its wisdom, has put the case back a week. A slight communication problem. Why am I the last to know? Back to the car and home to Montacute. I'd paid for four hours' parking, too. Still, I'll look on the time left in the day as a bonus, pop down the DIY store, and pick up a load of laminated beech flooring. We have decided to re-do the bathroom and a new floor is the first item. It is necessary to allow the boards to acclimatise for 48 hours in the environment in which they are to be laid, so I can't put them down today. What I can do, though, is the preparation. Isn't that always the boring bit? I rip up the old carpet and underlay, and observe the creaking floorboards underneath. The instructions on the new floor state that all nail heads must be buried in order not to muck up the new underlay. Armed with my trusty hammer, I duly hit the old nails as if they are heads in a Macclesfield forward line. There's one board that is loose and needs securing. Like an arrow, a new nail flies into the pine board, but as admire my handiwork, I wonder where that fizzing sound is coming from. Funny, it looks a little damp around the nail head. Prat that I am, I have punctured one of the main copper pipes, and water is now spurting out all over the place. I rip up the floorboard and the water smacks me in the face. This doesn't happen on *Changing Rooms!* Fortunately, the room below the bathroom is a utility room with a tiled floor, so I punch a hole in the ceiling to enable the water to cascade down. Panic? I'm like a headless chicken. What the hell do I do now? I turn various stopcocks, but the waterfall keeps on flowing. I try binding the pipe with tape, but the water squirts out in a different direction. This is worse than a leaking defence, and I can't plug it. The answer, when I can get myself together, is to phone my solicitor. When you want a plumber, where else would you turn? One of the secretaries is married to that man in a million who can come to my assistance and save me from drowning.

Mike Heather, ace plumber, arrives in a flash, complete with his two children, Rian and Abbey. Rian was one of the mascots at the Northampton game a week ago and takes my mind off the disaster by telling me all about the excitement he felt running out with his favourite player, Chris Weale, in front of some 6,000 people. Abbey is hoping to get her first hooped shirt for Saturday's encounter with the Swansea Jacks. Sanity returns to the Owen household and I can eventually put away the buckets that have been catching the deluge in the lower room. I feel like a limp rag. Mike has kindly agreed to undertake the necessary work when the new bathroom suite arrives. You didn't think I was going to do it myself after all this, did you?

The news from the club during the week is mixed. Good news that we have signed Ronnie Bull from Millwall on a month's loan. Apparently, Gary Johnson has had his eye on this lad since his days at Watford academy. Seems he might be able to put a bit of beef into the team. But as that little ray of sunshine breaks through, another cloud scuds across our sky in the form of the Welsh under-21 team. They are insisting that Kevin Gall must join their squad and be prepared to sit on his arse in the dug-out, or play left wing back, in an unimportant European game on Friday night, which means that Gally will miss out on Saturday's fixture with Swansea. It means that Adam Stansfield will probably get his first start of the season, and I hope and pray that he plays a blinder, but I think the Welsh have a bloody cheek insisting that one of our star strikers should turn into a full back! In fact, I shall go further than that and say that I think it stinks. After all, Swansea City are a Welsh club. How convenient to have Gally nicely tucked up and out of the way.

To make matters worse, that trendy laminate flooring that has been breathing and acclimatising for the past couple of days, turns out to be unsuitable for bathrooms. It's back to the DIY store to load up with the correct stuff. I've just about knackered myself from carrying it up and down stairs, and to and from the store, and I haven't even taken it out of the wrappers. I shall be glad when this week is over. Bring on Saturday; bring on the Swans, or the Jacks, or whoever they are. Come on, Yeovil. You can stuff this lot. You know you can. I shall be giving it everything from the stands.

What extra ingredient can I introduce to the match-day routine that will give the lads the edge this afternoon? Lin swiftly supplied the answer when I took up two mugs of coffee while her ladyship continued to recline in bed. She has never taken to the two new Yeovil mugs that I bought. Too chunky, wrong colour green and horrible old-gold lettering. She finds them depressing and has come to the conclusion that our recent run of defeats is associated with the purchase of these rogue drinking vessels. As soon as the coffee was drunk she leapt from the bed and went to the open window. She hurled her mug down on to the patio slabs below and watched as the offending beaker shattered into a myriad of pieces. I was taken aback at first, but soon joined her with my mug, which, with equal delight, I lobbed from the upstairs window. The spell was broken. We felt the relief pour over us. Look very carefully at that brooding jinx that you may have hiding in your cupboard and, if you think that it may be contributing to adverse results, give it the boot – smash the little bugger, and set yourself free.

It is a 1pm kick-off today because… well, I'm not sure why. England are playing an international against Macedonia. Perhaps that interferes with a 3pm kick-off, or perhaps the police have insisted upon it – like they seem to be insisting on everything else at Huish Park at the moment. It may be that they don't want the Swansea fans to have too much drinking time before the game. I just don't know.

What I do know is that it is becoming difficult to cross over from the Main Stand entrance of HP to the Bartlett Stand. Now that we have the new zoo cage in position, it is necessary to file your way through what is now the away supporters' car park, via the grass, to get round to the proper turnstile. It is not so bad at this time of the year, but when the autumn and winter rains are with us we could lose a few fans in the mud. Will Yeovil be supplying hooped wellies?

There is a great atmosphere in the ground this afternoon. The away end is almost stuffed to capacity, with about 1,500 Taffs/Jacks in position. There are still a lot of seats vacant in the Main Stand, which is confirmed later in the afternoon when the 'gate' is given as 6,600. Only around 5,100 Glovers fans. Don't the faint-hearted drop off quickly? A couple of bad results and they decide that a shopping trip to Matalan is more fun. Oh, ye of little faith.

This is a mighty fixture; we need a result of some kind just to steady the ship. A draw against the current League leaders would be fine, but it might be one of those games where either side could stuff the other. Swansea have the likes of Trundle and Nugent up front, and they have been firing goals at will so far. We have our Adam Stansfield. Every Yeovil fan is wishing him the very best for his first League start since 17 August 2002. I have never broken my leg, but I can imagine that it must be very difficult to have total confidence long after the break has mended. Hopefully, Adam will prove to us all that he has fully recovered.

Swansea are in their away strip of black. Blackjacks – I like it. But it is Yeovil who hold most of the aces. They start in a determined fashion, attacking with force and defending superbly, but Swansea are not here for the ride and soon show why they are top. Chris Weale pulls off a couple of great saves to deny them the lead. New boy Ronnie Bull settles well in the left back position, and keeps things under control down that flank. On 39 minutes a beautiful ball from Lee Johnson to the far post is met by Adam Stansfield, who heads it into the back of the net. Huish Park goes mad. The Elmore Kid is back.

It is 1-0 at half-time, and I couldn't ask for more. In the second half the boys in green and white give another demonstration in fighting hard for the ball. They are like a pack of terriers – snap, snap, snapping away at Swansea. A great through ball on 55 minutes, and Kirk Jackson beats the defenders and the keeper to it, and slots it into the Westland End net. Oh joy, oh bliss, oh happiness. What a beautiful day. Perhaps we should always kick off at one o'clock. Resolute defending sees us through, and even gives us the opportunity to strike the Swansea woodwork on two occasions. One effort by Gavin Williams, who ran half the length of the pitch, taking on all-comers, deserved a better fate. These three points will have done the boys the world of good. Morale, if it had slipped at all, will be restored.

No work for me come Monday morning so, naturally, I gravitate towards Huish Park. I hope to bump into G.J. so that I can congratulate him and the lads. As luck would have it, they were just about to start a training session on the pitch. The sun is shining and I have an hour to kill, so I take up a viewpoint from one of the 5,000-odd empty seats and enjoy watching the squad go through their paces. It is obviously hard work, but there is plenty of laughter going on. The two keepers, Weale and Collis, work out together before joining the others in a team game of three attackers against two defenders. The effort that is going into this very competitive match is tiring me out. They obviously give 100 per cent and seem to love every minute of it. Well, I suppose they should. How many of us would give our right arms to be kicking a football around rather than being stuck in a factory, shop or office?

I return home, make a cup of tea, and flop down in front of the TV to watch the Champions video that I just bought from the club shop. I'm having a great day, and, just to round it off in style, I receive an invitation to travel with the players on the team coach to Doncaster next week and stay overnight in their hotel. It doesn't get much better than this. Lin is pig sick when I tell her the news. I would love to take her with me, but someone has to keep working to keep me in the style that I am accustomed to. I think I just might position myself down near a corner flag at the Belle Vue Stadium. I reckon when the 'Scottish Player' takes a corner or two, I shall be able to express my opinion of him within his full earshot. Yes I know, you don't have to tell me. It is childish and should be beneath me. You're right. It would be a laugh, though. I'll see how I feel on the night.

Yet another top award comes Yeovil's way. Not only did we win the Conference silverware, but Ron Pippard has just won Conference Groundsman of the Year at a presentation at Windsor Racecourse. After all those years of mud and water, we now have a 21st century, state-of-the-art, greensward.

I had to travel down to Exeter on Thursday morning. It still amazes me that a city of this size has just seen its football club slip out of the Football League. How the tables have turned. We have always seen it as a feather in our cap when we beat them in pre-season friendlies, but now we would be embarrassed if we didn't. A friend, who for his sins is a Stevenage fan, travelled to their away fixture with Exeter on Saturday and although Exeter won 1-0, expressed the view that they were so poor that they had little chance of regaining their League status this season. Ah, well, it will probably do them a power of good to sample the delights of the lower reaches for a year or two.

My purpose in visiting the city was to interview a client who is presently languishing in the prison. Gaining entrance through the small wooden door in the large wooden door was quite nerve-wracking. Inside, it is all keys and gates clanging, I.D. checking, form filling. In fact, it was just like going through the season-ticket turnstile in the Bartlett Stand. I thought it seemed familiar. But, once inside, it is not like Huish Park at all. No lush grass in here. Brick, concrete and bars crowd in on all sides. While I was only doing porridge for about an hour-and-a-half, the relief when I eventually stepped back through the wooden opening was tremendous. What a thing freedom is. Most of us take it for granted. The freedom to go to a home game, or on an away trip. Thank goodness I had my get-out-of-jail-free card. Those Monopoly sets come in useful, you know.

Last Saturday it was the mugs. Today, Saturday 13 September, Lin is having jitters about wearing the shirt! After it was purchased, we had our three straight defeats, so, last week, she wore the green Champions T-shirt and we won. Today she is uncomfortable about donning the hoops again and declares that she will once again wear the T-shirt. I scoff at the idea, but, deep down, I think she is probably right to stick with it. If she goes back to the team shirt and we lose this afternoon, I think we would both feel pretty sick and pretty guilty. Anyway, it is a beautiful, sunny and warm day, and a T-shirt will do just fine.

Another step into the history books today (well, perhaps into the *Trivia Sporting Quizbook* or *A Question of Sport*). "Fingers on the buzzers. When was the first time that two League teams whose names both start with the letter Y played each other? Yes, Ally McCoist?"

"Well, Sue, it was in 2003, when the famous Yeovil Town met York City."
"Correct. Everyone knew it was Yeovil, but you did well to name the other side."

We are in for an experience of the Kettle kind today. Our old mate, Trevor, who refereed so poorly/badly/bloody terribly (choose which one you think applies) in the Conference, has followed us up into the big time. And, of course, a big stage calls for a big performance. Last week he hit the headlines by awarding three penalties and making seven bookings. Never a dull moment with our 'look at me, I'm in charge' official. Just have to keep my fingers crossed that Colin Pluck survives the afternoon.

The away end is sparsely populated, certainly compared with the Swansea gathering last week. A few red shirts are dotted around, but, on the whole, this lot don't look as passionate as the Jacks. It is, of course, a hell of a long way from York, and, perhaps, they are feeling a little weary after the long coach trip. York have been through the wringer lately – not just poor performances on the pitch, but all manner of nasty business behind the scenes. Once again 'property developer' is the phrase that jumps out and hits you. Bootham Crescent somehow got parted from the football club, and is presently under threat of concrete and brick from the housebuilders. It is a worrying time for all City fans, so perhaps that is why they look a little jaded this afternoon.

No worries about the lads and lassies at the other end. As always, a sea of green-and-white hoops sweeps from corner to corner of the Westland Stand. The sound of the drum, trumpet, back panels of the stand and a couple of thousand voices boom out as the boys appear from the tunnel.

Yeovil get into their stride first and attack the away end with some style. Several corners result, and York are finding it difficult to get out of their half. There is something majestic about Kirk Jackson when he jumps for a ball in the penalty box, and today is no exception. On 21 minutes he rises like a bird of prey, hovers in the air and then punches the ball home with his head. Wham! The Huish faithful are doing their own impression of a Jackson leap. That's two in two for Jacko. There had been a few mutterings that perhaps he wasn't going to make the step up into this standard of football – a little too slow, not positioning himself correctly for passes, that sort of thing. I don't think we shall hear any more of that from now on. Well done, Kirk. Great stuff.

"Anything you can do…" is possibly in the mind of Colin Pluck when he roars into the box for a corner, smacks the ball with his head and powers it sharply down under the diving keeper. Here we are at 34 minutes in complete control of this game. The Yeovil machine is purring again.

Second half, York take a long time to come from the dressing room and, obviously, the extended team talk has done some good. They have a lot more about them and Yeovil do well to keep them at arm's length. Three substitutes give York fresh legs as the heat of the afternoon begins to tell on both sides. The Glovers' new-style back four stand firm and, with the exception of one fine save by Chris Weale, the goal is fairly untroubled.

Towards the end, G.J. brings on Jake Edwards and Jamie Gosling, then, right at the death, Adam Stansfield. The fourth official signalled three extra minutes and Lin said: "Just time for Adam to score, then." As if by magic, the three substitutes conspire together in a beautiful move, allowing Stansfield the honour of tapping in from a yard out. Timing is everything. Three-nil to the boys in green and white puts us up to fifth place behind Oxford, Hull, Bristol Rovers and Swansea. Donny are next on Tuesday night, losers today to Hull City, but going well. Oh, and our favourite referee? Well, on the Kettleometer he scores fairly well. Only one chant of "You don't know what you're doing!" Shame he made a cock-up over what would have been a goal for Kevin Gall, but at least he didn't send any of our lads off. I'm thankful for small mercies.

Sunday morning and I am like a kid waiting for Christmas Day to arrive. I have never had any involvement in any capacity with Yeovil Town. I turn up for the game, I go home again. I do a bit of mooching around Huish Park and say hello to whoever may be up there. That's about it. But now, with my invitation to travel with the club, I shall become an ambassador for Yeovil Town. What shall I wear? I can't sport my hooped shirt on the coach while all the lads and management are decked out in... well, presumably, shirt and tie and smart jackets. I don't know. I've never seen them off to a match. Perhaps they wear the team tracksuits. I'm not sure. I think I'll have to take a big overnight bag to contain the various outfits that will suit the moment. One thing I cannot do is watch the match in a suit and tie. That is just beyond the call of duty. I must have the hoops, denim jeans and the desert boots. I have some self-respect. What do they all do on a long coach journey? Should I take a good book and sit quietly near the front? And what about coming back – hopefully, with the three points? Will we all be singing?

We are due to leave at 5.30 on Monday evening. So what can I do to pass the time? I decide I need to go up into the loft and find something. The hatch is in the bathroom and I put the ladder up to climb in. Just as I reach the trap door I get this nasty sinking feeling as the feet of the ladder begin to slip away on that new laminated floor that I have laid in the bathroom. Down it crashes, with me still clinging to it. My face bounced on one of the rungs and I immediately felt bits of broken tooth in my mouth as I was laid out on the floor with pains in my chest and blood running down my arm. Fortunately, my son, Tim, was in the house and came running to my assistance. He assured me that my broken front tooth didn't look as bad as it felt. I wonder if I am going to be fit to join the team and take that long journey north. This is a chance in a lifetime as far as I am concerned and it will take a bit more than a broken rib or whatever to stop me.

I'm at Huish Park well before the deadline. In my smart suit, crisp shirt and tie, I immediately see that I'm over-dressed. The team all arrive in regulation white polo shirts, black tracksuit bottoms and gleaming white trainers. The coach, all £150,000 of it, is probably the best I have ever travelled in. Leg room? You could seat a Hugo Rodrigues with comfort. Tables, electric points, fridge, microwave – a proper little home from home. I am assigned a seat with a table, near the front, facing towards the rest of the coach so that, as G.J. put it, "You can see what they all get up to on the journey." Gary is not travelling with us, as he has an engagement in Taunton before he can drive up to the hotel. He is giving a talk to businessmen on the subject of motivation.

Bumping over the speed hump on the HP access road seems to act as a signal to a number of the squad to start eating. A queue forms at the microwave as packs of bacon, chicken and pasta, almost anything, is shoved in – ping – pulled out and devoured. I have never seen so much food shovelled away in so short a time. I ask Steve Thompson about it. I thought that there would be a strict diet for each of them to observe, but I am assured that, because they burn up so much energy in training, they need to replace it with all kinds of food. The only things they have to avoid are items that will actually build up fat. Alcohol is the prime example and, because it is a potential problem in more ways than one, the squad abstain for 48 hours before games. Steve and I talk about the old days in football when there was a culture of heavy drinking. He tells me that those days are long gone and, as far as Yeovil Town is concerned, there is not a sniff of a problem. The only other 'food' off limits seems to burgers, at least on the way to matches.

A couple of lap-top computers are plugged in, and games of pool and snooker are commenced with as much zeal as you would expect from this group of fired-up lads. Darren Way, Kevin Gall, Gavin Williams and Roy O'Brien, laugh, exclaim, squabble and joke their way through a mini-tournament down at my end, while Skivo, Locky, Paul Terry and others are doing something similar further back. In the midst of all this, however, Nicky Crittenden manages to read a book, and Abdul El Kholti is tucked up with his pillow, fast asleep.

A short stop at the M42 services near Tamworth sees a rush to the pick-and-mix counter, where most players stock up with big bags of sweets. Back on the coach, an inquiry starts into an allegation that Jake Edwards was seen buying a burger. In his defence, he claims that it was all right because Thommo was in the queue as well. "Only for a coffee," Thommo splutters. It is down to Terry Skiverton, as club captain, to decide on Jake's fate. A small fine is imposed. I felt a little sorry for Jake. After all, he has been playing his football in America until recently, and I'm sure that burgers before games are compulsory there.

My room at the hotel is excellent, but I don't spend long in it. A quick change of clothing and I'm in the bar having a drink and a chat with Thommo, Maurice O'Donnell, Tony Farmer (the physio), and Ken (the coach driver). After midnight Gary and Fat Harry join our little band, and Gary immediately wants to discuss the approach he should take in the team talk next day with regard to McIndoe. I sit there, fascinated, while various views are expressed, and I feel very privileged to be party to the inner workings of my football club.

I slept like a log, waking only once to the sound of a banging door somewhere up the corridor. At breakfast next morning I learnt that there had been some casualties in the night. Adam Lockwood and Gavin Williams had been sharing a room directly beneath the hotel's swimming pool. There was such a smell of chlorine that their eyes were running. It got so bad that they dragged their mattresses into another room and slept on the floor. They wanted to know if swimming goggles could be provided next time. That banging door, however, was attributed to Gary Johnson who, at five o'clock in the morning, had received a mobile call from Lee to say he was suffering from severe stomach cramps. Gary had to drive him to the all-night chemist in Doncaster to get some tablets. Unfortunately, things did not improve for Lee, and a discussion took place about seeking medical advice. A doctor could not attend for at least two hours and a decision was made that Adrian Hopper, the publicity manager, should drive Lee to hospital.

Meanwhile the rest of the squad got ready for a training session. As luck would have it, a suitable piece of ground was found just round the corner at Warmsworth Lions Football and Cricket Club. For the price of a drink, the groundsman was prepared to give us the run of the place, though Stephen Reed ran on the cricket square that was being re-laid that day and had to be hauled off.

Walking down the lane, with all the lads in their kit, bags of footballs and marker cones, reminded me of days at primary school when we all trooped out of the school gates and down to the local recreation ground, football boots scrunching on the pavements, laughing and messing about, without a care in the world.

The sun shone brightly on the session, which consisted of warm-ups, running and various team games, including foot volleyball. I was roped in to adjudicate on dodgy line-calls. The competitive spirit came through, with either howls of complaint or great cheers, depending on which way I called. I loved it. It certainly beat working. G.J. drew a round of applause by demonstrating one of the moves he wanted them to do, executing a flying volley perfectly with a mobile phone stuck down his sock. He has obviously not lost his touch. He then used the mobile in a more conventional fashion to phone Lee at the hospital. There was only one doctor on duty and the waiting room was full. It could take hours. "Get up to that reception desk and tell em you're in agony," Gary advised. Lee replied that there are 20 or 30 people all doing the same. Good old NHS!

At 2pm we sat down to a specially-prepared meal of chicken, pasta, eggs, tomatoes and new potatoes, washed down with fruit juice. This would replace all the energy used up on the training field. After a full English breakfast, now this, and no energy used up, I shall shortly be turning into a complete lard arse. Still, I couldn't say no, could I? It would have been rude.

Lee Johnson had not returned, and Gary was, not unnaturally, a little concerned with only five-and-half-hours to kick-off. Meanwhile the knock-about fun between the other lads continued. They bounced remarks off one another, wind-ups, put-downs, all the time obviously enjoying one another's company. Someone spotted that Hugo was wearing flip-flops (well, it would have been difficult not to, with the size of his feet) and pointed out that he was in breach of the dress code, which requires players to wear the club trainers. The cry went up that there should be a fine imposed, but Hugo, in his charming Portuguese accent, disputed it vigorously. He pleaded that he had asked his room-mate, Abdoo, if it would be okay to wear ze flip-flops. Howls of derision followed. It seems that Abdoo picks up more fines than anyone, so he should have been the last person to consult. For the sake of a tenner this dispute was hard-fought.

Just as the dishes were cleared away, Lee and Fat Harry returned. Lee looked washed out and complained of feeling dizzy after being given a tablet at the hospital. He took a couple of bread rolls and, as he went to his room, Terry Skiverton gave a second medical opinion. He looked down at Lee and suggested that it was a bad case of 'midgetitis'. Even Lee allowed himself a little grin. Tony Farmer followed him to his room, gave him a stomach massage, and tucked him up in bed. Gary decided to leave the decision on whether to play him or not until the last possible moment.

Gary invited me to share a pot of tea with him in the lounge and we talked all things football for an hour or so. It was so pleasant, sitting there with Sir Gary, sharing all the ins and outs of my beloved football club. Frankly, I was amazed by some of the tales that he recounted (though not about Yeovil Town players). My jaw dropped when he told me of a player who came to him and said that he couldn't play for the team the following day as he had to leave the town swiftly. When asked to explain why, the player stated that there was a woman he knew who was about to give birth in the maternity ward whose husband might be more than surprised at the colour of the baby. Gary quickly put together a video of this player's best attributes (well, not all of them) and sent it to a manager of another club. On the strength of the video, the player was transferred to his new club in a matter of days. It puts a whole new meaning on a transfer request.

Before the next meal of tea and toast, I had the time to wallow in a hot bath with a good book and soothe some of the aches and pains that I was still feeling from the ladder accident. This had to be the height of luxury. By five o'clock I had donned my hoops and wandered down to the foyer. My blood ran cold as

I looked over to the reception desk. The 'Scottish Player' was standing there, the size of life and twice as ugly. What should I do? Go in double footed and saw him off at the kneecaps? Offer him a hot tip for the Doncaster races? Ignore him? I chose the latter. I had visions of the newspaper headlines if I attacked him. 'LUNATIC IN HOOPS ASSAULTS STAR FROM BIGGER CLUB' or 'FIRST DIVISION HOPEFUL MAIMED'. The prison sentence wouldn't be worth it for the little squirt. Oh, and by the way, it looked as if he had been back to the mad barber's shop again. Very short with tramlines.

Gary invited me into the conference room to hear his team talk to the lads. Gary likens himself to being a teacher in front of his class. Two boys slip in a few seconds late and have a ball of paper thrown at them in place of the blackboard rubber. Humour over, the whole squad become very serious and focused on Gary and Mark, the psychologist, who has arrived at the hotel. G.J. advises them that, with this match tonight, they reach another point in the development of themselves as a team – a team that wants to see how far it can go together. He refers to McIndoe and the comments that he has made in this morning's papers. McIndoe claims there is more pressure on the Yeovil players than on himself, and he is glad that he is up against Adam Lockwood and Gavin Williams. Gary then shows them another newspaper article from a Yorkshire paper and reads a few chosen sentences attributed to Macca. 'Donny have a history of league soccer – they are a bigger club and a better squad' etc. Some quotes, Gary says, he will save until after the game. He expresses the hope and confidence that should anyone in the room "and that includes Brendon" leave the club that they would not be so disloyal as to say the sort of things that McIndoe has said. You can trust me, Gary; I'm Yeovil 'til I die!

The coach pulls up at the Belle Vue ground and there is a knot of Yeovil supporters outside the players' entrance. A few quizzical looks come my way as I descend the steps, but I just grin and make my way through to the inner sanctum. Adrenalin is pumping now that we have arrived and I want the match to start while G.J's words are still ringing in the ears. I know I'm up for it.

I must admit to having little experience of football club dressing rooms. I have seen T.V. footage of Arsenal's and the Millennium Stadium's, but neither prepared me for this. Old, tatty, without the room to swing a cat, and with a shower area you could fit into a cupboard under your stairs. By the time the squad, the kit box and bottled water is shoe-horned in, I am feeling quite claustrophobic. Fortunately, we were all ordered out to inspect the pitch while the kit was hung up on the pegs.

I must just recount a little story that Gary told me about a scene in this very dressing room during the quarter-final of the F.A.Trophy in 2002. Yeovil were

2-0 down at half-time and Gary was not too pleased with the performance. Someone had left a kit bag lying in the middle of the floor and he had tripped over it while explaining a few things to a player. As he went to talk to another he tripped again, and, in his anger, he picked up the bag by its drawstring, swung it round, and accidentally let it fly. Unfortunately, Steve Thompson, who was sitting with an ice-pack on his thigh, caught the full force of the bag in the face. Gary felt that he couldn't just say, "Oh, sorry, Steve" and lose the momentum, so he marched up to him, pointed to the ice-pack and demanded to know if he was fit to continue. Steve was taken aback and blurted out that perhaps he couldn't go on after all. Gary told him to get off then, and let him put someone on who was fit. Despite going a further goal behind, the lads ran out winners 5-4 and, of course, they went on to win the Trophy at Villa Park. That, in turn, was the foundation for winning the Conference last year. All from one little kit bag. Throw a few more, G.J.

So I'm out of the tunnel at a sprint (well, a pretty fast walk). The roar of the crowd nearly knocks me off my feet, or perhaps it was the two stewards barring my way. But I get there. I'm on the pitch – that very pitch where our dreams came true only a few short months ago. I gravitate towards the home-end goal. I stand where Johnno took the quick free-kick, where Darren scored his first goal of the season and where Chris Weale put the icing on the cake with his penalty save. The memories are flooding back. I look up to the away end and remember all of our banners tied to the metal railings. There are none there tonight. In fact, I think Donny have added some more advertisement hoardings along that section. They've also added a fresh chunk of terracing at our end, where the grass was; they must be expecting more guests this year. As the players leave the pitch to get changed I take the opportunity of sitting in the dug-out. I see now why Gary Johnson stands throughout the game. All you can see from down there are ankles and knees. How anyone could tell what was happening is beyond me. I don't think I'll watch the game from here. Sorry, Gary, you will have to do without my words of advice.

Yeovil fans are beginning to filter on to the terracing, so I decide it is time to go and join the members of my tribe. It's hard to tell, but I reckon on between 150 and 200 of us – not bad for a Tuesday night in Yorkshire. I sit and have a chat with *Ciderspace*'s own HHH's Dad, Adrian, and reflect on that afternoon when this end was full to the brim with green and white. We both agree that it was away at Halifax last season when we knew we were going to win the Conference. Let's hope tonight can be just as exciting, if perhaps not quite so nerve-wracking. Just then, I spot a chap I stood with at that Halifax game and I go down and stand next to him again. You never know, it might work.

From the kick-off, Yeovil look secure, despite Donny pushing hard in the first few minutes. Yeovil are kicking towards us and I am right in line as Gally powers a shot that just skims the top of the bar. A few inches to the right and I think it would have taken me through the back railings. Adam Lockwood is playing a blinder. He's marking some Scottish winger bloke and has him stitched up like a kipper. As always, Yeovil's speed is causing problems for the Rovers' defence and, on 35 minutes, the breakthrough comes. A would-be Scottish international gets beaten to a challenge by Nicky Critts, and the ball runs out to Gavin Williams. Cool as you like, he runs forward and strikes the ball across the Donny keeper into the far corner of the net. One thing to be said for plenty of space on the terracing is that it allows us fans to run up and down the steps in delight. Now the chants begin in earnest. I hope the 'Scottish Player' had his ears pinned back in order to hear every word. "One-nil to the smaller club, one-nil to the smaller club" was a particular favourite of mine and, as I found out later, to the players and Gary Johnson. "Macca for Weymuff" and "You'll never play for Scotland" were sung with feeling, as was the rather less polite: "You can stick your Macca up your arse." Nobody said the fans had to act professionally, only the players. And they do. Not once in the whole game was there an unwarranted challenge on the lad. All of them were stars, I thought, especially Lee Johnson, who, despite all that lost sleep, pain and boredom at the hospital, played as well as ever.

Second half, Doncaster press harder and harder as a hint of desperation sets in. They are beginning to hoof the ball up the park in the hope that Fortune-West can get something on it. He certainly got something on Adam Lockwood's head. In fact, it was an elbow. For once, the guy with the flag who generally spoils the game with dubious offside decisions is spot on. After a short consultation the ref sends F-W off. Now Yeovil only need to hold the line and play out time. In fact, they go a bit further than that and almost score with a couple of good efforts. In the 93rd minute McIndoe has the last word. Well, the last kick anyway. I'll call it a mis-timed tackle by the corner flag. He got booked. As Gary had rightly said, this was about coming here and securing a win and three valuable points. In the press conference he said: "It was a fantastic result and a fantastic performance. We didn't put together too many good moves in the first half but we scored a great goal and I thought we finished worthy winners. There were some real heroes out there, and credit to all of them, because it is not easy to come to Doncaster and win."

My problem now was getting back from the away end to join up with the team under the Main Stand. I approached a steward, said that I was with the official party, and, without a blink of an eye he kindly let me on to the perimeter path and escorted me towards the tunnel. What a gentleman. Somehow I can't see the Westland Stand stewards being quite as helpful.

The dressing room is like a Turkish bath. Steam is swirling all around and so, ladies, I regret that I cannot tell you anything about the naked bodies that were jumping in and out of the showers and hollering with joy. Eventually I make my way out to the car park where the coach is parked. A group of Yeovil lads are stood waiting to see the players, and one or two greet me. Seb, the joint editor of the fanzine *On to Victory* shakes my hand and I congratulate him on a great edition. John Hartley, who wrote a very kind review of *Yeovil 'til I Die!* is there as well. We are all so happy with the win. Everyone is buzzing. They all want to know how I have blagged the trip on the coach, and some decide on the spot that they, too, will write a book in order to get the perks. I go off to join the players in the hospitality suite, where two chefs are offering a choice of beef bourguignon or chicken chasseur. Yes, it's nosh time again, folks. We watch TV for the other results. Most of them have gone our way, and we think that we have gone up a place or two to third or fourth. I'll settle for that at the end of the season.

The ride back home almost mirrored the trip up. The laptops came out and the pool and snooker were played again. Just for variation, though, Darren put on a *Family Fortunes* quiz game and I joined a team with Gary, Lee, Dazza and Thommo against the Welsh Wizards and a couple of others. Every answer given by the Welsh team seemed to involve sheep.

Gary showed me the reports from scouts that he sends to matches. I read the ones relating to Donny Rovers, and had to laugh when, under a certain person's name, it said: "He will insist on taking all free-kicks and corners." No change there, then.

A bizarre thing happened to the coach as we hared down the motorway in the early hours. About ten feet of metal window surround became detached and was waving about and creating a danger for vehicles on the nearside. We pulled on to the hard shoulder, and Ken the driver tried to push it back into place. A couple of players got out to give him a hand, including Darren Way. Laughter burst out among the others when he found he could not reach high enough to grab the metal strip. Shouts of "At four foot six, what are you doing out there." That's Darren – busy, busy all the time. He is the same off the pitch as on it. In the end, the offending strip was snapped off and laid along the aisle of the coach until we got home. At 3.15 we arrived back at Huish Park. Thommo had been up and down the coach, telling those who didn't play that he wants them back at Huish Park for noon. There is a reserve game at Plymouth at three o'clock, and they are playing. See, it is not all a piece of cake being a professional footballer. I offered my heartfelt thanks to Gary for letting me take this magical ride, and bid my fond farewells. The rest of the day was a blank. I slept or wandered around like a zombie – but a zombie with a great big grin on his face. We have won three on the trot, no goals conceded and it looks as if we have well and truly settled into the Football League.

Before I know it the Mansfield away game is upon us. If I had thought earlier I could have phoned and bought cheaper tickets, but I have let it slip and will have to pay through the nose at the turnstile. I half expected Lin to make a last desperate attempt at that trip to Bude, but she surprised me by being the first to suggest we go to Field Mill instead. On Friday I fill the car with the cheapest petrol I can find, and check the air pressure in the tyres. After all, it is a long old haul on the motorways and, again, we have left it too late to get a seat on the coach. But to show I am on top of my game, I pull the directions to the ground off the *Ciderspace* website. I read them carefully including: 'Past the KFC on the left-hand side and straight through the second set of lights'. I just hope they're green! If we survive that, it's plain sailing into Quarry Lane, which is the away end. A friend, Kate, phones and asks if she can join us for the trip. I am more than happy, as she will give Lin someone else to natter to on the 390-mile round trip.

We go to bed at a reasonable hour with a long day ahead. I take a couple of tablets for a headache that has developed during the evening – can't be too careful. By three in the morning I am in agony, and migraine pills won't touch it. I slept fitfully, knowing, as time ticked on, that I wasn't going to be a travelling Glovers' fan that day. I am bitterly disappointed but the pain is keeping me well and truly laid out. I disappear under the duvet until ten minutes to three, at which time I have convinced myself that I feel a little better, and would feel better still for hearing the dulcet tones of Phil Tottle broadcasting live from Field Mill, Mansfield. At this point I want to stress that I am not a hypochondriac. Apart from my injuries from the ladder, and now this, I have not complained about any illnesses since my bad back at the start of last season. I'm sorry, I just wanted you to know.

Despite my fragile state I get engrossed in the play and am pleased to hear young Andy Lindigaard acting as match expert next to Mr Tottle. For the fourth match on the trot, Yeovil are keeping it very tight at the back, attacking in numbers and pushing The Stags on to the back hoof, as it were. No matter how good the commentary is, I find it difficult to stick with it. My head is pounding, I'm uptight, and there is certainly no chance of me relaxing for the next 90 minutes. Frankly, it is no fun at all. After 20 minutes or so, Lin decides that sitting in the same room as me is a mistake. Half grunts have greeted just about every comment she has made, and so she decamps out through the French doors and listens from the comfort of her sun lounger. I continue to grip the arm of the sofa, bite my lip and wish for a goal. On 43 minutes Capt. Kirk guides the Enterprise home for Yeovil to take the lead: Jacko side-foots in from a mêlée following a corner. I heard the roar from the Yeovil fans, I heard Tottle say it was in the back of the net, but still it took an unusual time to register with my brain that we had scored. By the time I had cheered and thrown my arms in the air, Lin had come in from the garden and given me a look. Half-time comes and goes, and then Yeovil put on a magnificent performance to hold their lead. It is gutsy and gritty, and I don't think anyone could ask for more. They defend from the front, with Gall and Jackson harrying Mansfield deep in their own half. The midfield fight for every inch of possession and the back four are superb. Oh, and there is the odd brilliant save from Chris Weale. Par for the course, really. Into added time, still rock solid. The commentator says that the Yeovil fans grouped behind the huge green-and-white flag behind the goal are rising and clapping their team. I hear the strains of "Stand up, if you love Yeovil" stream through the airwaves. I stand in my living room, a proud, proud Glover. At last the whistle goes. Drained, exhausted, totally shattered… and that's only me. Goodness knows how the lads feel and the gallant band of 450 in Gary Johnson's Green-and-White Army. We have won again, this time against a club that last year played in the Second Division. Yeovil are coming of age.

Third in the Third. Wow! Only Swansea City and Hull City above us; Oxford City and York City just below us. One little town holding its own among four great cities. It says something. Staying with the theme of cities for a moment, it must be said that Hereford are off to a flying start in the Conference. Win after win has taken them to the top. I've had a little grin today, though, when I see that Burton Albion beat them 4-1 on Friday night. That's more like it.

A bad week has followed; the fall from the ladder has done me more harm than I first thought. A trip to the chiropractor reveals that I have two misaligned ribs, which are thumped back into place with an implement that has the effect of a lump hammer. Not content with that, my neck was twisted and cracked until he said it was correct. I reckon I shall be able to stand with my back to a game and still be able to watch it, so far round has my head been jerked. Yes, if you want to know, I am feeling bloody sorry for myself. The only thing that brings a smile to my face has to wait until *Points West* on Friday evening. An item on Yeovil reveals that G.J.'s new defensive strategy is called 'Mum-in-the-goal defending'. Apparently, the team have to pretend that it is their mum who is in goal, and then they have to work that little bit harder, as they don't want her to get hit. I like it, but will it work? On *Ciderspace*, questions are being asked. Is

Chris Weale's mum confused about this tactic? Will Chris Weale be expecting a Mother's Day card?

There is nothing like a Saturday for expectation. It is like no other day of the week. Hope is bursting from my chest. A desire to win envelops me from the moment I lift my head from the pillow. The added impetus today is the thought of a local derby. An all-West Country clash. Those Devon dumplings who call themselves The Gulls will be swooping down from Torquay this afternoon, accompanied, we are told, by a large number of supporters. Usually under-achievers, they seem to be making more of a fist of it in the last season or so. They narrowly missed out on the play-offs last time round, and they have signalled their intentions of doing even better this year with a solid start. A win over Torquay today would do us no harm at all. Come on, my beauties. This is what we have been waiting for all these years. A chance to show that we are as good, if not better, than our West Country cousins.

A crowd of 7,718, with a large number in yellow on the away end, makes for a great atmosphere. I turn in my seat and acknowledge Frank the Optimist – "The lads will do it today." I also acknowledge, in the next seat, Frank the Pessimist – "It's gonna be hard today, we'll be lucky to win." I side with the Optimist. I have 100 per cent confidence in our boys. Okay, so I know nothing about the opposition. What do I need to know? They are just unlucky players who haven't had the good fortune to join a club like Yeovil. Well, you've got to start as you mean to continue. A win, making five in row, and we might even be at the top of the heap come five o'clock. It was a year ago that Gary Johnson celebrated his birthday by going top of the Conference. As we all know, we never dropped from that position. Tomorrow is G.J.'s birthday. It would be nice to repeat the trick.

Yeovil come out and immediately go for the jugular. For the first 15 minutes or so Torquay hardly get out of their half. Smooth, free-flowing passing creates numerous corners and a lot of pressure, but nothing in the way of real chances. Inevitably the whole team gets sucked further up the field All of a sudden there is a break on. Two lively forwards are sprinting down towards Chris Weale with a minimum of defensive options to hand. A neat pass and the ball is settling in the back of the net. Sod, sod, sod! My mind settles on an unnerving statistic – when Yeovil have gone behind this season we have lost every time. Still, plenty of time to put that right this afternoon. The same thought strikes me again after Kevin Gall has put in an inch-perfect centre and Kirk Jackson has met it well with his foot, only to see the goalkeeper's legs keep us from equalising. We go in at half-time 1-0 down.

There is plenty of good football in the second half. Yeovil are still playing it sensibly along the floor, pushing hard but finding things tough in the opposition penalty box. The aerial battle is intense, as Colin Pluck found out the hard way. Up for a corner, he tangles with their captain. Both go down in a heap and there is obvious worry from Colin's team mates. In fact, both sides are urging their respective physios to get on as quickly as possible and signalling for the St. John's stretcher. Someone near us in the stand gasps, "Look at the blood on Kevin Gall's hands!" A few minutes of frantic activity, and Plucky is up on his feet. He's a tough nut, all right. He is led off with his head covered in swabs and to much applause. The Torquay lad is fixed up on the pitch with a head bandage, which makes him look like Basil Fawlty in the moose story. Big Hugo comes on, followed by Jamie Gosling, and we revert to playing three at the back. Within a blink of an eye, Torquay have made the Yeovil by-line and a wicked cross is converted, giving Chris Weale no chance. Despite constant effort, Yeovil can find no way back. They hit the net twice, temporarily exciting a desperate crowd, but both are ruled out, one for a foul and one for offside. Torquay fans go wild as their team and manager parade before them. Full credit to them. They supported their team well and deserved their success. Hopefully we shall be turning the tables when we visit Plainmoor in the spring.

Over a pint in the tent, talk swings from praise for Torquay – "Best side we've seen at HP this year" to "Our midfield are too small, they were all over us". I feel sad, naturally, that we lost, but I can't bring myself to criticise any of the players. I thought they had all played pretty well. We have a chance to get back in the saddle with the arrival of another home match on Tuesday night. Boston 'Cheats' United are our visitors. Should be interesting.

G.J. was obviously more disappointed with Saturday's performance than I was. After the game he said: "I didn't enjoy our team's performance today and I've let them know that. We are much better than that. There are dribblers that are better, then there are strikers that are better, midfielders that are better. Then there are defenders who are better than that. I felt that they (Torquay) were clever in all departments and you've got to take a lesson when it is given to you. We are in tomorrow (Sunday) morning and afternoon, so some grannies will be upset when their grandsons are not around for lunch. We are in every morning and afternoon. That wasn't anywhere near how we can perform. We are going to work hard and make sure we show a bit more mental toughness when we go 1-0 down." Get the picture? I think the players do.

I find a Sunday after a defeat a particularly difficult time. I wake with the joys of spring and immediately a scoreline flashes up in my mind. Not a good start to the day. We usually have a Sunday newspaper, which I pick up at the local garage, but when we have lost I deliberately avoid the place and ignore what's going on in the rest of the world. I console myself with a visit to *Ciderspace* and wallow in the self-pity of other sufferers. Today, major concerns are raised about the quality of the service at the tea bars, the fact that the players do not use the old club bar and can we have it back, please? Worst of all, have you noticed that the fuzzy red 'Bradfords' logo is beginning to wash off the shirts when they are put through the washing machine a few times? I sense a direct correlation of incidental problems to the number of goals scored against.Oh, and the park-and-ride bus took an hour from Westlands. It gives me a warm glow to be part of such a neurotic bunch of worriers.

Seriously though, that 'Bradfords' logo is beginning to fade. I've just checked my shirt, which was purchased a while before Lin's, and, low and behold, mine is pink while Lin's is still red. I have also noticed that I have a couple of snags in the hoop section. I may never be sartorially elegant in my extra-large, but, the way things are going, by Christmas I shall look a right ragbag.

Still, if all I've got to worry about is a pink logo, it can't be bad. I could be a Leyton Orient fan! Poor devils, just one win under their belt (why did it have to be us?) and the chairman gives the manager until Christmas to sort it out. That was a week ago. Obviously Christmas comes early in the East and Mr Brush has been given the chop. I guess the O's will be looking for a new broom!

Life is not much better for Northampton supporters, who also have just one win under their belts (why did it have..., etc, etc). Having spent a rumoured £300,000 in the close season, I guess their board expected a better start. Exit the manager. Don't get any funny ideas, Mr Fry.

Tuesday 30 September is the anniversary of my being shown the door by my old employers. I can look back on a glorious year with no regrets at all. My redundancy was a mutually agreed thing. I got lots of money, and they got an empty desk. Perfect all round. Well, for me anyway. A few months later the employer had to take on two new members of staff (one to make the coffee and the other to wash up the mugs; I used to do both). The freedom that I have gained is the greatest benefit. I am now my own boss and choose what to do and when I do it. If I want to spend all day annoying people at Huish Park, then I can. If I want to write a book about my favourite football team, I have the time.

So, Boston at home, and, I hope, a happy anniversary. I love evening games. With the days shortening fast, the floodlights are switched on well before kick-off, bathing the whole ground and surrounding area in a magical, silvery light. Somehow, the stadium looks bigger, perhaps because of the huge shadows that rear up from the back of the stands, or perhaps because people simply look smaller in the dark. Except for those of us in hoops, that is. We all stand big and tall. Tonight, this includes Lin, who has finished the experiment with the Champions T-shirt. She accepts that the previous run of three defeats was not down to her hoops and can now wear them again without guilt. The line-up sees a start for Hugo Rodrigues; in for the injured Colin Pluck. Also sidelined is Saturday's man of the match, Nicky Crittenden. An ankle injury forces him to concede his place to Abdul El Kholti. 5,093 spectators, bar a handful of Boston fans, are dying to see Yeovil take the Pilgrims apart. It is obvious from the first few minutes that Boston are no Torquay. They do not have the speed, skill or physical presence that The Gulls brought with them. Thank God for that! Yeovil soon get on top and force Boston back in their own half for long periods. One delightful long-range lob from Kirk Jackson bounces off the cross-bar to safety with the keeper well beaten. It was one of those shots that brought me half way out of my seat in preparation of a major celebration, but then I sunk down again with a deep sigh. Minutes later, I'm up again when there is an obvious handball in the Boston penalty area.

The lad could have been playing basketball, so neat a pat down was it. I don't think the referee saw it, but, fortunately, we had one of the rare breed of linesmen who knows what he is meant to do with his flag. Gavin Williams strolled up and stuck the penalty away. Twenty-one minutes, 1-0. My heart is happy; I'm back on the statistics again. When we have gone one up we have won all our games. This football is such an easy sport. Go one up and win, go one down and lose. Simple.

Yeovil continue to dominate, Boston have little to offer up front, in midfield or from the away end. Very quiet all round. In the 38th minute Ronnie Bull puts in one of the best crosses of the night and it is met by a high-jumping Adam Lockwood. The ball sails majestically into the top left-hand corner, despite a valiant effort by the keeper. I'm ready for a romping win now; a cricket score is in prospect. If only Kevin Gall and Kirk can find their shooting boots.

Boston United are, of course, the club that made a mockery of the Conference two seasons ago. Financial irregularities caused them to be fined and docked four points from their first season in the Third Division. Their cheating denied Dagenham and Redbridge their rightful place in the Football League. Tonight was the first time that Boston have faced a team from that Conference farce. It was only right, therefore, that they should be reminded of their felony. Loud, healthy chants of "You only win when you're cheatin'" and "We should be playing the Daggers!" ring out from the Westland Stand. Unlike the F.A., we have long memories.

Unfortunately, the landslide of goals fails to materialise. Yeovil seem to lose their momentum in the second half and the whole game deteriorates into a scrappy affair. One brilliant opportunity presented itself when 'Garree' El Kholti whipped in an unplayable ball, parallel with the goal line. Well, it was unplayable for Kirk Jackson. I don't know if he was surprised or mesmerised that the ball was just waiting to be tapped in, but he failed to react and the chance was gone.

Other results have gone our way tonight, and we are in third place. Happy chatter accompanies us back to the car on the Houndstone Estate. It is a contented warble, coming from every direction. How different to that morose silence that follows a defeat.

CHAPTER 3

A SPOT OF BOTHER

O ctober is blowing in with news and gossip a-plenty. Gary Johnson is the Nationwide Manager of the Month for September. Was there anyone else in contention? Jake Edwards has signed a contract for the rest of the season. Now we want to see what he can do. To date, he has had the shortest of periods on the Park but he has shown some nice touches. If he gets a little longer on the pitch, we may have a new star on our hands (not that I'm trying to tell you how you should play him, Mr Manager of the Month). More good news is that Ronnie Bull, our Millwall loanee, is to stay with us for at least another month. News on the transfer of Paul Parry from Hereford seems to be dwindling. Despite a rumoured offer of £25,000 plus either El Kholti or Andy Lindegaard, silence seems to be the order of the day from the Welsh Borders. I have a sneaking suspicion that Hereford's owner/manager, Graham Turner, is wrestling with a personal problem over Yeovil snapping up his best players. Let's face it, Hereford is merely our feeder club these days. Time they admitted it, and let Parry have the chance of better football.

If ever I needed to be reminded that we still have a universe to cross to rule the football world, the lesson was delivered to me by a ten-year-old boy the other day. Now that I have all this leisure time I thought it might be nice to 'give something back to the community', so, for the past few months, I have been an unpaid teacher working with school parties visiting Montacute House. The National Trust property is used by the children to help them understand a little of Tudor history. I was explaining something about heraldry to a group of about eight primary school kids and, in an attempt to bring it up to date, I pointed at my Yeovil Town Independent Supporters' Association (Y.T.I.S.A.) black fleece, bearing the proud logo of Yeovil Town. One little lad looked carefully at the name and said, "Why don't you support a professional team?" I was so shocked that I could only lamely ask which team he supported. "My dad takes me to watch Premier matches," was his superior reply. He was right, of course. In the eyes of many impressionable kids it is only the Manchester Uniteds and Arsenals of this world who carry any clout. It is unlikely that Yeovil will ever achieve such status. We will never have half of Asia screaming our name as we do our pre-season tour. Our shirts may not be worn on the furthest flung atoll in the Pacific. We may not aspire to our own brand of beer selling in every downtown bar in the Philippines. Thank God for that. Give me my individual club, with our home-grown supporters, any time. And if I see that kid again, I'll give him a clip round the ear!

I have bought our passports to Whaddon Road, Cheltenham. It was very quiet down at the all-singing, all-confusing ticket office. The chap in front of me was enquiring about tickets for the next home game. He wanted one ticket for the Bartlett Stand for his missus to sit down, and one ticket for himself in the Westland Stand. Isn't that nice? A husband and wife enjoying a sporting event together.

I have indulged myself today, 1 October, by buying a copy of Jimmy Greaves' autobiography *Greavsie* from Ottakers bookshop. The best bit was getting it signed by the great man himself. As I approached the table at which he was sitting, he looked up and said, "I wondered when I'd see one of those" – referring to the fact that I was wearing a Yeovil Town fleece. We had a good old chat about the two occasions that he played against Yeovil at the old Huish ground. The first was in 1976, for Chelmsford City, and the season after for Barnet. He also remembered that Yeovil lost to both of them. I told him that he was the reason I started supporting Yeovil in 1976 when I turned up to watch him play. He was very pleasant, looked fit, and said he was pleased that Yeovil had started the season so well.

Saturday 4 October, and we take the relatively short run up the motorway to the delights of Gloucestershire. A pint in a pub, a short stroll through Pitville Park, lined with some beautiful Regency houses, and then into the community centre at the ground. It is full of Yeovil fans, of course, and we greet many of them, share a drink and cast an eye towards the TV. Arsenal are leading 2-1 at Anfield in the lunchtime game. All very pleasant.

Cheltenham have done no improvements to the away end since their impressive rise from the Conference a few seasons ago. Despite reaching the heady heights of the Second Division, the facilities for fans are distinctly non-League. I would rather watch from the terraces at Clevedon. Okay, I know I would need extremely good eyesight to see this game from Clevedon, but you know what I mean. Although we have given ourselves a good half-hour to find a reasonable spot, as is so often the case, Lin and I end up with a rusty old girder blocking off half the view of one of the goals. I reckon that, with a decent gust of wind, the flimsy little roof that is being held up by this obstruction would be off and away. There are about 1,500 of us squeezed in here, out of a crowd of just under 5,000.

Just as the referee is about to get the match underway, a group of about four or five men, in their thirties I should estimate, muscle their way on to the steps just behind us. The area was already full, and this move has the effect of virtually pinning the last row of fans against the back wall and totally blocking their view. Lin has been squeezed forward by the bulk of the one directly behind her, and she is looking at me with more than a little alarm. I manage to pull her further my way, so that this guy's belly can have the room that it obviously needs. They wear no identifiable Yeovil symbols, for which I am grateful, because as soon as they arrive the big, fat ugly one (and they all fitted that description) behind Lin, chanted, "There's a monkey at the back." My blood turned to ice as I realised I was in the company of a racist moron. I turned and looked at him, but I guess he only had eyes for the Cheltenham full back. Together they started to shout "F**k off, Cheltenham" and other equally pathetic rubbish. Here we were, trapped in this grotty concrete hellhole, with a bunch of Neanderthals. I had hardly registered that play was going on until I spotted the ball go past Roy O'Brien and Ronnie Bull without either of them making any obvious attempt to get to it, and a Cheltenham forward sprinting in behind and slamming it past Chris Weale. Four minutes gone, and it was not turning out to be a good day, on or of the field.

Minutes later the ball has come down to our end of the pitch and a cry has gone up for a handball in the penalty box, but this is waved away by the referee, and play continues. The idiot behind Lin launches himself forward down the terracing, pushing and scattering her and others. He is screaming a torrent of foul-mouthed abuse at the linesman. Lin cries out in surprise and protest, and I bellow in his face, but he is totally oblivious to everything and everybody. People around are obviously worried but dare not say or do anything because of the number of his friends. I look for a steward or police officer, but, don't you just know it, they are all grouped up by the corner flag. We did the easiest thing and moved well away. We had a worse view than before, but at least we could do what we had come to do, and watch the football. To be honest though, the fun of the afternoon had been spoilt. I think when you are young and single you can put up with most of this sort of boorish behaviour, although no one should ever put up with the racist taunts. When you are older and have your wife with you it is not possible to ignore it. We are broadminded (let's face it, we wouldn't be away supporters if we weren't), but sometimes...

Meanwhile, back at the football match, Yeovil go two down in 15 minutes. I couldn't really see what was happening at the far end of the pitch, but I spotted Wealey desperately clawing at the ball as it seemed to come off the inside of the post. We appear to be falling victim to Cheltenham's hoof-it-up-the-park tactics but, having said that, Yeovil start to come back into it with some nice work on the ground. That's the only way we will have a chance. Several corners come and go before Kevin Gall lashes the ball into the net and we are back in contention. The last 15 minutes have been all one-way traffic, so it bodes well for the second period.

I notice at half-time that the 'Gang of Five' have left the terracing and have moved on to create mayhem somewhere else. Lin and I return to our original place and receive numerous raised eyebrows and weak smiles from those who remained. It is difficult to deal with a problem element like this one; a fist in the face is the likely result for voicing too much protest. I'm not sure how it can be rooted out. In fairness, this is the first time that we have bumped into this sort of nonsense in many a long year. I think that more than 99 per cent of Yeovil fans are good, honest supporters, who do not show up their club. We just feel a bit gloomy at this point and even 'Whodney Robin', Cheltenham's mascot, and the curvy cheerleaders, do little to buck us up.

All I need to say about the second half is that it was poor. On 55 seconds Cheltenham hit us on the break as we push up, and a one-on-one ended with the ball being slipped through the legs of the keeper. 3-1 it becomes, and 3-1 it stays. Yeovil have offered very little in attack. Just when you were dying for someone to have a poke, the result seemed to be a little sideways pass to someone else.

As we journeyed home Lin and I discussed the day. It was a black spot in our otherwise enjoyable adventures following Yeovil Town. She was obviously upset and shaken by the shove in the back and she is telling me that she doesn't want to travel away anymore. I can fully understand how she feels but, hopefully, with a bit of time, she will come round. I will travel with the others on the Independents' coach, but I shall miss her company very much. I shall also keep an eye out for that miserable sod and, if I get the chance to shop him, I will.

Gary Johnson talks about lack of consistency with some of the players and I think he's got it about right. We seem to be blowing hot and cold at the moment, which is a bit difficult to handle. Talking of consistency, you have to hand it to the linesman who, on four or five occasions, flagged Kevin Gall offside. When questioned about a few of his decisions afterwards, he admitted that he hadn't been too sure about them because the sun was shining in his eyes! It is real quality in the Third Division.

It is Tuesday night, 6 October. You can't have forgotten the Somerset Premier Cup First Round against Bristol City. Despite a day of slaving away at Bristol Crown Court, I suggest to Lin that she might like a breath of fresh air this evening and accompany me to the delights of the Main Stand, HP. To my surprise, she says she will. What can I say about the event? For some reason the stand lights were left on for the whole of the match. It annoys me when the lights are left on for a few minutes after play has got underway, but when they stay on continuously it is a real pain. We had a cup of Bovril at half-time to keep out the chill of what was turning out to be not just fresh air but freezing cold stuff. We left at full-time and drove back home. Those were the highlights, anyway. On the pitch, a couple of teams, one in green and one in red, played out a boring, training-type game, which Bristol City won 3-2. No excitement of a final against Taunton at the Hand Stadium, Clevedon, for us then. Still, we can't have everything.

Lin has the next week off, so we had been discussing what to do and where to go. We started by pouring over the travel brochures and checking out the cards in the window of the agents for late deals. I had resigned myself to missing out Oxford away, Bournemouth in the LDV Trophy and Darlington at home. Quite a sacrifice. In the end, though, we whittled it down to either a break in Paris or London, and that was no contest, really – it had to be London. We have been to Paris before and never quite experienced the romance that some say is to be found in that city. Lin is a south London girl by birth and it might seem a little strange to go there for a holiday. It is often the way, though, that when you are born and brought up in a place, you overlook the treasures that are all around. Things are taken for granted and almost ignored. It is a bit like at home. Somerset is full of wonderful places to see, but somehow we rarely visit them, with the exception of Huish Park, of course, which is now the Mecca of the West.

Bright and early on a glorious sunny Saturday morning we catch the train from Yeovil Junction to the capital. We have pushed the boat out and decided to stay at a swanky hotel in Kensington. Culture, West End theatre and top nosh is the plan for the next four days. I'm wearing my Y.T.I.S.A. fleece, though, just in case I meet a like-minded football enthusiast.

It is 11 October, and the Glovers are away to Oxford United. They have conceded very few goals at home, and so I am hoping that we can put one away early and do a similar job to that done at Donny and Mansfield. I'm not sure what is going on with Kevin Gall at the moment. He has been called up for the Welsh side again, and I presume that he played last night, but, barring injury, he is likely to play again this afternoon. I know that he can run and run, but how can you give everything twice in less than 24 hours?

Some 1,300 fans are due to make the trip to Kassam Stadium to give us a fighting chance and, fortunately for me, one of them, John Jeanes, is going to keep in mobile phone link with me as the game progresses. We dumped our cases at the hotel and made for the Victoria and Albert Museum. Now that the admission charges have been swept away it is a great place to visit. Miles of marble corridors link hundreds of rooms packed with fascinating objects. Although the place is full of tourists, it gives off an air of tranquillity. People seem to talk in hushed tones as they view one marvel after another, treading softly from room to room so as not to disturb each other. At precisely 3.15pm, as I am studying an exquisite oil painting of Elizabeth I, my mobile trills out the theme tune to *The Great Escape*. I put the phone to my ear and receive a cacophony of sound from chanting Yeovil supporters. JJ is doing his best to shout over them. I, in turn, begin to shout back. Lin is glaring at me as dozens of faces turn away from the Tudor monarch and focus on me. "One-nil down from a free-kick." If I was rude in my response, I apologise to the Japanese, French and whoever else was there. Still, a bit of old Anglo-Saxon wouldn't do them any harm.

JJ gives me a half-time round-up, which doesn't fill me with much hope for the second half. He says that we were poor throughout the first, and Kevin Gall, as I suspected, is not galloping around at his usual pace. Still, there are 45 minutes to put all this right. Ten minutes later, Lin and I have gravitated to Victorian costumes. I'm staring at a mannequin dressed in a great frothy white dress trimmed in, yes, you guessed it, green. The phone goes and I know, even before I answer it, that the dress is a Yeovil omen and we have equalised. Give it to me, JJ. "Playing much better this half, but still don't look like scoring. I'll let you know if we do." Oh, right, thanks for that. The clock ticks round to a quarter to five and the phone stays as silent as the grave, or in our case, a first century BC Chinese cremation box. We've lost again. It's that first goal thing again. We just don't seem to be able to pull it back. Later, JJ tells me that we put in a good strong second half, but, even if we had played into the night, we wouldn't have scored. Hugo had a good game though. Let's be thankful for small mercies – or, in his case, bloody great big ones.

At breakfast next morning a commotion breaks out at the buffet bar as several youngsters mob a tall good-looking couple. I focused on the pretty girl and wondered if she was perhaps a pop singer or an actress. I hadn't really bothered with her companion in his hooped shirt. After all, it wasn't green and white, so I wouldn't be interested. A Dutch family at the next table got very excited when one of their sons came back with a napkin with the autograph 'Rivaldo' across it. I'm still not sure who he plays for. After all, these Brazilians are two-a-penny. I wonder if Gary Johnson would have wanted me to get his signature.

By Tuesday we have done just about all things we had planned. We saw the musical *Mamma Mia* at The Prince Edward theatre. It's amazing how those old Abba tunes get people singing and clapping. The Dress Circle resembled the Westland Stand by the end. Lin swears blind that she saw the Queen – no, not in the Dress Circle singing *Waterloo*, but being driven in a Range Rover flanked by two big black cars turning off just before Harrods. I missed that, but I did see Tani Grey, the Olympic athlete, in the hotel foyer. We ate fancy fruit tarts in an Italian patisserie, we hopped on and off the buses and tubes, peered in the gay bars in Soho and ventured into one or two of those comical sex shops. Well, you've got to, haven't you? We had a great time but, by Tuesday evening, my thoughts were turning to Huish Park and two empty seats in the Bartlett. I could almost hear the regulars asking each other where we were. My battery has gone down on the mobile, so I am out of touch with the situation. We have visited Lin's mum for the night, and there is no Sky TV or internet for me to check the score on. It's just like the old days, when all that could be relied upon was the next morning's newspaper. I was just going to have to wait. The reward, of course, was a 2-0 victory over Bournemouth, with Jake Edwards scoring his first senior goal for the Town and a penalty from Gavin Williams. The crowd of just over 5,000 was the largest gate for the whole of the Northern and Southern Section of the round. Yeah, that's my Yeo. Cup giants again. Just what we needed. Come on, Saturday. I want to be back at my favourite place. I want to see Yeovil thrash Darlington.

Ronnie Bull has returned to Millwall with his knee injury. I guess that makes sense – there is no point in keeping the guy down in Yeovil and paying his wages, only to see him hobble around until his loan period expires.

The draw for the Second Round of the LDV Trophy gives us another home tie, this time against Colchester. Oh, happy memories of the last time we met them. It was in the F.A. Cup, and we won 5-1 – one of my all-time greats. Let's hope we can get close to a repeat. The tie is to be played the week commencing 3 November, and then, on 8 November, we've got the First Round of the real, all-singing all-dancing, cup competition. We will know who we have drawn come next Saturday afternoon, but meanwhile we have a league tussle with the Quakers to deal with. This is what I love about football. We have two consecutive defeats in the league but, come the next Saturday, that spring and bounce come leaping back. I feel like the Mr Wobbly toy. As soon as you knock him down, boing, up he jumps. The optimism just oozes from me; I feel so up for this one. If the team feel half the enthusiasm then we could get into double figures. Preparations for the day go well. Coffee and a cuddle turn into a long lie-in. Well, let's face it, I don't have to observe any rules about abstinence on the morning of a match. Later, I return to the scene of my recent accident, the bathroom, and manage to fit a new set of lights without mishap. It has got to be my day if I can manage that. A light lunch is taken to ensure maximum lift from the seat when the goals go in. After all, I am forecasting a hatful and I want to be able to jump in a delirious state after each.

Here we are then Saturday 18 October. We stop to buy the latest *On To Victory* fanzine, which contains an article about kicking racism out of the game. I hope the slob we met the other week has learnt to read in the interim and can perhaps comprehend the points made. Fat chance.

Darlo have brought two coach-loads of fans with them from the wilds of the north-east. You have to salute them coming such a long distance, especially with the internal strife that they are having at the moment. It seems that their chairman has taken against a lad who ran a fans' internet site, and has barred him from all home games. This, in turn, has caused protests from other suppporters. It is sad that a guy who loves his club so much that he is prepared to give masses of his time and efforts in establishing a forum for other fans, should be hounded out by someone who seems incapable of accepting a little criticism.

Darlington could have run out in clowns' outfits and nobody would have turned a hair. Their performance, especially in the first 20 minutes, was hilarious. Why have one defender jump for a high ball when two crashing into each other would be much funnier? What a hoot to put your own keeper under tremendous pressure with hard and high back passes, one of which he had to deal with like a seal balancing a beach ball on its nose. And did I laugh when, on four minutes, one of them wanted to play beach volleyball. Unfortunately for him, he was standing in the penalty box at the time. Thank you very much said Gavin Williams as he slotted the penalty away for a 1-0 lead. If we can keep scoring at this rate, we should run in 22 goals by a quarter to five. Yeovil, though, have other ideas. They obviously decide that such a one-sided affair would be too boring for the supporters and they gradually come down to the comical level of the visitors. By half-time I think we must have had ten corners with which we did nothing, one jinking run from Kevin Gall, which ended with him flashing his shot wide, and some huffing and puffing from Jake Edwards, who made his first League start. Darlington just contributed the jokes.

Second half and Yeovil have settled into the knockabout routine and are trading custard pies with the best of them. As the half drags on and Jake Edwards misses the easiest tap-in ever offered, Darlington begin to realise that they are not going to be thrashed and, if they could just remember the purpose of the long drive down, they might be in line for a point. I hate to say this, but Yeovil really began to sag and buckle. Now we have two players leaping for the same ball with potentially disastrous consequences. For the last 20 minutes we are all over the place and, if it wasn't for the likes of Colin Pluck and Darren Way, it could have been curtains. Having said that, I think the statistics will confirm that Darlington failed to get a single shot on target all afternoon. They finish this evening in twentieth position, while, with the three points eventually safely in the bag, we are in a pleasant sixth. Some games are going to be like that. Football? What football? But THREE BLOODY MARVELLOUS POINTS.

As we leave the ground my thoughts are already turning to Tuesday evening. We host Huddersfield Town. What can you say? This is why we have been looking forward so much to joining the League.Huddersfield have been one the country's giants – champions of the whole pyramid of football on three occasions and, here we are, on the same stage. Rise to the occasion, Yeovil.

You would think, from hearing the post-match comments of the two managers, that Gary Johnson had been on the losing side. Darlo's gaffer praised his team for their commitment and hard work and felt they deserved something out of the game. All I can say is that he has very low expectations this season. Gary, on the other hand, was not happy with Town's efforts. He said that "sometimes you may get half a dozen players who are not completely on song, but you seldom get the whole lot who are having an off day. But we've got a 1-0 and no one will remember how we played at the end of the season." Not unless they read this book!

Spooky or what? Another team played, and another manager departs. This time it is Bobby Gould of Cheltenham. I did worry for him when I saw him at Whaddon Road. Even with his side winning, he had the appearance of a demented chicken. Up and down the touchline, shouting, complaining – the whole 'I'm a stressed out manager' thing. Put your feet up for a while, Bobby, calm down, start a llama farm, anything – but don't go and muck up anyone else's football club. Another casualty at management level is Ian Britton of Kidderminster. His board of directors couldn't even wait for us to play them. Ah, well, it will give us the chance to see that nice Jan Molby back in action in the dug-out.

They say a week is a long time in politics but that is as nothing compared to the ups and downs of a football team. Here we are on Tuesday night, 21 October, and my spirits are soaring as we approach Huish Park. The temperature is dropping fast, the light has gone and winter football is with us. We snuggle into our seats – I say snuggle, because several people seem to be contesting the same seat numbers and we are all squeezed up in a huddle. Eventually, the difference between seats 15 and 18 dawns on one of the parties and some semblance of order is restored. Steam from hot coffee is drifting about from many sources in the stand. It is like being in one of those national parks in America, where they have hot mud pools that give off little puffs of sulphur. Not that I'm saying that HP coffee smells of anything other than the real thing. Someone nearby has bought chips. Even though I've just eaten, my taste buds are crying out for a sliced King Edward with ketchup. This cold weather certainly gives me an appetite.

Huddersfield have brought a couple of hundred fans for the occasion, one completely bare-chested. Their team wear an unusual strip for a night game – virtually all black, with just one white sleeve. Interesting. The officials change into canary yellow. It makes it easier for us to give them the bird. However, it is Terry Skiverton who does the flying as he soars through the air to meet a perfect free-kick into the box. Three minutes gone and we are up and running. The guy next to me, who, until now, has sat nursing his empty paper cup with a face that accuses the world of stealing the contents, becomes almost animated. I don't know if it is my influence as I bounce up and down howling like a banshee, but I could have sworn that he clapped. Modestly, of course. That has got to rate as goal of the season so far. Nice to have you back, Terry.

Huddersfield are a different kettle of fish to Darlington. Fast, inventive, determined. Yeovil have to be really on top of their game tonight to pull this one off. On the way in, Lin asked if I would be happy with a draw tonight. I would never like to settle for a draw, but I hesitate before replying that I would give an answer in an hour's time. We haven't had a draw yet and, while I would prefer it if we drew away, it wouldn't be the end of the world if it came this evening.

Suddenly it looks as if the referee is doing his damnedest to help Huddersfield get that result. Hugo Rodrigues makes an inch-perfect tackle just outside the penalty box, foot to the ball first and into touch, and the official gives a free-kick. The wall lines up – one of those small walls you don't need planning permission for, containing Darren Way and Lee Johnson. The ball is pushed to the right and belted past Chris Weale. I'm not sure if it took a slight deflection or not, but I was a little surprised to see it beat him. A loud drum beats from the away end and the Yorkshire Tykes are bellowing into the night air. They sense that something might be on here. The game swings from one end of the pitch to the other. Yeovil put together some great moves, but the strikers are not putting the chances away. On one occasion, Kevin Gall races through the defence but shoots too early and strikes the advancing keeper. Surely, with his pace, he should try and take it round the keeper. Chances are that he will succeed or be brought down in the attempt. At the other end, Weale makes a brilliant close-range stop that is hacked away by Skivo for a corner.

The second half begins as the first finished. Both teams are committed to attack, both believing that the game is there to be won. Lee Johnson thinks so, as he meets a cross from the right and heads it past the disbelieving keeper. I'm not surprised he was disbelieving. When was the last time Lee scored with his head? Normally the ball tends to bounce over him. He is ecstatic as he poses in front of a boiling Westland Stand crowd. "Two-one to the Yeovil" booms out the message to the away supporters. Their drum has perhaps developed a fault, because I can't hear it any more. The quality of the football continues to be first rate as both teams power on, Yeovil trying to extend their lead and Huddersfield giving everything to level. Kirk Jackson replaces Jake Edwards, who has had an anonymous game. Terry Skiverton takes a knock and hobbles off to the applause of the faithful. Paul Terry slots into the back four. Jacko has the chance of the night when he bursts through a Huddersfield defence that has had to push far up the field. He gallops on and on with just the keeper to beat. Unfortunately, he has been watching Kevin Gall and adopts the same manoeuvre with the same result. The keeper spreads himself, and the shot strikes him firmly in the body. A collective groan is emitted. Still, the chances are being made and Yeovil see out the nail-biting remainder of the game playing attractive, slick football. What a cheer greets the referee's whistle. I hold my scarf aloft and salute a bunch of very happy players and one contented manager.

Perceptions of a game vary so much. It obviously depends firstly if you've won or lost. Lin and I chat about it being a fantastic game with two good football-playing sides, as we sup a pint in the tent (Captain Scott couldn't have felt much colder in his Antarctic equivalent). Next to us were a group of Huddersfield lads, bemoaning what they deemed to be their "chuffing bloody useless lot. Forty bloody years supporting this lot. Still we're gonna drink more than you tonight." I'll happily allow them that pleasure. We watch the evening scores come up on the TV, and note that leaders Hull are held to a draw and second-placed Swansea suffer a home defeat. Oxford also draw, but Doncaster Rovers win again, and are up into third place ,with us one point behind in fifth. One of the Huddersfield lads phones a Donny friend and, after a short conversation, he offers me the phone. The first thing the Donny lad says is what a difference M.M. the 'Scottish Player' has made. I ask him if he scored this evening and was pleased when he said no. He is obviously the best thing since sliced bread up there.

Gary Johnson is naturally very pleased with the team's performance. He acknowledged that Huddersfield were possibly the biggest club we had played in the league, with some very expensive and experienced players in their squad, and we did very well to come out on top. He made me laugh when commenting on his son Lee's goal: "He only scores with his head in the garden." You can see it, can't you, complete with mini goal-posts.

I had to pop down to the club to pick up a ticket for Meet the Manager night next week, and pay my next contribution to the Glovers Gold Bond scheme. I usually wait for someone from the club to call at my house before I part with the monthly instalment, but as I had received a winning cheque for £10 this week, I felt the least I could do was pay on time. I just happened to wander down to the players' entrance as I was there and bumped into Chris Weale. We had a chat about the Huddersfield goal and he confirmed that it had taken a slight deflection off Terry Skiverton. Wealey was disappointed to have let it in, and felt that he should have done a little better. Still, we were both delighted with the win. Next, I saw Hugo Rodrigues in the corridor. Well, it was hard to miss him. We nattered on about the game and his contribution for quite a while. He, not unnaturally, was unaware of the historical size of our last opponents. When I pointed out that they had won the First Division Championship three years running, albeit a few years ago now, he was very surprised. Is that the same as the Premiership now?" he asked. I likened them to Manchester United, and he was amazed. Perhaps it is just as well he didn't know before the game. He might have been overawed.

What I like about G.J. is that he will always find time to have a chat. I stuck my head round his office door and he greeted me like an old friend. We discussed the contrast between the Darlo and Huddersfield games, and other topics. I suggested that there should be extra one-on-one with the keeper training for Kev Gall and Jacko. No, I didn't really. I might have been out of that door on my arse if I had.

Things have gone well this week. Not only three lovely points, but Mike the plumber has been and installed our new bathroom suite. Well, almost. The only thing that is missing is the toilet cistern handle. I returned to the DIY store to remonstrate with them and I was informed that I had not ordered one. It comes as a separate item from the rest of the toilet. Silly me, I should have known that. Not everybody would want to have a handle, would they? Far better to keep taking the lid off the cistern and pulling the plunger up with your fingers. Still the missing item is on its way – from Northampton, or Northumberland, or somewhere!

Am I stupid? Some few months ago I had a phone call from the National

Trust at Montacute House. They were planning a volunteers' recruitment day and asked if I would be prepared to help out and show a group how we teach the Tudor history to the children. I was quite surprised and flattered that they should ask me, as I have only been doing this sort of work for a short while. The date suggested was so far off that I failed to check either my diary or the fixture list. And here we are, Saturday 25 October. Yeovil are playing away to crowds at Cambridge, and I am playing to an audience at Montacute. I just hope my involvement only runs to a morning session. I may be able to salvage something from the day by listening to the live commentary on Somerset Sound.

I'm in luck. Released from my duties at the house, I am comfortably seated on the new toilet seat in the bathroom, radio on, waiting for the match to begin. I can't just sit in an armchair and calmly listen to a match (the nerves are too great for that). I have to have something to do, so I'm in the bathroom tiling and grouting, stopping dead every now and again as the action builds to some exciting point. And boy, does it build.

Gary Johnson is returning to one of his old clubs. He had considerable success with Cambridge United and, by the generous applause that the fans at the Abbey Stadium give him before kick-off, they have a soft spot for him still. I am sure we will be the same if, say in a few years' time, Sir Gary is invited by the Russian oil billionaire to manage Chelsea (after all, only the best will do) and he were to return to Huish Park in the F.A.Cup. We would give him a huge ovation and then, hopefully, go on to knock his team out of the competition.

Yeovil start like a rocket, ripping straight into a Cambridge side that seem to be coming into form, having won away at Bristol Rovers last Saturday. From the off, the pace of Kevin Gall and the intelligent play of Jake Edwards is causing all sorts of problems at the back, and the 500-plus Town fans can be heard loud and clear over the radio, backing the boys. On 16 minutes Gally supplies a cutting through ball with the precision of a surgeon's knife and Jake is in acres of space, with only the keeper to beat. The radio commentary seems to go into slow motion as Edwards approaches. I hear the roar first before the commentator confirms that he has coolly slotted the ball into the net. Jake's first League goal for Yeovil. Fantastic! I knew he was worth persevering with. Perhaps this will unlock the floodgates and he will become a star.

Stung into action, Cambridge come back into the game and pressure the Yeovil goal. Skivo, Hugo, Locky and Colin Pluck all seem to be playing well this afternoon, protecting Chris Weale's goal from any serious attempts. The name Kitson crops up more than a little, but he is Cambridge's leading scorer this season with seven goals, so he is bound to be a danger

Half-time approaches and the border tiles are complete around the bath.

Things are looking good at home and away. On 44 minutes, Terry Skiverton and Hugo Rodrigues both step up and allow Kitson to slip between them and give Wealey no chance as he hits his eighth. In sympathy, a tile springs away from the wall and slides into the bath.

Half-time, then, it is 1-1. The statistic that has followed us all season comes back to my mind. We have scored first in all of our nine League victories and conceded the first goal in all of our six defeats. As we don't do draws, it is obvious that we are going to go on and win the game in the second half. No problem. And so the prophecy was fulfilled. On 59 minutes Edwards doubles his League tally with another one-on-one with the keeper. Two minutes later and it is 'anything you can do' as Kevin Gall slams home number three. Yeeeess! The fans can be heard singing their hearts out as Yeovil rampage across the pitch. I'm singing at the top of my voice. Not a pretty sound, I will admit, even in the acoustically-tiled bathroom, but I don't care. "WE LOVE YOU YEOVIL, WE LOVE THE GREEN AND WHITES..."

Tiling finished, I unplug the radio and run down the stairs and plug it in again, so that I can watch all the scores and goal flashes on TV. Just as I do, Darren Way grabs a piece of the action and smashes in the final nail in Cambridge's coffin. DARREN WAY, WAY, WAY. 4-1 to the mighty Yeo. What a brilliant afternoon. Thanks, lads.

It's all go today. Having just caught my breath from the wonderful win, it is now time to watch those black balls slip from the velvet bag into the plastic bowl – F.A.Cup First-Round draw is with us again. We don't have too long to wait. Mark Lawrenson dips in to pull the home ball, Yeovil Town, and the away ball is... Wrexham. This could be some clash. Huish Park should be full to capacity. With our other Cup game against Colchester in the same week, this is good practice for when we make the Second Division!

The strange thing about moving up from the Conference is the lack of live-TV coverage from Huish Park. By this stage of the season we would normally have featured on Sky, but this year, nothing. All is put right, however, by our high-profile Cup draw with the Welsh side. Sky are going to cover our game for the live evening kick-off at 5.35pm. £50,000 will go into the club's coffers.

Following the F.A.'s well-advertised intentions of getting tough with those who bring the game into disrepute, a mere 14 months have skipped by and they have brought Graham Westley, former manager of Farnborough Town, to book for his disgraceful performance at our temporary home at The Avenue, Dorchester, last season. If you recall, he had to be carried out of the ground by stewards following a particularly petulant display. Had Arsene Wenger or Alex Ferguson behaved in such a way, the nation would have been near to meltdown.

However, the F.A. have come down on Mr W. like a ton of bricks – a reprimand and a £500 fine. That's telling him.

The curse of Yeovil has struck again on the manager front. This time it is David Moss of Macclesfield. Watch out for the gaffers of Torquay, Oxford, and, especially, Darlington. I had to chuckle when I read that Max Griggs, chairman of Rushden & Diamonds, has decided that enough is enough. Having taken The Annies to the Second Division he obviously feels that, with gates of only 4,000, he can go no further. I believe that he is willing to give away the football club, but will be selling the stadium and all of the other facilities. Does this mean the decline of the moneybags?

When I took voluntary redundancy and early retirement last year, I told myself that this was merely a change in career direction. I had no intention of vegetating. After all, the thought of me lounging around at home would be more than Lin could bear, and a list of chores as long as your arm would soon have appeared. No, I wanted to balance my free time with a little part-time work. At first, the free time was overwhelming and very little work came my way. I didn't exactly panic, but I had a few doubts about whether I had made the right move. Here I am, one year on, and that little bit of part-time work has swamped the free time. I have spent the whole of this week perched on what must rank as the most uncomfortable seating in the south-west, as a trial has unfolded at the Crown Court. My backside has screamed out for relief as hour after hour has passed by. The upshot of this is that I cannot face sitting down for several hours and driving to Bury on Saturday. As much as I would love to be there, just click my fingers and be at the ground is the only way I could contemplate travelling. So once again I shall be at the tender mercies of Somerset Sound.

I did manage to ease my aching rear into a vice president's chair on Wednesday evening for the 'Meet the Manager' session. Held in the VPs' lounge rather than the advertised marquee, it was certainly comfortable for those who could get in. The first floor at HP is not user-friendly for the disabled, and at least one fan was unable to gain access with his wheelchair. Not unnaturally, this caused more than a little upset and annoyance. It was all the more ironic given the fact that the entrance fee for the evening was to be donated to the disabled supporters' group.

Gary Johnson and his compere, Geoff Twentyman, from Radio Bristol, gave a smooth performance in front of 100 or so 'friends'. There were no nasty or aggressive questions about his team-handling. Most of us would be hard pressed to think of any at the present time. G.J. was quite candid with many of his replies, and gave many there an insight into his football philosophies. He often said "this is off the record" or "just between us" and I believe that he had sufficient trust in those present to expect those comments to remain between the four walls of HP. What he did say for public consumption was that he was very pleased to have Steve Collis as second keeper at the club, for he thought it only a matter of time before Chris Weale was making great saves in the Premiership. A question about the need to fill the void left by the 'Scottish Player' produced the response that he would bide his time. He reiterated what he had told me at Doncaster, that it was important not only to get in a player who was good at his game, but also a person who had the personality and character to blend with the rest of the squad. Having said that, he was able to confirm that Lee Elam, who presently plays for Halifax, but would be better known to Yeovil fans as a thorn in our flesh whilst playing for Southport, was on trial for a couple of days. Later in the week it was confirmed that he would be with us on a month's loan. Gary said that he wanted to have a long look at him, and the loan suits both parties. Fingers crossed that this winger, who can play on either side, is the answer to the minor problem we have had.

Comfortingly, Gary also informed his idolising audience that "Everything I want is here right now at this football club". Long may that continue. He did add, though, that if Tottenham Hotspur made an inquiry...

CHAPTER 4

'TIL HULL FREEZES OVER...

I t is Saturday 1 November, it is three in the afternoon, and once again I find myself far from the action. My passion is as great as ever, and my heart is with the lads at Gigg Lane, but somehow I can't face those long motorway journeys week in, week out, especially now that Lin has been turned off the idea. I have, however, set my sights on a trip to Hull City later this month and perhaps that will revitalise me. Someone, during the summer break, accused me of being seriously obsessive about Yeovil Town. I laughed it off, but, when a totally independent source said something similar, I did sit back and wonder if it was true. Is it obsessive to be totally committed to a cause? To spend an extraordinary amount of time travelling to witness 90 minutes of pleasure (or pain)? To desire success with a vengeance? The need to know all the daily ins and outs of a favourite pastime? Yes, it probably is, and I probably am. But perhaps I have unconsciously taken on board what I took to be criticism and have pulled back a little. That is why I find myself once again in my bathroom, boxing in the pipework, rather than standing on the terraces.

Last Saturday the commentary from Cambridge was not only upbeat about the skills, flair and teamwork of Yeovil, but also singularly silent in major mention of the referee. Quietly doing a good job throughout the game, he needed no mention. How different this afternoon. It sounds to me as if the man in black is centre stage for most of the proceedings. Right from the off Mr Jones stamps his authority on the game. Three bookings in no time at all, for what the commentator says required just a quiet word with each offender. He's obviously going to be a pain in the neck.

Listening to the match on the radio requires quite a bit of visual imagination.

Not knowing what the configuration of the stadium looks like, I have to construct my own terracing and seating and place the Yeovil fans behind one of my goals. The commentator helpfully says that Yeovil are playing left to right. Now is that left to right from the bath to the wash basin or from the radiator to the linen basket? "The grass has been left long," he proclaims. A vision of Darren Way's blond mop just poking out from the top of the lush greensward pops into mind. A mental lawnmower has to be employed to return the pitch to a reasonable state. "Yeovil are playing in their familiar green-and-white stripes." I beg your pardon. Stripes? Shirts from the past swim in front of my now befuddled mind. He obviously doesn't know his hoops from his stripes. This is all hard work. There's hardly time to concentrate on the actual football.

Having said that, though, according to our lad at the scene the football is not of the highest quality. Scrappy is the word that he and his co-accused, sorry commentator, use over and over again. Yeovil have been forced to make several changes for the game. Paul Terry and Stephen Reed come in for injured Terry Skiverton (dead leg in training) and suspended Hugo Rodrigues. Young Reedy, at 18 years old, makes his League debut and immediately seems to settle in. I've said it before (but I'll say it again): I think this boy has got what it takes to make it all the way in the game. Not only does he have natural talent, self-confidence and the right psyche, but I think he has that other necessary ingredient to go far – a footballing brain. Good luck, Stephen.

The referee is obviously not as impressed as I am and books him quite early on for an innocuous challenge, probably more youthful exuberance than anything else. Still, that is what we've got to put up with today. It is also unfortunate that Gavin Williams is forced to retire hurt, also with a dead leg, after only ten minutes and is replaced by Lee Elam. Didn't take him long to break into the team.

Three big defenders ensure that Bury keep the forward line at bay and most of the play seems to ping-pong about in the central third of the pitch. Bury don't appear to have a lot of skill and appear to be content just to keep Yeovil out. The break comes on 31 minutes when Jake Edwards has a strike on goal and the ball deflects off a 'Shaker' into the net. I do a whoop and a war dance and then settle down to listen to Yeovil romp all over them. The second goal comes shortly afterwards when, in a defensive clearance, the ball is belted up the backside of a fellow defender and the forward nips in and says thank you very much. It would have been bloody funny if it hadn't been a Bury goal. 1-1 at half-time. But again we've scored the first goal, so we will surely win.

More scrappy stuff, in fact even scrappier I'm told, in the second half. Kevin Gall has a golden opportunity with a one-on-one but fires from 25 yards out and misses the target. The referee decides that Steven Reed's tackling is so ferocious that he has to hand out a second yellow card and makes the lad trudge off the field. I slump down on the toilet seat and groan. Incidentally, on Wednesday night Gary Johnson had commented on our good disciplinary record and the fact that we had not picked up any red cards this season. I feel so sorry for Reed; I just hope it doesn't knock his confidence. Bury scent blood, and throw everything into the final few minutes. Finally, up pops the lad who Reedy would have been marking at the back post and heads past Chris Weale. Little time remains and Yeovil don't get another sniff. Beaten by a sucker punch. I switch the radio off quickly. I'm not into post-match analysis at the moment, thank you. I immerse myself in my DIY. The boxing of the pipes is coming along very nicely, the grain of the wood is most attractive and the brass screws look most fetching. Bugger, bugger, bugger. I feel sorry for the 449 Glovers' fans who now have to make the long trip back home. Still, we only slip to sixth in the table, although I notice with a little distaste that Doncaster Rovers have won 1-0 against Torquay and move up to second behind Hull, with only one point separating them. And I've still not received the toilet cistern handle. What a shitty day!

Gary Johnson was bitterly disappointed when I met him on Tuesday morning. I went to watch the lads training on the top pitch and, to keep out the cold wind, I slipped into one of those perspex dug-outs that they have now got up there. Gary came and had a chat whilst he kept a beady eye on two French lads who were being given a trial. He used the words 'robbed' and 'violated' in describing how Bury snatched the points from us. I don't think he was too impressed by the lads from La Belle France either. I doubt that we shall see them sporting les hoops.

We can take a breather this week from the hurly-burly of League football and enjoy the delights of the LDV Trophy followed by the F.A.Cup. Two Second Divison teams in one week. This will certainly be some sort of test to see how far our boys have come, although it is difficult in a one-off to gauge the ability of a team against higher division opponents. When we last met Colchester, our Tuesday-night opponents in the LDV, we thrashed them five-one in the F.A.Cup. Our team on the day was magnificent but there is little doubt that they would have been slaughtered week in week out in the Second Division. Still, it's all good fun and we shall see how it goes.

Our first test then tonight, Tuesday 4 November, against the bright orange shirts of Colchester United. I counted 26 fans on the away end and 11 flags. Not a bad ratio. I think others must have been sitting in the stand, because they had two coaches parked out the back. It has been a wet day, but now, in the mild night air, Huish Park seems to be misty and muggy, and the playing surface, damp and fast. Just over 3,000 punters have got excited enough over this fixture to attend. I guess with two all-paying games in a week, there is a considerable outlay for many people and a lot of prioritising to do. LDV versus FA. It has to be the world's oldest and favourite cup that will win out.

Both Skivo and Gavin Williams are back, having fully recovered from their dead legs. Nick Crittenden is also back from his ankle injury and starts in place of El Kholti. Throughout the years, Yeovil Town have never been respectors of higher league opposition and tonight is no different. From the first whistle it is Yeovil, Yeovil, Yeovil. They immediately get into their stride and produce some great one-touch passing that dissects the Colchester defence and leads to some good efforts on goal. Jake Edwards and Kevin Gall have begun to work well together, and it is no surprise that, in the eleventh minute, Edwards finds himself with some room in the penalty box and lashes the ball into the net. Yeovil do not sit back on this early lead. Well, let's face it, that's just not their style. Attack, attack, attack. They stream forward time and time again and only some heroic efforts by United's keeper keep the score to one. Some of our football is scintillating and I am on my feet again when Kevin Gall chips the keeper from 25 yards. I am sure that it is goal-bound but fall back in my seat as the ball skims just over the bar.

Then all the good work is undone in one moment's madness. A long ball bounces up near Town's penalty box and Terry Skiverton, with the Colchester number eight, Andrews, inches behind him, goes to head back to Chris Weale. The whole scene seems to take on a slow-motion effect. The header from Skivo has little weight to it and Andrews skips past the captain and gives Wealy no chance as he races off his line. 1-1 and the half-time whistle blows, four minutes later. I can't believe that the two sides can be going down the tunnel all square. We had superiority in heaps and here we are on level terms. Sometimes there is no justice in football.

The second half is a little more even, but with the crowd singing "We're going to win five-one" (a reference to our previous meeting). I have confidence in abundance that we are going to get a good result. It's Kevin Gall, to whom I had spoken in the morning (and who, in my opinion, sounded a little short on confidence), who sets Huish Park alight. On 66 minutes a typical Gally run brings him one-on-one, and this time he makes no mistake, placing the ball away from the outstretched arm of the keeper into the far corner. He stands like a gladiator before the rampant fans on the Westland Stand, letting the adulation flood over him and allowing that confidence to soar once again. Right, we are back on track. Let's have another and finish this lot off. Jake Edwards comes off and Adam Stansfield is applauded all around the ground as he springs on to the park. Colin Pluck has also left the scene, limping slightly, and Stephen Reed gets his second game on the trot. As I expected, he slots straight into position and looks as if he's always been there.

Eleven minutes later and it is becoming 'be generous to Colchester night' as we give them another lifeline. A hopeful punt into the penalty box results in a defender and Chris Weale standing rooted to the spot and looking at each other while substitute McGleish gets up and nods it in the back of the net. This is getting silly! What's the point of playing all that good football, over-running the opposition, only to gift them two crazy goals?

Extra time it is. I am just hoping and praying that we can somehow get the 'silver goal' in the first 15 minutes and save ourselves the nerve-wracking experience of the penalty shoot-out. I don't normally bite my nails, but this evening I am making a right mess of them. No silver goal appears, and we play through the second period with huff and puff but little else. The boys look dead on their feet. They huddle together on the pitch as the referee and linesmen work out the details of the shoot-out. He seems to toss a coin several times to decide which end should be used. I don't know if the captains have demanded best out of three. The Westland End it is, and the cacophony of noise builds to fever pitch. I feel sick, Lin can hardly watch, faces everywhere are tense with nerves. Gavin Williams steps up to take the first ever penalty in a shoot-out at Huish Park. And there is man of the match Simon Brown to make a fine save. The pendulum has swung away from us. Colchester make no mistake with their first, sending Chris Weale the wrong way. Nicky Crittenden restores some hope by crashing the ball into the net for 1-1. United clinically put away their second and up steps Adam Lockwood. What's he going to do? My instinct tells me that a full back will usually smash the ball either straight in or high and wide. Adam takes the softly, softly approach and taps it to the keeper's right. He saves it only to be penalised for coming off his line. Next time Adam makes no mistake. Colchester make it 3-2 and hearts are sinking fast. Darren Way marches forward with a purpose but does not have a shot to match. Easily saved and United only need to score now to win. Chris Weale is beaten again and the whole thing flops into an anti-climax. The 20-odd fans at the away end naturally run around like headless chickens, while the rest of us stumble dejectedly from the terraces wondering how that one got away.

I'm not taking this defeat very well. I fume and cuss all the way back to the car, kicking piles of wet leaves in frustration. It is not the fact that we have lost, although I always hate that, but the way in which we have crashed out of a competition that we could have done very well in. So much effort, so much brilliant football, all lost in the space of two split seconds.

I can't say I feel much better in the morning. I had a miserable night's sleep. I must have replayed the game a dozen times and still we kept losing on those damn penalties. It's like having a hangover without the pleasure of the alcohol.

I read in the paper that Southend United have decided to part company with Steve Wignall, their manager for all of six months. Only two wins out of the last 12 games has convinced the chairman, Ron Martin, that he had to go. "I did not see the passion in his eyes," he laments. What will he see in the eyes of fourth-time caretaker-manager Dave Webb? I hope it's not a victory at Yeovil in a fortnight's time.

Come Wednesday evening, I have got over the blues of defeat and am now working myself up into a state over the forthcoming clash in the F.A. Cup with Wrexham. I note that they are playing this evening in their Second Round LDV Vans Trophy game at Stockport. I am hoping that they also get taken the distance and have to play out extra-time. There is no reason why they shouldn't be as knackered as our lads were 24 hours earlier. It might just give us an edge. Oh, the Cup, the Cup. I love it. My blood tingles at the thought of this great competition. David versus Goliath, with all the attendant giant-killing that goes on. I am pleased that we weren't drawn against some minnow and are risking being giant-killed ourselves.

Stockport do help us out a little bit by drawing 4-4 with Wrexham and taking it to a silver goal, which they scored in the first half of extra time. So the Welsh boyos had to run for an extra 15 minutes and then feel the disappointment of being beaten. Every little helps.

Saturday 8 November dawns grey and cool. It is going to be a long day, with the kick-off not until 5.35pm, and so a training schedule is arranged. Coffee (Yeovil mugs obviously), papers, lie-in. All rather essential today, following a night at Bridgwater Carnival. Three hours of standing pressed into a prickly hedge watching huge floats with some of the most energetic people imaginable, having my ears assaulted by the loudest of music and frozen to the bone. Still, Lin enjoyed it.

I'm keeping a special watch out for the Farnborough v Weston-super-Mare tussle this afternoon. W-s-M is the place of my birth, and I feel duty-bound to support them at this stage. If, of course, we meet them in Round Two, then all links are severed. Within five minutes of kick-off Billy Clark scores for Weston, and we are treated to a little-known fact by Geoff Stilling on Sky Sport that Weston have never lost in the cup to a team beginning with the letter F. TV is so educational these days.

It seems strange to be turning up at Huish Park at a time when we are all usually leaving the place. Instead of half-time scores being broadcast, it is the full-time results that are being cheered or groaned at. A big cheer for Scarborough, who have dumped Doncaster Rovers. A fair-size cheer for the demise of Hereford, and I detect a little cheer for Weston, who ran out 1-0 winners The Gas, the Gulls and Plymouth Argyle all flopped, leaving only Bristol City, Weston and Yeovil still in with a West Country interest.

Let those cameras roll! This is the first time the nation has had the opportunity of seeing the Yeovil All Stars perform on stage in hoops. Let's hope they are impressed. I can imagine the scene in bars and clubs across north Wales, where the Wrexham faithful must be gathered. I say they must be there, because there are so few of them congregated on the away end. A couple of hundred have ventured far from their mountains and valleys to enjoy live football. The rest are tucked up with a satellite dish and a sheep. Never mind, this is going to be our party anyway.

You can tell this is an important game for us because the Jolly Green Giant is wearing his new XXXXL hooped shirt, and very fetching it looks. Not only that, but we have revolving advertising boards! This is almost Champions League standard. I'm not sure if our boards are powered by electricity or a small child running on a treadmill, but I am impressed. Any more of this and we can expect to have hot meat pies available throughout the game. Silly me, I'm getting carried away now.

Paul Terry makes a start in place of Hugo Rodrigues. I understand that Hugo has been suffering from a cold, so is on the bench. Mary, one of our little clique in the Bartlett Stand, is offering to run across the pitch and rub his chest better. Hold her down, someone.

5,049 lucky souls settle down for the first-ever clash between the two clubs. The atmosphere has been ratcheted up from the normal League level, so much so that I can almost reach out and touch the expectancy and anticipation that we share. We all love this competition; after all, we are the famous, the famous Yeovil.

Wrexham, in all red, kick off towards their own supporters and in the first few minutes indicate that they are here to win, a good shot being desperately palmed away for a corner by Chris Weale. A Welsh dragon flag flaps in the stiffening breeze, and the boyos are getting excited by the prospect of the corner. This is easily dealt with and Yeovil stream down the pitch. Gavin Williams combines well with Kevin Gall and Jake Edwards, and opportunities open for the Town. Gally is flying tonight. I've never seen him run so fast. Defenders are being left for dead and those that get near him are fouling him. A great chance comes as Kevin breaks free on the right and slams in a cross for Jake Edwards. Only a heroic effort by the keeper, Andy Dibble, prevents his touch hitting the back of the net.

Yeovil have grabbed this early period of the game by the scruff of the neck. On 39 minutes Lee Johnson rips down the right and whips in an inch-perfect cross, which is met by 'Road Runner' Gall. Gally stands firm and heads the ball past the despairing Dibble. There is an eruption from the western end of Yeovil, which must have been felt down in the town centre. Bouncing, leaping, screaming, clapping, waving lunatics are everywhere. We are on our way. Wrexham snap back, but the 1-0 score holds at half-time. I fancy that the queue for the toilets is much longer than usual. Must be all the excitement. Still, it passes a quarter of an hour.

We have just sat down after clapping the lads back on the field for the second half when Nicky Crittenden loops in a beautiful ball, which Gavin Williams gratefully side-foots into the goal. Suddenly, Wrexham have no answers and Yeovil are turning it on with exhibition moves involving six or seven players. There has been some criticism lately that we do nothing with our corners. All that was put right on 59 minutes when a Lee Johnson kick flies towards the back post and Colin the 'Quiet Assassin' Pluck leaps high and powers the ball under the desperate Dibble. It's party time at Huish Park. "Oo-arr, it's a massacre" rings out from three sides and "Can we play you every week?" makes people chuckle. The trumpet boy, who is obviously seeking a musical audition thanks to Sky TV, is having a good game. I was a little disappointed with his performance on Tuesday against Colchester, but I reckon he has been training hard since

It gets better and better. On 66 minutes Darren Way, who has, as always, run his heart out, slips through the defence and squares a ball to Jake Edwards. Jake, an ex-Wrexham player, delights in slotting the ball past Dibble. Many of the Wrexham fans are now wishing they had stayed at home and begin to head for the exits. Being a friendly lot, we wave and sing "Cheerio, cheerio, cheeerio." As seems customary on these big F.A. Cup occasions we have to inquire if someone or other is watching. In 1993 it was Jimmy Hill as his Fulham were beaten. Often it is our old adversaries from Weymouth who we wish to witness our happiness. Tonight it could only be one person. Dumped from the competition by a non-League club, the chant goes out: "Are you watching, McIndoe?" I wonder if he was. I heard a rumour today that he may be going back to north of the border with a transfer to Hearts.

Having acknowledged his own song, G.J. takes off the three strikers, Gall, Edwards and Crittenden, and brings on Adam Stansfield, Kirk Jackson and Abdelhalim El Kholti. It's only fair that they should have a bit of fun, after all.

GREEN PARTY: The travelling faithful await the kick-off of Yeovil's first ever League match at Rochdale.

HISTORY BOOK: The line-ups printed in the programme from that opening match.

ROCHDALE A.F.C. V YEOVIL TOWN — MATCHDAY TEAMS
9TH AUGUST 2003

	ROCHDALE		YEOVIL TOWN
13	Matthew Gilks	1	Chris Weale
2	Wayne Evans	4	Adam Lockwood
3	Michael Simpkins	5	Colin Pluck
4	Sean McClare	6	Darren Way
6	Darryl Burgess	8	Lee Johnson
7	Leo Bertos	9	Kevin Gall
8	Chris Beech	10	Nick Crittenden
9	Chris Shuker	14	Roy O'Brien
17	Patrick McCourt	18	Kirk Jackson
26	Simon Grand	20	Gavin Williams
27	Paul Connor	23	Jamie Gosling
1	Neil Edwards	3	Abdul El Kholti
15	Robert Betts	4	Adam Stansfield
19	Kevin Townson	12	Hugo Rodrigues
5	Lee McEvilly	13	Steve Collis
10	Matthew Doughty	16	Andy Lindergaard

Referee: Mr MR Warren
Assistant Referee: Mr RJ Holdsworth
Assistant Referee: Mr M Matador
Fourth Official: Mr JD Stokes
www.rochdaleafc.co.uk

MAGIC MOMENT: *Kevin Gall turns to celebrate after scoring Yeovil's first League goal at Rochdale.*

LEE-WHIZZ: *Lee Johnson is mobbed after scoring goal number two. The first took 108 years to arrrive, the second just 29 more minutes.*

BACK TO FRONT: Defender Adam Lockwood moving forward at Rochdale.

AWAY DAY: You put your left leg in... training before the Doncaster game.

Gavin Williams in training. Lee Johnson (right) still looks unwell as he prepares to board the coach on the way to the game.

HUNGRY FOR SUCCESS: Skipper Terry Skiverton prepares to enjoy yet another meal before the match.

DRESSED FOR THE SEASIDE: That's Lin and me all set for the away game at Southend.

WAY AHEAD:
Darren Way
celebrates scoring
goal number four
in the victory at
Cambridge.

FRESH LEGS:
New signing Lee
Elam in action
against Bury.

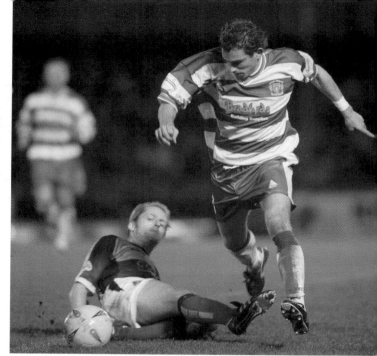

GAS LEAK: Nick Crittenden rounds a Bristol Rovers defender before scoring a wonder winner at the Memorial Ground.

NICK KNACK: Crittenden is mobbed by team mates seconds after scoring.

SPOT ON: Gavin Williams puts away a penalty in the F.A. Cup Second Round victory over Barnet. Now bring on Liverpool...

But instead of adding to our total, with our customary kindness we gift a goal to Wrexham two minutes from time. A little bit of casualness at the back allows the former Spurs striker Chris Armstrong to chip the ball over Chris Weale. Jubilation and celebrations at the final whistle. Happy, happy, people everywhere.

Lin and I have no time to drink the success in the marquee tonight, though. We have been invited to a surprise birthday party at The King's Arms, Montacute. We should be there at 7.30 ready for the birthday girl's entrance at eight, and I've been asked to take the photographs of her as she arrives. With the final whistle blowing at 7.25pm, we've got our work cut out to get there in time. We race from the ground and dash to the car. I could have flown there, as I am as high as a kite, re-living the great goals and the superb skills of the 14 Yeovil heroes. Back to the house, change into party kit and run up the street to the King's. Camera out, click, just at the moment a large curtain is pulled aside revealing the party guests to the unsuspecting lady. No sweat, it's all in the timing. Just like Yeovil Town, really.

I allow myself the indulgence of a Sunday newspaper today. Well, after all, we won, didn't we? Just a short report, but using those nice words 'stunned' and 'thrashed'. That'll do for me. Looking at the results, I see, as always, that the Cup has thrown up some unlikely successes. Burton Albion away at Torquay, Stevenage at home to Stockport, and Thurrock holding Luton Town! The one I want to watch on TV this afternoon is Accrington Stanley and Huddersfield. What a clash. Flat caps as far as the eye can see. As it turns out, not only caps are on display – the first-half streaker gives everyone a laugh. You should have seen the size of his goose pimples. It's not Huddersfield's day. Come to think of it, it's not been their decade, has it? Reduced to ten men, they battle valiantly until, two minutes from time, they are forced to substitute their keeper through injury. The first touch the replacement makes is to pick the ball from the back of the net following an opportunistic strike from a Stanley substitute, who himself has only been on the park for a couple of minutes. Great stuff.

Minutes later and Lin and I are perched on the edge of the sofa shouting 'Yeovil' every time the home ball is pulled out in the Second Round draw. We are left until late, but our patience is rewarded. Home to Barnet or Stalybridge Celtic. I'm not going to count any chickens or make any regrettable predictions, as I still have Burscough at the back of my mind, but let's say it could be worse. Accrington Stanley, for their endeavours, have Bournemouth away, Weston have Northampton away, Burton Albion draw Hartlepool, and Stevenage will have to travel to Swansea. Not easy.

The *Ciderspace* forum is swamped by fans from just about every corner of the globe. The match was shown live in the United States, so a good few saw the excitement. Mac from Oz was internet-watching at 2.20am on Sunday morning. Guys from Borneo, France and Sweden joined in the fun and swapped messages as the match progressed. What did we do before the modern wonders of technology? The lads abroad would probably have to wait for pony express or whatever to deliver the letter from home. With that sort of time scale, Mac would just about be celebrating the Conference championship!

The post-match comments from Gary Johnson were, of course, full of praise for the fantastic performance. In his words, he "found it very hard to be humble, because I really enjoyed it." Humble? Who wants to be humble? Let it flow, Gary. Dennis Smith, the Wrexham manager, was a little more sombre when he said: "Anyone who has seen us play will know we don't let goals in and yet by the end of this match we were almost happy to have only four against. It is an embarrassing performance, to be honest." That's how it goes, Dennis, when you meet the mighty Yeovil.

Gary and the lads have become the major celebrities in Yeovil this year. Invited to switch on the only Christmas lights to rival Regent Street in London, they were besieged by the town's population, which included more than a few impressionable young ladies who got carried away at being so close to such handsome young sports stars. The only disappointment of the ceremony was that Gary needed the aid of electricity rather than clicking his fingers and saying "Let there be light." So he is mortal, after all.

We now have to put the excitement of the Cup to one side and strive to maintain our position near the top of the table. Southend, Hull and Lincoln are all looming. Hull is away, and we can't wait to go to their Kingston Communications Stadium with a whopping great crowd. We've booked our accommodation at an old coaching inn in the village of Howden. Sounds very nice. Apparently we will be able to wander down the old cobbled streets that surround the twelfth-century minster, and enjoy the peace and quiet, although only a stone's throw from the motorway. Peace and quiet? What we want is wall-to-wall chanting and deafening noise. We need to be surrounded by 20,000 others, a fair percentage of whom we will wish to be from Yeovil. Still, it will be nice to have somewhere pleasant to retire to after a stonking victory.

I'm getting ahead of myself here. Before we meet the table-toppers, we have the potential banana-skin clash with Southend United at home. The Blues are currently in twenty-second place in the division and lurching from one game to another. And they have lost their manager. These are dangerous ingredients, in my opinion. I notice that most teams that wave farewell to the gaffer go on to win the next few games under their caretaker. And, as we know, they now have some caretaker. Our old mate, Dave Webb, will, no doubt, be pulling out all the stops to get a win and allay any suggestion that he may have left us a little too early to join the Thames Estuary outfit. Saturday will also be a personal clash for me. Having been initiated into the joys of football with Southend at the tender age of 13 and followed them until Lin and I left Essex to set up home in Yeovil, I have always wondered what this day would be like. I have been waiting 27 years to have my two teams face each other. Had they met in the League, say, 26 years ago, no doubt I would have been shouting for United. But as the years have gone by, my love and allegiance to Yeovil has grown and grown, and I now have no doubts in my mind or in my heart as to who I want to win. That doesn't mean I don't still have a soft spot for the old club; I look out for their results and still take a mild interest in who is transferring in and out. Up until this year I have been able to compartmentalise the two cubs – Yeovil, my joyous non-League team, and Southend, a team to keep an eye on in the League. Now the compartment is the same and my wonderful Yeovil are about to trash them.

To make matters even more complicated, we have been harbouring two Southenders under our roof these past couple of days. Fortunately, they are not face-painted, shirt-wearing, flag-waving hooligans come down early for the game, but my mum and dad. They have now lived in the town for some 40 years but the mysteries of all things football and Southend United are as great to them today as they ever were. The nearest they get to entering Roots Hall is to attend the weekly market in the car park. No danger there, then, of learning the off-side rule. While the Southend fans will be bombing down the A303 to Huish Park, my parents will be travelling in the opposite direction back home, having declined our kind offer of buying them a couple of tickets for the away end. We have a little banter over breakfast. Being full of the Saturday excitement, I suggest that we will win 6-0. Playing with fire, I know, but that's what it's all about. I practise the "Oo-arr it's a massacre" song until they decide they have had enough and beetle off home. See you at Easter, when we visit as away fans. Hopefully, we shall all be doing the conga up the pier as we near automatic promotion or the play-offs. Again, I'm tempting fate, but I like it.

Memories flood back as I notice that the Southend supporters still travel with the same coach company that I had the pleasure of breaking down with on many a long trip. As a young lad, I treated it as all part of the fun day. Now I would probably freeze to death, standing at the side of the road for hours, waiting for a replacement. Three coach loads have arrived – not bad for a team that is far from well supported at home, and near the bottom of the League. To my surprise, the team runs out in red shirts and black shorts, not the familiar blue that I remember. Ah, those lace-up shirts and baggy knee-length shorts. The calf-high brown boots and heavy leather ball. Cor blimey, guvnor, I remember when the sea used to come up to the goal posts in the second half. This unfamiliar strip has turned them into just another set of opponents. Nothing special about them. I turn my attention to the faces on the away end. I scour the terraces looking to see if any of the lads I used to run with are there. They would be the ones with the long hair and flared jeans. Nope, there's nobody there that I know. Just a few bald ones with beer bellies. That couldn't be them, could it?

The opening ten minutes are like a re-run of the battle of Waterloo. Webby has obviously sent his team out to do some serious damage to our lads. Break up their free-flowing pattern of play, must have been the instructions. Boots, elbows and anything else handy go flying in from the Shrimpers. I've never seen such a violent bunch of shrimps in all my life. However, once Yeovil have adjusted to leaping three feet into the air to avoid the scything tackles, the clever stuff begins. The team begin to string some great moves together and Southend are beginning to look decidedly ragged. With right-footed Nicky Crittenden on the left wing and left-footed Lee Elam starting on the right, Yeovil have them foxed. However, it is not until the 32nd minute, that Yeovil take the lead following a Lee Johnson corner. Lee Elam, playing in place of Gavin Williams, who was injured in the warm-up, slams in his first goal for the Town, with just a little help from a slight deflection. Celebrate, my son, this could give you a Yeovil contract. Just eight minutes later and another telling through ball from Johno to an advancing Darren Way allows him to accelerate into the penalty box and rip the ball past the keeper. Easy, Dazza, you've doubled your goal tally for last season and we haven't reached Christmas yet. Two minutes after that, Johno decides he's had enough of being goal provider and takes a free-kick five yards outside the penalty box. Calm as you like, he curls it into the top of the net. At this point I thought I caught sight of the chairman of the anti-Lee Johnson club faint and fall to the floor.

It's bubble, bubble, chatter, chatter from the fans at half-time. There is some surprise that Dave Webb hasn't shown himself and given us a wave. He never was one for the dug-out, or for the fans, though, and on reflection, today would be a better day to hide rather than do a lap of the pitch. Shortly into the second half and an obvious handball in the penalty box is spotted by an alert lino, and Yeovil are awarded a penalty. The Southend players and their fans are a little upset, to put it mildly, and, while the players race from the pitch to touchline, the supporters pour down from the terraces and confront the ref. The only one who keeps his head is Lee Johnson, who, after all the fuss has died down, smashes the ball past the keeper. 4-0 on the hour, thank you very much. To add to Southend's woes, Jenkins, who has obviously argued far too much about the incident, is sent off. They are not happy up the away end and, probably because of that, they missed the most beautiful sunset over the Main Stand. The reds and golds filtering through the thin clouds were something to behold. You see, even in times of pumping adrenalin, nature can eclipse everything and take your breath away. But it can only do that, of course, if you are 4-0 up.

As so often happens, the backs-to-the-wall, ten-man outfit find some inner strength and manage to pull their game together, though not enough to threaten the Yeovil goal. That was some thrashing and I'm glad I had practised "Oo-ar" etc., because it was. Thirty-three points, fifth place and only three points behind Hull, who lost 3-1 at Huddersfield. Doncaster lost, and Oxford drew. Swansea play on Monday night. It's all pretty tight at the top.

For the second Saturday running, Lin and I find ourselves at The King's Arms in Montacute. This week it's the cricket club's presentation and piss-up night. While ordering the umpteenth beer, I am advised by the barman that there is a Southend fan dining in another part of the inn. Curiosity gets the better of me, and I contrive a reason to meet him. Only to see if I knew him from the old days, you understand. Not to gloat or anything. I didn't know him, of course, but we had a fair difference of opinions on the game. He blamed everything on the ref. It was never a penalty, the guy should never have been sent off and Lee Johnson's free-kick should never have been given. It is funny how you can get such a warped perspective of a match just by supporting the other side. So I did have a good old gloat, and laughed at his preposterous theory that Southend were the better side for the first ten minutes and, had they scored when denied by a Chris Weale special, the match would have been theirs for the taking. He was not amused when I suggested that I thought they were relegation fodder and soon United could be my favourite Conference team. It was so nice to exchange views in such an unbiased way.

Roy O'Brien has had an operation on his ankle and will be sidelined for the rest of the year. That is a great pity for Roy, as he has fought so hard to make a place in the starting 11. Someone else who has worked tirelessly to hold a place in the team, Andy Lindigaard, is off to the seaside to play some competitive football with the Weymuff. Can't be easy for a Yeovil boy, born and bred, to go and join the Scummers, but he is a true professional and will do a good job, I'm sure. It is only a loan period and this could do his chances of a place back at Huish Park a world of good.

Monday morning, and it is good news for the Lockwood family. Adam and Jolene are delivered of an 8lb 6oz son, Joshua Adam. Congratulations. Not such good news for the Owen family. The postman has not delivered the long overdue bathroom toilet handle. Four weeks! I chide the DIY salesman. A phone call to the warehouse in Bolton (I thought it was in Northampton) brings news that two have been sent and presumably lost, and that another will be sent by special courier. I've worked it out now. It's Bolton. They've not forgiven us for humiliating them with that magic Warren Patmore goal at the Reebok Stadium in 2001. They've seen my address and want revenge. Am I becoming paranoid?

Still, things are on the up. I picked up my long-awaited hoops mobile phone cover this morning. Very smart it looks, too. Only thing was, when I tried to fit it, the casing was too small. I have it with the packaging ready to take back to the shop tomorrow. Fortunately, Tim, my son, saved me from huge embarrassment by explaining that you have to take the old cover off before putting the new one on. I knew that, just testing to see if he could do it. Phew!

The TV football has been good this week. Monday saw Swansea fall at the hands of Northampton Town, who looked as good as I remembered them from their visit to Huish Park in August. I am just surprised that they are not doing better in the League. Wednesday night provided a choice of Wales v Russia in the European Cup play-offs, which unfortunately they lost, or the First Round F.A. Cup replay between Canvey Island and Southend United. I chose the later and was thrilled to see that Trevor Kettle was the man in charge. He didn't disappoint. Nine yellow cards and one red. In fact, he wanted to make it three reds, but had forgotten firstly who he had given yellows to and then picked on the wrong player before realising his error. A right horlicks. Chris Kamara was one of the commentators and says that the squadron leader (I didn't know Mr K was a squadron leader, did you?), is in his first year in the Football League and is going to have to learn to allow more advantage and stop booking people for ordinary fouls. Tell us about it. Still, it was all very entertaining, and Southend ran out 3-2 winners after a cracking game.

Meanwhile, on Tuesday night, Stalybridge Celtic and Barnet fought it out for the privilege of meeting us on 6 December. It was that man Giuliano Grazioli who ensured that it will be Barnet we face. Released by that great talent spotter, Ray Graydon from Bristol Rovers, at the end of last season, Grazioli has been setting the Conference alight with 19 goals already. He was certainly a Yeovil favourite back in the 95/96 season, when he banged in 16 in only 13 starts. I remember he was so popular that he was presented with a shirt when he left. I think we'd better have that back, Mr G, if you don't mind, just in case you do something nasty to us.

Yeovil have had videos, national press coverage and some bloke has written a book about them. What next? Well, it looks like Yeovil Town will be the subject of a theatrical performance. Entitled, for the moment, Up the Glovers, the Peter

Quince Theatre Production Company are planning to produce an hour-long play, in which they will join the domestic lives of two people to the ups and downs of Yeovil in their first year in the Football League. I had lunch with one of the writers, Nick White, the other day and we discussed the plot and characters. Penny and Yandle – after Yandle's Garage, Martock, of course – are a young couple whose relationship ebbs and flows with the fortunes of the Town. There's a good chance that Yeovil will make it, but will Penny and Yandle? The world premiere is scheduled for 23 July 2004 at the Octagon Theatre, Yeovil (a good venue that – having previously been called the Johnson Hall). The plan is that this first night will be for charity, with the company moving on to the Edinburgh festival for a couple of weeks. Nick tells me that the average audience for a fringe production is four, but that this company has averaged 14 with another play. Let us hope there are a few Celtic supporters in Edinburgh, with a curiosity for their adopted English club.

Right. It's Hull. The big one. *Ciderspace* forum users have been building up all week for this one. How many coaches will be going? What pubs can we drink in? Will it be the biggest crowd that Yeovil have ever played before in the League? Are the Hull fans worried that their team will lose? All these thing, and the meaning of life, have been discussed at length. Hull fans in their turn have been chipping in with the usual jibes of carrot crunchers and yokels. It is a bit like the hype that is surrounding the Rugby World Cup final between Australia and England on Saturday. I never thought I would be writing about egg chasers but hey, it is a World Cup final and even if England are playing tiddly winks we will get behind them and wish them well. Due to the time difference down at the other end of the world, the Green-and-White Army will be on the motorway at the time the match is on television. Perhaps that will be good for us – after all, if the nation is watching the match, the roads should be quiet. From the weather forecast, it looks as if we could do with some help. Heavy rain in the south and thick fog in the Midlands and north. But what do the weathermen know?

It is dark, it is wet, very wet. Okay, so Michael Fish gets it right sometimes. It is Saturday 22 November and we make our way towards the biggest League game we have ever played. Gary Johnson has issued a rallying call in the *Western Gazette*. The gaffer says "This game is another experience exercise for our players and, although we know we cannot beg people from Yeovil to travel, it would be nice to see some green and white up there. I am sure it will be a great game for those who do come, no matter whether we win, lose or draw." I read that the GWSC are taking four coaches, and we have been following a coach from Dorset up to the motorway at Bridgwater. Cary Glovers have one, and I know that Mark Kelly will be taking one with the Independents. I think the rule of thumb is that a third of supporters travel by coach, so if we have 250-300 in the coaches, we should have more than 750 in total. With apologies to AC/DC, *Highway to Hull* blasts out from the car as we splash our way up through Gloucestershire. Having warmed up on that, we then switch to Radio Five Live for this World Cup thing. To tell you the truth, the next two hours are so nail-bitingly tense that I hardly realise I am driving at all. Punching the air alternates with smacking the steering wheel as England roar into a lead, only to let it slip in the last minute. Extra time, with the prospect of a drop-kick shoot-out at the end makes it almost as nerve-wracking as Colchester in the LDV Vans Trophy. Then up steps our hero with 20 seconds remaining and drop kicks the ball to win the Cup. Jonny Wilkinson will live forever in the folklore of sport. Ever thought of taking up proper football, Jonny? We might be able to find a place for you. You would have to learn to keep the ball down, though.

We race under the Humber Bridge, a huge grey shape looming out of the mist on the Estuary like some mighty colossus guarding the approaches to Kingston upon Hull. Had they heard that the Green-and-White Army were on the march?

Lin and I opt for the well-signposted park-and-ride scheme. We find a well-laid-out, spacious car park with an inviting bus terminal and more than one bus! Perhaps the powers that be in Yeovil could note that. We are swiftly deposited at the entrance to a large grassed open space upon which has been built the Kingston Communications Stadium. It is magnificent. No, it is better than that. It is breathtaking. My pulse begins to race as we near this beautiful construction. Through tinted windows I can see a huge social club or restaurant/lounge, an education centre, equipped like a library, and a very imposing reception area. This is class. Inside, the facilities for the fans are very much like at Bolton. Large serving areas dispensing beer, meat and potato pies (hot), sausage rolls and hot dogs – and all within sight of televisions showing Sky Sports. Yeovil fans are congregating in large numbers, all enjoying the Yorkshire hospitality.

Up the steps and into the arena. Wow! 25,000 seats are set out in a gracious bowl. We are in the South Stand where every seat gives a great view of the pitch. There must be something approaching that 750 figure, all decked out in our green and white. It would be nice just to be able to dash down to the other end for a few minutes to look back and appreciate the turn-out. Hull have had between 13,000-21,000 gates this season, but as I gaze out across the acres of seats at 2.50pm, I am thinking that they must have stayed away today. Frightened of witnessing a Yeovil win? Five minutes later, they have arrived, all 14,367 of them. The huge East Stand is obviously the place where the noise will come from and, as if to demonstrate this, in answer to a "Good afternooooon,

East Stand" from the tannoy, a mighty roar rolls out from under the high roof. Not to be out done, when the tannoy welcomes Yeovil fans to the K.C. Stadium, we send out a defiant chant of "We are the famous, the famous Yeovil". This is just like a cup tie atmosphere. We have felt this at Reading, Bolton and, of course, the Trophy final at Villa Park, but we have never played an ordinary League match at such a venue. Did I say ordinary? There is nothing ordinary about today. This shows us all how far our club has come. We are in First Division surroundings, and I could get used to this. Lin and I are so glad that we have made the effort to come this far to witness this great spectacle. To see our lads strutting their stuff and hopefully scoring a goal or two will be the pinnacle of our sporting season to date. Come on, you Greens!

No Darren Way, reportedly injured in training. It must be bad for Darren to cry off. Paul Terry slots into his midfield place and Hugo Rodrigues comes into central defence. The game is played at a cracking pace, end-to-end stuff with neither team being able to get the upper hand. Yeovil have to be extra vigilant when Lee Johnson leaves the pitch for 15 minutes to have a head wound sorted. The determination of the players is visible. Every one of them is working like mad, and every Glovers fan is singing and chanting to keep them going. Hull are dangerous in attack, but Lockwood, Skiverton, Pluck and Hugo keep them at bay. The roar of the Tigers fans is only intermittent – no defined songs that I can hear, only a response to action on the pitch.

We did not have too many chances in the first half, the only notable shot coming from Jake Edwards. Having said that, this game is fantastic. Gavin Williams is all over the park, tearing into the Hull half and frightening them to death. Similarly, their right winger is fast and dangerous, and certainly frightening me. 0-0 at half time and all to play for. One goal could decide this.

On 55 minutes Lee Johnson, with his head bandaged from earlier, floats a great free-kick towards the back post and our own giant, Hugo, launches himself high with the goalkeeper and beats him. The ball loops up and lands on top of the bar, then falls away on to the netting. The collision with the keeper leaves Hugo struggling on the ground, and, for some inexplicable reason, the referee waves away the physio. Being the tough guy that he is, Hugo pulls himself up and hurries to the other end, where he is immediately involved in a last-ditch tackle, which sees the ball go into touch. Down he goes again and this time it is for good. Jamie Gosling is called into the defence as Hugo is helped down the tunnel, clutching his back. This cannot be easy for Jamie. Thrust into this most competitive cauldron, with little League experience, he proves he is man enough for the job. Despite some heart-stopping moments and thanks to two world-class saves by Chris Weale, Yeovil hang on to a well-earned point. We sang our hearts out and were rewarded, not just with a point, but with the sight of our team performing at the highest level and taking the League leaders all the way. I have the feeling that Gary Johnson and all the boys really did appreciate our support this afternoon.

As we wait for the park-and-ride bus after the game, I look back through the dark at the stadium. It stands, bathed in powerful white and mauve lights, like a giant spaceship destined to speed off to some alien planet. It is beautiful. I'm sure that, at a cost of £43million, the people of Hull are rightly proud. One day, Yeovil, one day.

I had wanted to finish with another groaning Hell/Hull joke, but 'to Hull and back' and 'Hull and high water' just didn't seem appropriate. How happy was I when, next morning, we awoke in our hotel to a glorious white frost. We could genuinely say that we had been there 'Until Hull freezes over'!

Ciderspace fans report in on Sunday morning that, when they pulled into a motorway service area, Gary and the boys arrived and spent quite a while chatting and discussing the match. They were so pleased that their club does this sort of thing. It may be only a little thing, but it makes friends for life. Thanks, Gary.

Monday lunchtime and I've been let out early by the Crown Court, so I rush up to Huish Park. I am still so puffed up with the whole weekend experience that I just wanted to thank the lads in person. On the top training pitch I found Chris Weale and Steve Collis being worked hard in training by Jon Sheffield. I watched them for the best part of an hour as they dived in all directions, coated from head to foot in mud and, towards the end, totally exhausted. I can see now why I never put myself forward to be a goalkeeper. Steve told me that Jon has been taking them for training on Mondays and Thursdays for the past fortnight, and that they were so pleased to have a professional coach. Steve said that they could see the difference already, and pointed to Chris's last couple of performances. He sighed and said that he wished he could just get a chance. I was quick to tell him that we were so lucky to have two class keepers and, at some stage, he was sure to get his opportunity.

I buttonholed Gary Johnson in his office and we discussed the game. I asked him how Lee's head was, and he said that the doctor at Hull had put four stitches into the wound. Lee had been urging him to hurry as fast as he could and, when he got back out on to the pitch, he called to Paul Terry "What's the score?" Paul shouted back that it was still 0-0 "but it's like the bloody Alamo out here." I told Gary that, towards the end of the game, I had become completely hoarse with all the shouting, and he confessed that he had as well. Because the dug-outs were so far back from the touchline, he spent almost every minute in the marked-out box on the edge of the pitch. He explained that the fourth official was happy for him to stay there as long as he was shouting instructions, but, as soon as he stopped, the official tried to usher him back to the dug-out. So, for almost 90 minutes, he had to shout at the top of his voice, and suffered as a consequence. I am informed that Hugo's back injury will be fine by next weekend, but the injury to Darren Way is not so easy. Darren is suffering from a stress fracture to his leg and, while 'Weasel' desperately wanted to play on Saturday, Gary said he wouldn't have forgiven himself if he had allowed him to and then seen him develop an even more serious injury. Better to have four weeks out and recover properly.

Still on the injury theme, he tells me that against Southend he named the substitue keeper as Steve Collis and had him sitting on the bench. In truth, if a second keeper had been required, Steve could not have gone on because he was suffering from a dislocated finger. It was kidology on Gary's part, so that Southend should not know that we had only one fit keeper. Had they known, he said, they would probably have clattered Wealey in the first five minutes. Fortunately, with the return of Jon Sheffield, we shall again have a third keeper.

Christmas must be coming, as the *Ciderspace* guys chat about green-and-white Santa hats. Ansford Glover has proposed the idea that the club might like to buy in a batch of these novelty hats with the logo 'Santa loves Yeovil' or just 'Yeovil Town F.C.' printed on them. Unfortunately, the club shop seem to be a bit on the Scrooge side of delighted. They are not proposing to take up the idea. Bah, humbug! Other more enterprising *Ciderspacers* have scoured the internet for suppliers and have come across a firm in America doing them at ten for seven dollars. We may yet see Ansford Glover doing a roaring trade from a little stall just off Huish Park. One of the lads says they would look nice at Stamford Bridge in the F. A. Cup Third Round. Another says, even better in the Fourth, having beaten Manchester United in front of 60,000 in Round Three.

As night follows day, Christmas and the New Year are followed by the village pantomime. This year Montacute is putting on one of the old favourites, Jack and the Beanstalk. Lin is playing the part of Jack's daft brother, Silly Billy. No comment, is probably the safest thing I can say. I am looking forward to all that thigh-slapping though. Thinking about it, Jack and the Beanstalk is very similar to Gary and the League. Gary, alias Jack, plants the magic beans and a huge Football League springs out of the Conference soil. Up and up he climbs and, in order to get right to the top, he has to slay the biggest team at the top. I'm not quite sure where the chopping down of the Football League (beanstalk) fits in, but it was going okay until then. Who said, "Oh, no, it wasn't"?

An early Christmas present has arrived – well, two actually. That special courier from Bolton has delivered my toilet cistern handle – and so has the postman. You never know when you might need a spare. Anyway, I'm now flushed with success! (I've already got my coat.)

Friday afternoon brings news on *Ciderspace* that the club have transfer-listed Abdelhalim El Kholti. I had the feeling that it was coming. He has not played a major role for some time, and only this week had to start in a reserve line-up comprised mostly of under-17s against Bristol Rovers at Mangotsfield. Gareee probably knew the writing was on the wall after that. G.J. says that Abdooo has not made the progress that he had hoped for and he no longer figures in his Division Three plans. On a personal note, I am sorry for the young Moroccan. On the occasions that I have chatted to him, I have found him to be a pleasant guy, although rather shy and quiet. I've put that down to language problems, but there is something of a mirror image on the field. Quick and skilful, yes, but lacking in the gritty, stick-your-face-in-it style that we have come to expect from a Yeovil team. The evening finds Lin and I going in separate directions. She heads into Yeovil for her staff Christmas party while I drive out to a country pub where a leaving party for a secretary at a client's firm is taking place. The lovely Katrina will no longer brighten up my visits to their offices but, fortunately, they still have Julie and Louise. You've got to have some perks in this job. The upshot of our partying is that we both get to bed rather late, which has the knock-on effect of producing two zombies on Saturday morning. I manage to get the correct mugs for the coffee, thereby ensuring a win this afternoon. I take this responsibility very seriously. The hopes of some 5,000 people are resting on whether or not I remember this little ritual. Yes, I know that everyone else has the same feeling of responsibility when they pull on the correct socks, eat the regulation lunchtime meal or wear that lucky T-shirt under the hoops, but I feel the pressure is all on me at a time like this.

Saturday morning is a bit of a non-event, to be honest, which is not a bad thing because the weather outside is bloody awful. Lashing rain and gale-force winds make us glad that we haven't got to get in the car and drive to the other end of the country. We should be able to manage the short trip to Huish Park without being blown off the road. As we approach three o'clock the storm has subsided. Now I'm not sure if that is a good thing or not. I have read that Lincoln City, our opponents today, favour the direct, up-in-the-air style of play, and I was rather hoping that the gale-force wind might spoil their game. On balance, though, it is better to have decent playing conditions, and for Yeovil to dominate with their more attractive passing method. That's the plan, anyway.

This fixture is an all-ticket game. It causes no problems to Lin and me, being season-ticket holders, but it seems to be causing difficulties for those who, for one reason or another, don't read the advance advertising and just turn up before the game to buy a ticket. Then they find that there are no ticket sales on the day. Why we create all these barriers to supporters coming to enjoy a game of football, I do not know. What's so special about the Lincoln game that it needs to be all-ticket? Are we likely to fill the ground and therefore don't want to run the risk of hundreds of people milling about outside desperate to get in? I don't think so. Is it the club or is it the police who are insisting on all this mucking about? Have the police had intelligence that Lincoln fans will be coming in their thousands, hell bent on trouble, and therefore fear a last-minute rush to the ground by Yeovil hooligans? All I do know is that some people will have been turned away from Huish Park disappointed and may never venture back. As it turns out, with an attendance of 4,800-odd, we can ill- afford to turn anyone away. I also note that at these all-ticket games (and today is no exception), there are enough stewards in the ground for us all to have one each. As for the police presence, you would think that George W. Bush was going to be guest of honour. What's going on?

Gary Johnson has rung the changes in the starting line-up. Jake Edwards has given way to Kirk Jackson as strike partner for Kevin Gall. Lee Elam gets the nod over Nick Crittenden on the wing. Big Hugo, his back suitably recovered, retains his place in defence in order to snuff out the long ball to the Lincoln forwards. Looking at the opposition I can see why they like to keep the ball in the air. Almost man for man they are quite a bit taller than our lads, with one of them, Ben Futcher, coming in at only an inch shorter than Hugo.

Both sides take a few minutes to settle down, each testing the other's style of play. On 11 minutes, Kirk Jackson receives a great through ball in the penalty box, and despite his first touch being a poor one, the keeper feels obliged to bring him down. Penalty. After what seems like an eternity, Lee Johnson is given the go-ahead by the referee to take it. How is it you can sometimes tell from the way a player runs up to take the kick that he is going to miss? I have that feeling with Lee, and so it is no surprise to see the keeper dive away to his left and make a fine save – no surprise, but a big disappointment. I'm not really complaining, because I can't remember the last time that Yeovil missed a penalty. It would have been nice to have scored, though.

For the rest of the first half the two sides scrap for the ball, but neither can put their mark on the game. Yeovil seem to be suffering from the hangover that is still affecting my wife. She is very quiet this afternoon and confides to me that she "can't really get into this." A little later, I realise why Yeovil are having a poor game. Lin whispers that she has got the wrong knickers on. Horror of horrors. Not wearing the lucky Yeovil knickers? All is lost! I just might have to give her a dressing down for that later.

It is 0-0 at half time, but the stalemate does not last long into the second period. On 50 minutes, Lincoln put together a series of short passes that open Yeovil up and Chris Weale has no chance to stop a short-range shot from their number 9, a player called Yeo, of all things. How could he? A nasty autumnal gloom seems to envelope the ground, despite strong sunshine from over the Westland Stand. While Yeovil, as always, are giving everything, nothing seems to be coming off. Nothing, that is, except Kevin Gall. An injury sustained in the first half forces him to leave the field shortly after the game resumes. It does, however, give Adam Stansfield a chance of a longer-than-usual run. Too many passes are going astray, giving Lincoln extra possession and putting unnecessary pressure on the back four. It is turning into a long afternoon. The Lincoln fans are singing with confidence now and I'm feeling more than a little edgy. This is an important match because Lincoln lie in sixth place just behind us, and have only lost once in the last 18 games.

Colin Pluck. I love you! The epitome of the Yeovil Town spirit. Never stops trying, never admits defeat, hard, fit and skilful. He is everything you could wish for and he scores some very useful goals. Up he pops at the far post in a crowded penalty area and – bang – it is in the back of the net on 54 minutes. Now things begin to change. Yeovil up it a gear, the crowd gets the scent and begin to howl. Chris Weale sends the pulses of 4,000 racing as he brings off a couple of superb saves, and, in the process, breaks Lincoln's heart. We are leaving this late if we want the win. 85 minutes have gone when Yeovil attack in numbers and a right old scrummage develops in the Lincoln penalty box. The ball is bouncing loose, knocked out, knocked back in, feet and legs hacking and kicking everywhere. One foot belongs to Adam Stansfield. Somehow – and from where I am sitting, I don't know how – he puts it in the goal. "You're not singing any more" booms out of the home end, with a certain amount of relief mixed in there. Five minutes to go and Lincoln are not giving up on this game. They are doing their best to salvage a point. They push high up the field and feed some good balls through to their forwards. Gary Johnson pulls off Kirk Jackson to replace him with an extra defender in Jamie Gosling. With what I am sure was his first touch of the ball, Jamie finds himself in space in the Lincoln half, racing towards the keeper. Cool as you like, he rounds the keeper, the ball running a little wide as he does so, chases on to it, and smacks it from the angle into the open net. The ground goes mad. My scarf is whirling round and round my head. Everyone is screaming and cheering. Too late for City to come back now. From the depths of despair to the heights of paradise in a few short minutes. Only football can do that. I love it, I love it.

CHAPTER 5

A WAY IN A MANGER

I used to hate Mondays – the start of another busy working week; the long drive down to the Weymouth office; problems waiting since Friday, snapping and snarling at your heels. And now? I wake to the sound of the lark, the palm trees swaying in the bright morning sunshine. I slip into the Olympic-size swimming pool while the maid prepares my fruit juice and croissant breakfast. She irons the newspaper that contains the back-page article on Yeovil topping the Premiership. Oh, I've been dreaming again. But hey, you never know. It may happen one day. I've just got to keep taking those rejuvenating pills long enough to see it come true. That may have been a dream, but, in reality, Mondays are still pretty good. I need to buy my Barnet Cup tickets today and, of course, I only need the slightest excuse to find my way up to Huish Park.

I find a couple of walking wounded in the dressing room. Darren Way is wearing a boot that either he could ski in, or it could be proudly worn by a storm trooper on the set of a *Star Wars* film. Frustration is oozing out of Dazza. He is so keen to be back in the fray, but is sensible enough to know that he still needs to rest the stress fracture that he has picked up. He played with it for a couple of weeks before it was diagnosed, and he could hardly walk at the end of the games. A couple more weeks and he should be back in contention. The other patient is Kevin Gall. It was his foot that got stamped on by an Imp on Saturday and he is only 50/50 to play against Barnet. He is frustrated at the thought of missing out on the F.A.Cup.

I manage to buttonhole Chairman John Fry for about an hour. We talk about the ticketing system and the fact that some 200-300 Yeovil fans had been turned away on Saturday afternoon because of the 'no tickets on a Saturday' policy. He shows me the wads of paperwork that relate to the safety of the stadium and the rules and regulations that seem to be pouring across his already-cluttered desk. There is a safety committee that consists of representatives of the club, local authority, fire authority and the police. It used to be two or three people in the Conference days, but now they need the vice-presidents' lounge to accommodate everyone who has input at these meetings. The bottom line seems to be that if the club ignores the advice of the police and something dreadful happens, there would be hell to pay for Yeovil Town. *Ciderspace* fans have suggested that all Yeovil fans should pay a nominal sum each season to have a numbered membership card. With this card they should be able to buy tickets on the day, thereby excluding any rogue away supporters who may be trying to infiltrate the home stands. At the present time Yeovil fans are being penalised in these all-ticket games for the potential attendance of undesirables from the other side. The bias should be in favour of the home supporters not against them. Can we afford to turn so many fans away? I expressed this view to the Chairman.

It is that time of the week when thoughts begin to stray (or gallop, if you're like me) towards the delights of the weekend ahead, especially when it's F.A.Cup time. My thoughts are sharpened by an item on Sky Sports' lunchtime football update. The Barnet squad are sitting in some peculiar positions chanting "Ommmmmmm." Their manager, 'Mad Dog' Martin Allen, believes that Yoga is going to help them overturn the Glovers in the Second Round. To add extra focus to their 'training', they are concentrating on an apple in the centre of the room. A green apple represents Yeovil and, at the end of each daily session, this unfortunate fruit is eaten. The core is thrown down and trampled on. In this way Barnet will vanquish Yeovil. I'm laughing like a drain now, 'Mad Dog'. I just hope I'm still laughing at five o'clock on Saturday.

I have certainly had the smile taken off my face today, Thursday. Under the headline 'Blow for Roy', Steve Sowden of the *Yeovil Express* reports that Roy O'Brien faces another operation next week to try to rectify his medial knee ligament problem. Gary Johnson is quoted as saying: "The operation will mean that Roy will be out for the rest of the season. It is a huge shame for Roy, because he has had his fair share of injury problems. They talk about the luck of the Irish, but Roy has been very unlucky. But he is young enough to recover." What can you say? When it goes against you, it goes with a vengeance. Roy has become such an important ingredient in the Yeovil squad. Dependable on the pitch, morale-boosting off it. A good guy to have around. Good luck to you, Roy. Yeovil fans will all wish you a speedy recovery.

As one door closes (hopefully only temporarily), another opens. Lee Elam, who nervously saw out his month on loan at Huish Park, has been rewarded with the offer of a contract. Halifax have agreed to an undisclosed fee for his services, and Gary Johnson predicts: "Lee will be a very good addition to the squad. He has come to a very confident group of people and that will do him good." He added: "What has impressed me is that he wants to be here 100 per cent. He has the right mentality. Flair players such as Lee need to feel comfortable and, now that he has signed, he should feel more at ease." Welcome to the gang, Lee. It is just a pity he has to sit out Saturday's game through being Cup-tied. Doors are swinging for two other squad members. Transfer-listed El Kholti and Chris Giles, who is returning from injury, are off to Stevenage to discuss a loan spell. Manager Graham Westley, he of the Dorchester fracas last season, has been in touch with Gary, and apologised. The air having been cleared, the two managers were able to get down to some mutual assistance. Chris Giles needs plenty of competitive matches to bring him back into contention at HP, and Abdou may find that Stevenage appreciate his undoubted talents. A little more consistency from him may make the gaffer change his mind about him. G.J. once said: "Abdou can be Maradona one week and Marado-nut the next."

Saturday 6 December starts as dull as ditchwater. Grey mists swirl around St. Michael's Hill in Montacute. Shadowy trees loom forward and fade back again. They could have filmed *Lord of the Rings* here. I'll just borrow Frodo's ring to create a little magic this afternoon. It is not dissimilar to a murky day almost a year ago when we hosted Barnet in the Conference. The game matched the conditions as The Bees ground out one of the most boring 0-0 draws in memory. Can they afford to play with such a negative attitude today? I think not. Players seem to have a different mind-set when it comes to the F.A.Cup. As supporters, we know how our pulses quicken, hearts race and heads spin just at the mention of some famous old victory, never mind being there and sucking in that adrenaline-pumping atmosphere. Why should it be any different for those lucky enough to be taking part?

I had a phone call out of the blue the other day from a lady living in Yeovil. She had been having a clear-out, and came across an old photo of a bygone Yeovil Town team. Knowing of my interest in all things Yeovil she offered me the photo, and I went to her home to collect it. She proudly told me that her father had been responsible for heating the boilers for the hot-water baths at the old Huish ground in the thirties. She remembered well the deep-tiled communal baths that the players would have gratefully slipped into at the end of a hard game. Her photograph, she believed, had been taken during this era. It wasn't hard to date the photo with the help of my favourite book of reference, *Hendford*

To Huish Park. On the reverse of the photograph were written the words 'Crystal Palace, Exeter and Liverpool.' Here it was in the book – the 1934/35 season. Crystal Palace beaten 3-0 at Huish in the First Round of the F.A.Cup. Exeter City visited on 8 December, 1934, and were beaten 4-1. Then, on 12 January, 1935, the mighty Liverpool arrived in Round Three and ended Yeovil's dreams with a 6-2 win. In order to reach those heady games, Yeovil had had to win through the qualifying rounds one to four, meeting Tiverton, Wells City, Glastonbury and good old Weymouth. Just think, if we go on a similar run of six wins and a defeat, we shall be in football heaven.

There is a Santa's convention this afternoon up the away end. Some 250 Barnet fans have come bedecked in seasonal costume. I hope they have brought their team with them – gift-wrapped.

From the off, it is presents all round. Barnet give to Yeovil, Yeovil give to Barnet. On nine minutes Colin Pluck unwraps the Barnet defence with a gorgeous looping header that pops into the top corner of the net. In return, seconds later, while most of the crowd are still settling back in their seats and listening to a tannoy message about a lost mascot, Yeovil offer a chance to the unmarked Beadle and he heads past an amazed Chris Weale. They'll be hanging mistletoe from the crossbars and swapping mince pies in a minute.

All of a sudden Christmas is cancelled. Yeovil go mental. Lee Johnson powers a ball into the penalty box and Maddix is unable to control it without the aid of his hand. Penalty. No mistake this week. Gavin Williams waits for the keeper to dive and coolly slots it in the other side to make it 2-1. If it is spectacular you want, look no further than Kevin Gall. Beating the offside trap, he sprints past the keeper, pushing the ball a little too deep for my liking, but with his acceleration he meets the ball by the by-line and smacks an inch-perfect centre for Gavin Williams to make it 3-1. YES! The ground is bouncing, whooping and cheering. We are on our way into the big round. Santa's little helpers at the other end are silenced. Lin says she feels sorry for them. I don't. I still remember their keeper bringing Andy Lindegaard down in the final minutes when they stole two points away from us last season. They don't call me Elephant Owen for no reason!

Half-time brings that warm glow of impending success. Barnet, to their credit, have come to fully contest the match, but that has been their downfall. Anyone who comes to Huish Park to play football is going to have to play extremely well to beat our lads. Barnet, bless them, are not in that league. I've also got a feeling that their Yoga apple wasn't the cider variety!

Plenty of good stuff takes place in the second half but it looks like it may stay 3-1. Once again, though, I have underestimated Kevin Gall. On 74 minutes the

Olympic sprinter hares off through the Barnet defence and cuts in on goal. Instead of taking the shot, he slips the ball square to an incoming Nicky Crittenden who blasts it into the top of the net. Whooaaa, bring it on. Jamie Gosling, on for Lee Johnson, refuses to be left out of the celebrations. Four minutes after Crit's goal, Jamie sends in a deep cross, which Kevin Gall volleys, the keeper beats it out, and Jake Edwards is on hand to slot the ball home as Gally is brought off to rapturous applause around the ground. What a star, what a talent. Just wish he had been able to pop one in himself. The singing is coming from all sides now. Happiness is Huish Park shaped. We have the golden team playing for us.

Who do we want? Well, I was quite looking forward to a day out at the seaside with a match against Weston, but they have fallen by the wayside. Telford, however, have swept Brentford aside 3-0, so I wouldn't mind another visit to the Buck's Head ground. Either anything that is eminently winnable, or something mega. I'm not asking much.

Number 59 is the ball to watch out for in the Third Round draw. George Cohen pulls us from the pot. Nerves jangle, hands are clenched in prayer. "Will play.......... LIVERPOOL." Yes, yes, yes, Liverpool. Michael Owen at Huish Park. Emile Heskey? Hugo can look after him. We have a chance, Liverpool are on the wobble. What am I saying? We are to play the mighty LIVERPOOL. ANFIELD, THE KOP, BILL SHANKLY, KENNY DALGLISH, IAN RUSH, THE LIVER BIRDS, BEATLES, MERSEY FERRY, DEREK HATTON. YOUR BOYS ARE GOING TO TAKE A HELL OF A BEATING.

What a reward we have got. It is the romantic tie of the round. Let us see if we can make it the banana skin game of the round. What I pray for is that the Yeovil winning goal replaces that sad old Ronnie Radford goal for Hereford on the television for the next 100 years. We've got to be live on Sky or the BBC with this one, and a quarter of a million quid in the bank. But now is not the time to be thinking about the money. This is the glory time, the rolling about in it like pigs in shit. I am all over the house, can't sit down, can't think of anything else. Roll on January. Bring on the Scousers!

Thank God that Lin and I are season-ticket holders. It will be panic, panic, panic from now until the long queues form. What will the club do? We have two home games before the match, Scunthorpe and Kidderminster. The club should give priority to those who attend both games in order that we get near sell-outs. Coincidentally, it was announced this week that it will be possible to buy a half-season ticket from the New Year. If the club advertises these as giving first claim on Liverpool tickets (after full season-ticket holders, of course) they should sell a bundle. Anything to get an advantage.

Now that I've calmed down a little I'm thinking how spooky it was that I should receive that old photo of the 1935 team that played Liverpool. It could have been any team photo, from any year, and yet it was the only time we have played them before. I don't know what to read into this, but I'll think of something. My love of omens is at work again. The night before the Barnet game, Lin and I went to the cinema and one of the adverts was for that hair product where all the people of a town had extraordinary styles. Just at the end, a sign came up which read 'Bad Barnet'. I growled my approval, knowing that this was a prediction that they would be poor and Yeovil would be fantastic.

Pride swells in my chest as I recline in bed and read Monday morning's national newspaper. Giant headlines hit me between the eyes. TOP TIE FOR YEOVIL. Pity it was accompanied by a photo of Hartlepool, but never mind. We are the centre of attraction. The nation wants to know about US!

On 'business', of course, I hurry to the club, eager to feel the atmosphere, grab a chance to congratulate a player or two, even have a word with G.J. I bump into John Fry, who is dashing to meet temporary-stand erectors. "If we could get another 3,000 or so on the away end that would be great," he enthuses. Hang on a moment. That'll be half the Kop accommodated. We don't want to be out-chanted. "But think of the revenue," he beams. Yeah, there is that.

I join a modest queue to get hold of some application forms for the half-season tickets for friends. This is where working part- time really comes into its own. I have the flexibility to be in the right place at the right time. How the nine-to-five brigade are going to cope with the complexities of the ticketing I do not know. Will they be camping out through the night? Will they have the time to queue to return their passport-size photos, returning some time later to queue to get their grubby little mitts on those precious tickets? Yes, of course they will. The more innocent and sheltered in the queue ask outright for two Liverpool tickets please. Patiently, the office staff explain that they are not on sale yet and the inquirer will have to jump through a number of hoops (preferably green and white) to get even one ticket. Things are just beginning to turn manic. Oh, the fun of the Cup.

The main purpose of my visit to HP is to see if I have been granted that rare privilege of an invitation to the Christmas party tonight. I had put in a suitably grovelling request the week before to the chairman, on the grounds that it would be essential research for this book. Fans want to know what happens at these events. Someone needs to be there to record such things for posterity. I thought this was a winning argument. Unfortunately Mr Fry didn't. Not enough room in the vice-presidents' lounge. Too many people invited already. Full sit-down do, and no space at the back for the likes of me. Okay, I get it. I'm not on the celebrity A-list, then. I take it well. Stiff upper lip and all that. Thanking him for his kind consideration, I return home and plot plan B! I know that the playwright Nick White has written a script for a comic Nativity play to be performed by the players. Surely he won't be able to organise everything on the night by himself. He'll need a little helper. Like me. When your luck's in, it all slots into place. A quick phone call ascertains that young Nick has been allocated three invitations for his theatre group. Only two can attend. "You would like me to come along? How kind. See you at 7.15 then." You see, a fellow writer understands the concept of research.

One hundred-odd people, including all the players, their wives, partners and girlfriends (none of them took all three, fortunately) the army of staff who keep Huish Park ticking, directors and one or two hangers-on (don't know who you mean) enjoy a smashing evening. Gary and the boys, in keeping with the highest traditions of thespians, perform *A Way in a Manger.* I'm thinking of signing them up en bloc for the Montacute panto, so good are they. The house is brought down with the arrival of the baby Darren Way, complete with nappy and dummy, carried in by his Virgin Mummy, Mary Skiverton! Other skits, involving Gary Johnson and Steve Thompson as The Two Ronnies, and Blind Date, with Fat Harry as one of the delightful lovelies on offer, have us rocking in the aisles. The heady mix of unusual talent and the continual buzz surrounding Liverpool has made me quite intoxicated. Time to phone my lovely chauffeuress to take me home.

One little tale that I can remember next day involved that now infamous green apple that so occupied the Barnet manager. While sitting in the dug-out during the game, Steve Collis, Yeovil's substitute goalkeeper, took the opportunity, following the fourth goal, to roll an apple into the Barnet dug-out. It happened to fall at the feet of Martin Allen, who, taking one look at it, kicked it to where Jamie Gosling was standing, waiting to come on to the pitch. He in turn kicked the apple back into the Barnet area, whereupon Mr Allen picked up the offending fruit and threw it down the tunnel. A case of an apple turning into sour grapes.

Great news comes through that, at the south-west Sports Awards in Bristol, Yeovil Town are voted the team of the year. Gary Johnson is the manager of the year, Kevin Gall player of the year and Hugo Rodrigues, best newcomer of the year. Not bad for a 'small pond' club, as described by Ray Graydon, then manager of Bristol Rovers, when explaining why Kevin Gall had done so well to become a 'big fish' when he left Rovers. A mighty ocean in comparison, are you? Let's talk about that after next Saturday.

Also good news is that Abdoo and Chrissy Giles have come winging straight back home from Stevenage. They obviously took one look at the delightful Mr Westley and said thanks, but no thanks. After all, they wouldn't want to miss out on the goings-on at HP, would they?

I had agreed with the club some time before that I would shadow Dave Linney, the commercial manager, and get to know what happens behind the scenes. The chosen day turned out to be one of the most chaotic and crazy ever experienced by the club The drama started at around 3am on Wednesday 10 December, with a call from the Fire Brigade to say that Huish Park was alight. To be more precise, the Portakabins containing the ticketing offices, were on fire. When I arrived some hours later, the area had been sealed off in order that fire damage experts could sift through the debris to determine the cause. It was a sorry sight. One cabin had been completely gutted, while the ticket office itself had suffered burning to the exterior wall and smoke and water damage. Fortunately, the many paper applications for the half-season tickets, complete with photos and cheques, had escaped with just a minor singeing. Computers and telephone cables had melted, and there was devastation all around. All this just 24 hours before the Liverpool tickets were due to go on sale. There are, of course, queues of people trying to get the qualification tickets and more of the half-season tickets, and so the show has to go on. At first, a table is manned outside in the freezing cold fog, until a temporary ticket office could be set up in the old Glovers' bar. With hardly a working telephone, difficulties were rearing their ugly heads.

I had planned to sit quietly in the office and observe a typical day at the club, but before long I had rolled up my sleeves and set to helping a hard-pressed bunch of people. Credit to them all for the way they pulled together to turn a disaster into a great recovery. By mid-afternoon I had been drafted on to the reception desk to field all those little queries relating to everything Liverpool. Can I do this? Or must I do that? How can I guarantee the other? A wave of humanity descended on HP. The queues for the ticket office stretched out of the bar, down the corridor and staircase and out into the street. The phone calls never stopped coming. People from Kent, Yorkshire, Liverpool, anywhere and everywhere, wanting to come to the match, and some not understanding why they couldn't. We are trying to pour a quart into a pint pot here. With a ground capacity of just under 10,000 I think the club could sell the seats three or four times over, such is the frenzy. I am worn to a frazzle, but at least I understand the pressures and problems that afflict the back-room staff. By the end of the day, the businesses of Yeovil had rallied round. Offers of new Portakabins, computers, staff, stationery and office accommodation had all arrived to raise the spirits. Another piece of good news was delivered by the fire authority. It was not a case of arson by a deranged, disgruntled individual, but a simple accident caused by a faulty power cable. Achieve by Unity is the motto. They did today.

Am I barking or what? I have agreed to help out again on Thursday. I take with me seven applications for the half-season tickets for friends. I also plan to get Liverpool tickets today for Lin and myself with our season tickets. Huge queues greet me as I approach the club. I can barely squeeze into the office door. I immediately start to work by answering the phone. The instructions are different today. No Scunthorpe or Kidderminster tickets will be on sale, in order to accommodate the large number of season-ticket holders claiming their Cup tickets. Further information needs to be given to the public regarding the half-season tickets. So great has the take-up been that the Main Stand and the Bartlett Stand are now completely sold out. Only Westland terracing is available. At this rate, every space in the ground will be claimed for every remaining home game this season. Desperate people are phoning with no idea of the enormity of their request for a couple of Liverpool tickets. Personal applications are the only way of getting anything, I tell the man phoning from Norway. I join the queue myself when the first rush has subsided. I continue to have the phone growing as an extension to my ear, which is causing amusement to others waiting. All of a sudden there is a call from Radio Five Live. "What's it like down there?" asks a voice. I think I replied "Bloody manic!" and the interview went downhill from there. I hate to think what they may have broadcast.

I'm at the front of the queue, my £40 has been handed over, and two beautiful green-and-gold tickets are going into the safety of my pocket. I sort out the applications for my friends and, to my surprise, I am offered the chance to buy their Liverpool tickets as well. I have no more money on me and have to politely decline. People look at me amazed, shocked even. I take away the distinction of being the only person to refuse a Liverpool ticket.

I return to my post in the reception area and, throughout the day, talk to dozens of smashing people who, for one reason or another, are running out of time in which to get the thing they crave most – a little paper ticket. Three teenage girls arrive, having trekked from the other side of the town, in order to buy Scunny and Kiddy tickets. Their faces fell when I had to tell them the sale had been suspended today. Fortunately, a car drew up outside the doors, and their attention was focused on the driver. Squeals of delight came from them as they recognised Gavin Williams. Their journey was not in vain. Gavin waved to them and they squealed again. Oh, to be young. Later on, I take a phone call from Mark Wright, the Chester Manager. He wants to talk to Gary Johnson, but he can't. Gary has gone to the dentist. "So, Mark, how are things at Chester, then? Still buying a player a week to try and climb out of the Conference?" I wish I had. Several beefy-looking guys come to reception and offer their services as stewards for the big day. Isn't that nice of them? Free of charge, too. That'll be inside the ground, then? Mothers phone just to ask if their child could be the mascot for the day. No, I won't make a note of your name and number. We have more than 100 potential mascots already.

Eventually, I stagger into the cold night air and head for home. Sad stories, and that never-ending ring tone, rattle round my brain. One lady phoned from North Yorkshire. She was very excited, and wanted to buy a magic ticket for her disabled son for Christmas. While not registered disabled, he lived in sheltered accommodation in Dorset. He had followed the Glovers for some 20 years and, while not a season-ticket holder, came regularly to Huish Park. She told me that he would always try to sit in the same seat near the exit in order that he could slip away just before the end to avoid the crowds. By the time our conversation finished she had gone from the high of the surprise present to the knowledge that her son would be unlikely to be able to watch another game this season. It was very sad, and I felt almost as miserable as she did. I am sure there are a multitude of supporters who will have a sorry tale to tell. That regular trip on a Saturday afternoon to watch our favourites is such an important aspect of many of our lives. To think that because of one high-profile game so many will have their pleasure denied them is hard to accept.

With all the goings-on, time has flown by and Friday is upon me before I've noticed. That only leaves a matter of a few hours before we head to the big city. Our moment has arrived. All those years of Bristol Rovers this and Bristol Rovers that. Every time the local television news mentioned football, it would be Bristol Bloody Rovers. Well, here we go. I hear a rumour that our coaches are to have a police escort into the city. That will be fun. I know that many Yeovil fans, unable to get a ticket in the away end, have been buying admission to the home stands. I guess as long as they do not flaunt their Yeovil colours and bite their lip when we score, they should be all right. This, however, is going to be a very volatile crowd with a charged atmosphere. I just hope nothing goes off. We relish a hard clash between the two teams, but not between the supporters.

Lin and I arrive early at Huish Park to travel on the Independents' coach. Like kids, we clamber upstairs on the double-decker. We are hoping, from such an elevated position, to have a good view of the countryside as we travel up through the Mendips to Bristol. It is not to be. The coach windows are covered in condensation as the rain lashes down outside. I think the forecast is for brighter later, which I hope is right, as I've just learnt that we are on the open terraces at the Memorial Ground. I had been working on the misunderstanding that it was a covered stand. I had assured Lin that it was, too.

We leave early, so that a stop can be made at a watering hole at Gurney Slade. Pity the driver drove straight past it. It took quite a lot of time, a good deal of skill and a watchful eye towards posts, walls and parked cars, to execute the three-point turn. Seventy-five people pile into the pub for a one-hour stop. Two bar staff and a tiny bar mean that, after half-an-hour, Lin and I decide we weren't thirsty anyway. We have our dignity.

We creep through the suburbs of Brizzle with no sign of the police outriders. Perhaps they are stuck in the Saturday afternoon traffic as well. Before too long, we sight the great landmark of the city, the place that draws people from far and wide. Yes, it is the unmistakable blue of the Ikea building. The Memorial Ground is just up the road. It is only a quarter to two. What shall we do? We could stroll down the city streets admiring the Victorian and Edwardian architecture, calling in at a welcoming corner public house and chatting to the customers about the forthcoming football match between two fine sides. Alternatively, we could find ourselves an attractive metal crush barrier in the away end and settle down in the freezing wind and spitting rain to wait for three o'clock. That's settled then. We pick up our free copies of the *Evening Post*, complete with cardboard cut-out face masks of Kevin Gall, and head for the turnstiles. By the time of the kick-off, I am frozen. Why did I leave off that extra layer of clothing that I normally wear under my hoops? Lin, on the other hand, took no chances and stands next to me looking like Nanuk of the North. The fur-trimmed hood that surrounds her face looks very appealing. I couldn't just borrow it for a couple of minutes, could I? I would hardly have to worry about the style police. I think they might be concentrating on the lads who are sporting large green Christmas tree hats, complete with flashing red lights. Wish I had one. I could warm my hands around the bulbs.

Almost 10,000 fans pack the Memorial Ground to witness the first-ever clash of the city slickers and the country yokels. Bring it on!

Yeovil kick off with the brisk, swirling wind in their favour and force the home side on to the back foot. Numerous corners are awarded, and Gavin Williams swings them in, causing all sorts of mayhem in the Rovers box. The advantage of big Hugo coming up for corners is that the opposition have to concentrate so hard on blocking him out that it often leaves an unmarked Yeovil player to create a chance. Today it was Colin Pluck, roaring through and unlucky to see his shot go wide. Rovers, to the accompaniment of their fans singing *Goodnight Irene*, scrap hard. With a skilful little winger in Williams, they create danger down the left flank and produce a couple of worrying moments in the Yeovil box. The play switches from end to end, with neither side being able to create a clear-cut chance, until a Rovers' defender rises high in the penalty box and directs a powerful header on to the crossbar. Nearly 1-0 to Yeovil. I would have enjoyed an own-goal this afternoon.

On 41 minutes, noticing that the half-time queue at the food kiosk has yet to materialise, I ask Lin if she would like a Bovril. She says she'll get them and slips away. On 43 minutes, Nicky Crittenden picks up the ball near the right touchline, cuts in and powers into the Bristol box. He unleashes a fantastic shot, which rifles into the back of the net. The contingent of travelling fans goes wild. Bodies are leaping, arms are raised to the heavens. The cheer splits through the wind and reverberates around the ground. ONE-NIL TO THE SMALL POND TEAM. Lin returns with two steaming drinks. "Did you see it, did you see it?" I bawl. Fortunately, she did. She had even danced with a policeman whom she fell against when she jumped. Any excuse, eh? Half-time, hot Bovril, warm hands, happy Green Army. Who could ask for more?

The second half is also devoid of clear-cut chances, which suits me fine. Kirk Jackson makes way for Jake Edwards up front, but within a few minutes he is off. Pushed in the back, he retaliates while on the ground and the referee produces the red card in a flash. An automatic three-match ban will rule Jake out of contention for the Liverpool game. I feel sorry for the lad. He has competed with Kirk Jackson all season, and now the big game is in sight he rules himself out of it. Nice touch on Saturday when Kirk, who had been substituted for Jake, ran round the pitch and down the tunnel to console a lonely player in the dressing room. It is backs-to-the-wall time for Yeovil, but I can't see anyone in the Rovers team that is going to get past our magnificent defence. Junior Agogo looks as if he is a Agonegone. They fail to seriously test Chris Weale, and the referee puts them out of their misery bang on the 90 minutes. A great win lads, 40 points on the board and up to fourth. It is all back on the coaches and yes, this time the blue lights are flashing all around us as we are taken for a victory parade through the streets of Bristol and up to the M5. Great fun whizzing through all the red traffic lights and holding up all the rest of the traffic. Time for a large gin and tonic, flopped out on the sofa, Britain's Best Read on the TV (is it *Yeovil 'til I Die!* – wishful thinking?) and the great notion that Yeovil could be in the automatic promotion places come May next year. Did I really say that?

All of a sudden I have become Mr Popular. Now there's a first. Years and years of watching, eating, sleeping and probably boring people about Yeovil Town have been registered. Phone calls. E-mails and letters from all sorts of people are arriving daily. They just happen to mention that if I could get a couple of Liverpool tickets, they would be very grateful. I'm expecting invitations to posh dinner parties pretty soon. Don't bother bringing a bottle of wine – just a couple of tickets will do. I haven't had any women throwing themselves at me as of today, but I live in hope. Of course, I haven't got any more clout than the next season-ticket holder, and it wouldn't be right if I had. I'm just a bog standard ordinary fan like thousands of other supporters, except I happen to be a lucky son of a gun with a season ticket and Sir Gary Johnson's telephone number on my mobile!

Despite the grumbles from some on *Ciderspace* about the allocation of tickets and the 'exorbitant' rip-off price, I think the club have been as fair as they could be. It is easy with hindsight to say they should have done this or that and perhaps they are learning lessons for the next big occasion, whenever it comes along. A lot of people are going to have to realise that we are no longer sleepy little Yeovil Town from the non-League backwaters. All of a sudden, in fact in the space of pulling two balls from the pot, we have been elevated to Premier League proportions. We have the enviable problems that face the likes of Arsenal, namely a ground that is too small and a vast number of people who wish to get in.

It seems that 9,800 people can be wrong. We all thought that Jake Edwards had been sent of for retaliating with a kick. But for Clive Penton the reason was dangerous use of an elbow in the earlier tackle with Adam Barrett. Mr P claims that it was flagged up by his assistant, but he chose not to ask him what he saw. I think the Rovers' centre-back, Barrett, sums it up nicely when he says after the game: "I think the ref made too much of it. It was nothing really. But I think because of the occasion and with the fans voicing their opinion, the ref got a bit carried away." The Club are to appeal against the red card. There is hope for you yet, Jakey boy.

Among the many threads relating to ticketing on the *Ciderspace* forum I have come across one to lighten the mood. Under the heading 'If we beat Liverpool I will...' various writers have contributed:

Buy a Weymouth shirt.

Apply for the vacant manger's job.

Predict that we get Scarborough in Round Four – and lose.

Run around Yeovil naked the Monday after.

Buy a Hereford season ticket.

Do a whole day's work without checking out *Ciderspace* once.

Blimey, the F.A. can move quickly, after all. Their appeals committee have apparently viewed Jake Edwards in action, found him guilty, and turned down his appeal. All done and dusted, it seems, before the referee, who agreed to look at the video evidence, had even got the package from the postman. Gary Johnson is fuming. He said that he was absolutely gutted by the panel's decision. "I would like to know what goes on in those video advisory panel meetings, because clearly, in this case, they have made the wrong decision. It is not just a case of losing the player for important games. The fact is, their decision is wrong and my player is innocent."

Another player taking no part in the Liverpool circus is, of course, Roy O'Brien. He has now had his operation to rectify the medial knee injury. He is on crutches, but all is well. He has got to let it heal and then start his rehabilitation. Next year then, Roy. Gary also mentions that Darren 'Weasel' Way is having a further X-ray today, 18 December, to see if he can step up his training and recovery regime. "He's chirpy, and comfortable with the way it is going. The New Year is about the time we would be looking at. That is the time everyone gave before the Liverpool tie came up. But there is a lot more he has to make sure about before then. Everything has got to be right." In other words, Darren will be snarling and spitting more like a feral cat than a weasel if he is not in contention for the starting 11.

I think the lads and Gary will need extra stamina exercises if they are to keep up the engagements that they are currently involved with. On almost every page of the *Western Gazette* and *Yeovil Express*, I see them grinning at some do or other. They open a new MRI scanner at the Yeovil Hospital. Gary Johnson judges a Christmas card competition at a local school. The team open the new Alpine slope at the ski centre. Gary Johnson is signed up by the Commerce of Trade to give an after-dinner speech on motivation. And, somehow, they are squeezing in a couple of football matches in their spare time. Go easy, fellas.

We have a big match coming up on Saturday. Scunthorpe are the visitors, and every ticket in the ground has now been sold. Well, not every ticket. There will be plenty of room up the away end. I can't see them bringing a huge number. Yeovil fans without the all-important ticket stub may well be tempted to put on a northern accent and become Scunny fans for the afternoon. I can't blame them. The opposition themselves are on an F.A.Cup roll of their own, having disposed of Sheffield Wednesday in a replay on a penalty shoot-out. That was on Wednesday evening. I wonder if their legs will still be feeling the effects of that extra-time come Saturday. I hope so.

Another amazing escape act has seen Andy Lindegaard scuttling back over the Downs and out of the clutches of the Seasiders. Gary Johnson is becoming a good shepherd at the moment, the way he is bringing his flock home. Joking apart, that month in the sea air will have done Lindy a power of good. The only way to come back after a long injury is to play really competitive football. With Weymuff riding on the crest of a wave in the Dr. Marten's Premier League, he will have had the opportunity of sharpening his skills against some good opposition. I'm not sure when we will see the lad in action, but it is good to have him back.

Right, that is the last of the Chrissy presents bought and wrapped. A power tool for Lin (lucky lady) and a DIY manual should set her up for those little jobs around the house in the New Year. After my clumsy efforts of late, we need someone who can do a decent job. I'll just sit and finish off the last of the orange and lemon slices and check the TV schedule. On the other hand, I might watch the *Champions* video again. No matter how many times I watch it, I well up and come near to tears. It is that wonderful moment at Doncaster that does it every time. What a lucky, lucky bunch of supporters we have been, and, of course, continue to be.

Three points this afternoon, Saturday 20 December, are so much more important than any result in the Liverpool game. Yes, it would be fantastic if we were to win or get a replay. The media would have a field day, Yeovil would be celebrated across the nation. But we would eventually go out to someone and then have to return to fighting for points in the League. If we have lost a couple of games while all the razzmatazz of the Cup is about us, we could find ourselves outside the play-off zone and playing catch-up. I rest assured in the knowledge that G.J. has all this in hand. He won't be letting the players take their eye off the league ball, I am sure.

Despite my faith in G.J., I wobble a little when I hear the line-up for this afternoon. No Way or Johnson. Well, that was known for some time. Lee Johnson has to serve a one-match ban for picking up five yellow cards. But, in addition, there is no Gavin Williams or Adam Lockwood. What is going on? Talking to the guys amongst the little pocket of Bartlett Stand experts, the theory is, as Messrs. Williams and Lockwood are currently on four yellow cards, they may constantly have the fear this afternoon of picking up another and therefore missing the Liverpool game. That fear may cause them to unconsciously bottle important tackles and hand the advantage to Scunthorpe. Okay, I'll run with that. Now is the time to see what depth we have in our squad. Jamie Gosling, Paul Terry, Lee Elam and Andy Lindegaard, none of whom were in a starting line-up a couple of months ago, are in. On the bench we have Kirk Jackson, Adam Stansfield, Stephen Reed and Steve Collis.

I won't detain you with a match report. Yeovil Town give everything as always. Effort and determination are in abundance. What is missing is the sharp, incisive, clever passing game that we have seen so often. Scunthorpe, who have drawn half of their away games so far this season and remain unbeaten in the last 14 matches, play hard and tight. Nothing about their team shouts class, but they all work hard for each other. At half-time the score is 0-1. A dodgy penalty decision from a dodgy ref (well, I would say that, wouldn't I?) has given Scunny the lead. We have had our chances, but failed to put them away. The second half does not bode well as Yeovil constantly give the ball away at vital attacking moments. We are not getting near the goal – at least until the introduction of Kirk Jackson and Adam Stansfield. Then Lindegaard puts in a peach of a centre and Jacko tucks it away with a well-placed header. I had been getting very edgy up to that point, but the relief of seeing the ball nestle in the back of the net floods over me and I whoop with delight. Fifteen minutes to go and Yeovil fans sense a whiff of victory. The singing belts out from all around. Colin Pluck, substituted for Stephen Reed, dances around the dug-out, as excited as the rest of the mentalists in the stands.

Lee Elam, a player who has covered every inch of the park all afternoon, plays in a great ball and yes, our own, our very own Andy Lindegaard is there to blast the ball in from close range. Huish Park erupts. Like molten lava, the cheers and cries roll down the terracing. HANG ON YEOVIL, HANG ON!

And they do. Every one of them a hero. Every one of them deserving of the applause ringing round the ground at the end. G.J. has pulled it off.

With Doncaster Rovers winning 3-1 against Swansea on Friday night, the table has changed a little. Donny are now on top, Oxford second and the mighty Yeo are nestling there in the third automatic promotion place. Mmmm, that tastes good. Mansfield move into fourth, having become the first team to take the three points off Hull at the K.C. Stadium.

Over a decidedly cool beer, a group of us discuss the presents we are hoping to receive in a few days' time. Lin and I confess that we have both made visits to the Club shop and some others nod in agreement. Someone suggests that we all wear whatever we have received on the Boxing Day match against Kidderminster. I think I'll be all right in a new scarf (possibly), but Lin is going to feel mighty chilly in her green-and-white sparkly thong.

I know it is a bit churlish of me even to mention the ticket situation again, after witnessing such a fine comeback job, but I am going to. Tickets are flavour of the month, after all. We knew that today's match and the Boxing Day game were sold out, So why did we only have a crowd of 5,700? Where did all those folk who presumably bought the tickets go? Obviously people have varying commitments, and not every one can attend every time, but if that attendance figure is correct, something like 1,500 or so who had bought tickets did not fill a seat. Now, looking from my position in the Bartlett Stand, I could see blocks of seats vacant in the Main Stand. What surprised me, though, was that they are the blocks of seats that are nearly always vacant. Has the club held them back and still announced a full house?

No Christmas for Yeovil Town, according to G.J. While he feels able to trust the lads, he thinks that a near-normal schedule of training is best. He says he doesn't need rules about drinking, because he knows the behaviour of his players so well that he can even tell when they have had an extra cup of tea. No repeat of Forest Green away last year, then – one of only three defeats, and it added to the gloomy statistics of previous Yeovil Christmases. Let us break a habit of a lifetime this year and stuff the Kidderminster turkey.

Don't get me wrong, I do like Christmas. But when you weigh up the effort that goes into producing the product that is Christmas Day, I have to wonder if it is worth it. Lin spends ages searching for what she hopes will be the right present for everyone, wrapping those presents, writing all those Christmas cards and buying in the mountain of food necessary to sustain an army. Then, within a few short hours, the presents are opened and piled up in the corner of the room, a huge dinner has been consumed, together with liquid refreshment, and all anyone is fit for is to slump in front of the box and fall asleep. Well, that was all I could manage, anyway. I awoke once to see a three-inch mouse in a suit being addressed as 'son' by a middle-class family living in New York. I wasn't sure if this was the result of my drinking too many bottles of strangely-named ales; you know the ones – Sheep Wash, Curate's Toenail and Wimborne Midge – or if this was one of the top-notch quality television programmes we have come to expect. Whatever it was, I slipped back into my slumbers and was soon running out of the tunnel at Anfield, about to score the winning goal at the Kop End. It all helps to bring Boxing Day that little bit nearer, and, with it, the chance to see some real entertainment.

It is a 'nothing day' weather wise, just mild and overcast with a light breeze. There has been no sudden overnight freeze, bringing with it six-foot snowdrifts, or iron-hard frosts.

Lin has had a pair of new-style Yeovil Town mugs from Father Christmas, so we decide to road-test them this morning in advance of the visit from Kidderminster Harriers. They are a much nicer green than the ill-fated pair that were dispatched earlier in the season. These have all together better vibes about them.

A pleasant morning is spent in the company of my parents, my sons and their respective wife and girlfriend. Lin provides more food. No, no, not more food, I can hardly fit into the hoops as it is. I do, however, sport a very nifty pair of sunglasses. James, my eldest, has given me a pair with 'Yeovil 'til I die!' printed across the lenses. I like them very much. Pity there is no sun today.

Walking to the ground, I casually remark to Lin that the wind seems to have got up quite a bit. In fact, it is blowing pretty hard, and by the time we have taken our seats, the rain is beginning to fall pretty hard as well. The few hardy

Kiddy fans on the open end are going to get soaked if this keeps up.

Little do we know that this game will virtually be decided on the toss of the coin in the centre circle. Who won the toss I don't know, but Yeovil are to have the wind in their faces in the first half. And what a wind it has become. It is howling straight down the ground, and bringing with it wave after wave of lashing rain. Still, it will be to our advantage in the second half. And with a pitch with a draining capacity of something like an inch an hour, no worries.

I could tell something was wrong with the day when, in the twelfth minute, Kiddy's number five decided to take Boxing Day literally. I'm not sure if it was a right hook or left upper cut, but whatever it was it floored Kevin Gall. Three sides of the ground gave identical advice to the referee. OFF! OFF! OFF! He took little action, while Gally was revived with the bucket and sponge. Once back on his feet, he was immediately yellow carded. Did I miss something? He then turned his attention to 'Mike Tyson', and merely gave another yellow card. I sit like a goldfish in the Bartlett, mouth wide open, thinking I must have forgotten something that went on ten seconds ago that would have influenced the ref into such a decision. I have always thought that if a player raises his hand to another, he is off. Perhaps if you go on to strike the other, the rules change. What is it with these Muppet referees we encounter? And who said the standard would be better in the Third? Bring back the Conference officials, especially Mr Singh.

As the rain hammers down on the roof, Yeovil find it more and more difficult to play their normal passing game. I should imagine they had difficulty seeing each other through the torrent that fell. Kiddy, on the other hand, with the gale at their backs, were pumping the ball forward in the hope of a lucky break. And it came. Just before half-time, with most Yeovil fans satisfied with 0-0 and the prospect of things changing in the second half, a slippery ball was slammed across from the right wing and a bedraggled creature slid in at the far post to put it in the net. Miserably wet Kiddy fans became bouncing lunatics as they danced up and down the terracing. Lin and I gritted our teeth and prayed for Yeovil to rip the guts out of them in the next 45 minutes.

During the interval the rain increased. People sitting in the first ten rows of the stands evacuated the area and moved back up under the shelter of the roof. Pity was taken on the Kiddiminster fans and a decision was made to rescue them from the elements and move them into the Bartlett. With only 5,640 people at the game, that luxury could be taken. Once again, where were all those people who had bought up every ticket for this game?

Beautiful though it is, and state-of-the art it may technically be, the pitch is becoming waterlogged. The goalmouths look like the shallow end of a swimming pool and, as the half kicks off, the true state becomes apparent. Every kick along the grass throws up great sprays of water and the ball refuses to travel any distance. This is becoming a total farce. Call it off, referee. Make one useful decision this afternoon. Yeovil's skilful, neat passing game, is being left for dead. Kidderminster, who appear to lack those same skills, are coping better. Is it my imagination, or has the rain eased? A crack appears in the dark sky and a patch of lighter colour opens up. The wind drops, as if the machine generating it has been turned off. Yeovil's advantage has just been removed. The storm has passed.

On 58 minutes, Kevin Gall roars through the water, mud and defenders to slam home the equaliser. How he kept his feet, at the speed he travelled, I shall never know. It was sheer brilliance. But it is not enough. At 78 minutes and a free-kick for Kidderminster results in a mud-bath scramble to clear the ball away. Unfortunately, it does not happen and we are 2-1 down. When the ball doesn't run for you, there is nothing that can be done. A Lee Johnson free-kick is palmed on to the cross-bar, Kevin Gall slips in the mud while about to tap the ball into a virtually empty net, and another shot is hacked off the line by a desperate defender. Kiddy waste time, and Hugo gets a booking for trying to hurry them up. Nothing goes right. Mother Nature has had a bloody good laugh at our expense today. Thank you very much. Why do we have to have Boxing Day in December? If it had been 26 August instead, chances are we would have had a beautiful sunny day, dry pitch and no wind. Yeovil would have torn Kidderminster apart. I feel very bitter. I can't remember the last time that the weather has played such a huge part in the proceedings. Three valuable points have literally gone down the drain. We slip to fifth, with Donny, Oxford, Mansfield and Hull all winning. Our Boxing Day jinx continues. Christmas? Bah. Bloody humbug!

I'm over it. Confidence has been restored. It is business as usual. We board the coach to travel to the land of my fathers and Swansea. Lin and I have never visited the south-west area of the principality before, and so we await with anticipation the delights to behold from the coach window. I am told that the Gower Peninsular is an area of natural beauty with much rugged coastline. Pity, then, that we only saw Port Talbot and the outskirts of Swansea. Never mind, we have, after all, come for the football and not to compile a *Wish You Were Here* holiday programme. Tales of festive excesses are swapped, as the last of the turkey sandwiches are eaten. Nights out in Yeovil and Crewkerne hint at all sorts of alcoholically-fuelled mischief. What did we do Christmas Eve, Lin? Oh yes, fell asleep in front of the television. Oh, to be young again!

From the coach it was only a stone's throw to the ground, which seemed to be the worry for some fans. Bricks became part of the conversation when discussing the welcome that could be expected from the Swansea Jacks. Fortunately, we saw no one who looked anything like a rock chucker and, while most headed in the direction of the nearest pub, which had been declared Yeovil-friendly, Lin and I took the opposite route out of the car park and walked on to the sea shore. We could see the hazy outline of the Devon coastline away in the distance, with a vast expanse of grey sea in between. Unfortunately we could still see the belching industrial works of Port Talbot down to our left. But, with a bit of imagination, I could just about conjure up a vision of sun loungers and bikini-clad girls in the summer. You have got to have something to keep you warm on a raw December day, after all.

The Vetch Field is a funny old ground. There is an old rickety wooden seating stand along one side, while on the opposite wing is an enormous bank of terracing that is partially closed off. The away end is similarly terraced and, at the home end, is a two-tiered affair that looks as if it was half built when they ran out of money. I understand that Swansea are in line to move to a new venue in the next couple of years, but perhaps they should have waited a while longer before they sold off parts of the old ground. Towards the corner of the park the stands end, and the back garden wall of a row of fairly new houses begin. I can imagine a player taking a corner on one side of the wall while, on the other, a householder is re-arranging their gnomes around the ornamental pond.

"Coffee, Lin?" After all, we have been standing for the best part of an hour before the game begins and, as she says, I know how to treat a girl. Take her to all the smart places and wine and dine her. I join a short queue outside a giant coffee mug that doubles as the burger bar. The attractiveness of it is somewhat spoilt by the large metal cage that surrounds it. In order to get the food, it is necessary to reach through a gap in the wire. Who were they expecting dressed in green? The Hulk? I wend my way back through the 800 or so Yeovil fans, with two polystyrene cups of wet and warm. I catch my foot on a rough bit of concrete and all of a sudden I am sent into a headlong trip along the terrace. As luck would have it, a guy walking the other way catches me before I hit the deck and, miraculously, I still have the cups in my hands. There is no longer any coffee in them, but I have the cups. Others said it wasn't worth drinking anyway.

Adam Stansfield makes a full start today in place of the suspended Jake Edwards. Darren Way is back, and named on the bench. I must say that his inclusion is a surprise to me. I think it may have been a surprise to the club as well. They have arrived in Swansea without Dazza's shirt! In the time-honoured tradition of "Is there a doctor in the house?", a call goes out to any fan with Darren's name and number on their hooped shirt. The call is answered by Andy

Bown of Langport, who can now proudly boast that his shirt has played for Yeovil Town. What is not such good news is that Lee Trundle is back from suspension for Swansea. He soon proves that he is a handful for any defence, even one as good as ours. After a pretty even start the Swans are awarded a penalty in the 29th minute, and Trundle strikes it into the corner, giving Chris Weale no chance. Swansea think they have doubled their lead shortly after when a free-kick is hammered into the net, only to be disallowed by the referee for a foul on the wall. My heart sinks into my boots at this point, and I become grateful we were still only one down. Swansea are fast in attack and keep Yeovil pinned back into their own half for much of the first 45 minutes. Nothing of any significance takes place up the other end. Stansfield is unable to win anything in the air and is not receiving anything on the floor. It is not looking good.

The second half sees our little dynamo Darren Way replacing Adam Lockwood and it makes a difference, as we dominate the midfield and hold the ball up a little more. Despite this, Swansea are still creating problems for us and we cannot get our usual flowing game going. Things go from bad to worse on 67 minutes when a failure to clear the ball away from the goal area results in a hopeful shot from the edge of the area finding its way into the back of the Yeovil net. Two down, and gloom is descending over the Yeovil contingent. But, as we all know, football is a game where anything can happen right down to the last kick. With Andy Lindegaard and Kirk Jackson both on, Yeovil seem to have woken up. Attacks with some purpose now begin, and on 73 minutes Gavin Williams is able to beat the keeper to the ball and lob it over his head to bring us back into the race. With one minute of normal time left and with the Yeovil fans in full cry, Kevin Gall heads the equaliser after some good work by Andy Lindegaard. The majority of the 9,800 crowd are stunned. In fact, I think we all are. Just seconds remain and Yeovil attack again. "We're gonna win three-two," had been the earlier tongue-in-cheek chant when we were two down, but now it looks like a reality. Then a hopeful punt down field towards the Yeovil corner flag finds Kevin Gall leaping high to cut the ball out. It drops conveniently at the feet of the chasing Swansea winger and his cross is eventually slammed into the roof of the net by Lee Trundle. Seconds later the final whistle blows. The points have been snatched from us, and I'm gutted. I feel cold, miserable and far from home. Get me back to England now. What a killer. Why do we do this to ourselves? I don't need this kind of pain. I could be doing a Christmas jigsaw on the dining room table back at home. Umm, perhaps not. It could be worse – I could be in the queue that we have heard has been forming since four o'clock this afternoon at Huish Park. The remaining Liverpool tickets go on sale tomorrow morning at nine and there are not going to be many to go round. When the coach arrives back at HP, there is a row of igloo tents along the front of the building and a lot of people with chairs wearing many layers of clothing. The moon is shining brightly upon them but, with the forecast of minus five degrees tonight, it is going to be a long old wait.

I can't resist the temptation on Monday morning to go down and look at the scene around the ticket office. Not only was it perishing cold during the night but there has also been a few hours of rain. But by the time I arrived, the tent village had gone, mission accomplished, tickets in hand, off home for hot food and bed, I should think. I met a few friends in the queue with rather blue noses, but they had only been there for four hours. Part-timers! The happy outcome is that everyone who was prepared to put himself out managed to get a ticket. It seems there was a good atmosphere built up during the dark hours before dawn and, according to some posts on *Ciderspace*, it was an occasion that people would remember forever. I feel almost jealous. As a season-ticket holder, I had no excitement when I strolled in and picked up my ticket. The earth certainly did not move for me.

Pop Idols they are not, but Gary and the boys have been slaving away in the recording studios this morning. To the tune of *Two Little Boys*, Mr Bobby K has penned Yeovil Town words. I have a feeling that the only chance this tune has of making the big time is if we thrash Liverpool on Sunday. I think the whole country could be singing it by Monday morning if we do. Why is it the F.A.Cup brings out the worst musical tastes in all of us?

The week has crawled its way into Tuesday. Will we never reach Sunday? I haven't slept well now for I don't know how long. I dream about being at the match, but nothing seems to happen on the pitch. Crowds are milling around, searching for Michael Owen. Is he playing? Is he on the bench? Has he retired from football? I keep waking up at all sorts of unearthly hours with thoughts going through my head as if in a tumble dryer. I am glad we only play one of these games once in a blue moon. My health just wouldn't be able to take any more.

To take my mind off the subject I have arranged to interview a prisoner down at Dorchester prison. I have to talk to him about burglaries he may or may not have committed. It is good to have something light-hearted to deal with while waiting for this serious football match. The prisoner turns out to be a scouser! Professional to the end, I avoid any mention of the big event. After all, being locked in a small cell, I may not have got out alive. While I am incarcerated in deepest Dorset, the F.A.Cup has paid a visit to Yeovil, proudly displayed in the Nationwide Building Society and then taken out to Huish Park for Gary and the lads to get their hands on it. Well, it is good practice for later, maybe.

News Year's Eve at last. A chance to look back at 2003. All I can say is thank you, Yeovil Town, for the most wonderful year. The memories will live with me forever. Can I just be a bit greedy and hope for something similar in 2004?

CHAPTER 6

UP FOR THE KOP

Walking through the town centre on New Year's Day, it is good to see so much green and white in the shop windows. Everyone is now entering into the spirit of the Cup. Down at the Top Ten Bingo Hall in Stars Lane, the foyer is decked with masses of shirts, scarves and all things Yeovil. Allegedly the management, based in Hull, have refused to allow the staff off for the day to watch the match, and so a television engineer has been brought in to tune all the bingo screens to *Match of the Day*. Houses all around the town have banners wishing Yeovil good luck.

There are still 53 hours to go to kick-off when I wake up on Friday morning. I would like to go down to the ground and breathe in the atmosphere, but I have to head off to Taunton for an appointment with the judge. I wear one of my Christmas presents from Lin. No, not the Yeovil v Liverpool hoops. I don't think His Honour would approve of such apparel. Instead, I sport the Yeovil Conference Champions tie with pride as I stand in the Crown Court foyer waiting for my client. Bless him, he never turns up. I can't say I'm surprised. Just think, if he has a ticket for the game, he wouldn't want to run the risk of being locked up and missing it. I'd certainly do a runner in his position. It gives me the chance to get away quickly from the Court and I head with all legal speed to Huish Park.

It is like walking into a film-set at Pinewood Studios. Scaffolders are busy erecting large towers at various points around the ground. Chippies are hammering and banging as they build commentary boxes on the roof and next to the Westland Stand. Camera crews are everywhere. Interviewers are two-a-penny. I recognise him from the Beeb. Oh, and him off Sky. That's the one that does the *Six o'Clock News*. Gary Johnson has a queue of reporters, note-pads in hand, eager to jot down his pearls of wisdom. Despite the frenzy that surrounds him. Gary still has time to walk over to me, shake my hand and wish me a Happy New Year. It makes me so proud to be a part of this great football club. I love you, Yeovil. I could burst.

I get invited up to the vice-presidents' lounge, where the players are gathered. In sweatshirts, baggy jeans and baseball caps they look like a rap band. On second thoughts, with *Yeovil True* still giving me nightmares, perhaps they don't. Dozens of people are up there, most of them from the press, all desperate to get a scoop. With a cup of tea in hand I do the room. All the lads seem to be taking the attention in their stride and are happy to chat to the hacks. I have a laugh with Hugo about him becoming a newspaper star over the last few days. He finds it all very amusing, and says that his family back in Portugal have become very excited about it all. I chat to Lee Johnson. Lee has just moved into a new house and has installed a water bed. We talk technicalities of too little or too much water for a good night's sleep. A reporter approaches and asks Lee if he could interview him for *The Sunday Times*. I grin at Lee and say that it makes a change from *The Yeovil Times*. He laughs and disappears to do his piece. Enjoy it, lads. Fame is fleeting, and it will soon be over. Memories are so precious. Try to hang on to them.

Saturday: football day. I feel like a spare whatsit at an orgy. Everyone else is involved in the Cup. Kidderminster are battling with Wolves, Telford are leading Crewe, and Gillingham are taking the mickey out of Charlton. All I can do is sit and wait. I'm not very good at it. I want to be at Huish Park now. There are still 21 hours to struggle through. Deep breathing, that's the answer. Time for a little mental yoga. Analyse the situation and deal with it logically. Okay, I'll give it a try. What we have is a game of football lasting 90 minutes between two teams of 11 men. I shall be sitting in a seat some yards from the pitch, watching what goes on, with a particular interest in the actions of one of those teams. At the end of the 90 minutes it is probable that one of the teams will have scored more goals than the other. If it is not the team that I have specifically watched, then I shall leave the ground, return home and continue with my normal day-to-day life. If it is the team that has attracted me, then I shall go ballistic, mental, crazy, wild and foolish. I may run naked down Middle Street with just body paint on. Drink every pub in Yeovil dry and then move on to the villages. Sing, dance, weep and hug. Swim the length of the Nine Springs lake, kissing every duck on the way. Hijack an open-top bus and demand it drives to a certain northern city and does a victory parade. Well, perhaps not the last one. After all, I want to live to see the Fourth Round. So the yoga doesn't work. What can I do next?

It's here, SUNDAY 4 JANUARY 2004. The lull before the storm. Montacute is ready. This momentous occasion has caused the owners of the petrol station and convenience store to close for two hours; between one o'clock and three there will be no service provided. This is the first time in living memory that the garage has ever shut. I think this shows the enormity of the situation.

The bottom line is that we are not playing for valuable points. The club has made a pile of cash from the event, enough to keep the place up and running for a while. There is little realistic chance of a Yeovil win and, even if we did, we would not go on to win the Cup. All we require is a contest we can be proud of; a celebration of the beautiful game. We have wonderful opponents, with a rich and magnificent history. It is just a question of bathing in all of this glory and national attention. Right, that's all the correct things to think and say. Now with all the passion at my command I want Yeovil to become world heroes. I want newspapers from Portsmouth to Peking, Weymouth to Washington to be shouting about the fantastic victory. I don't care what the score is. I just want to win. A single goal in the first minute, the last minute or deep into stoppage time. It's all the same to me. A Nicky Crittenden blaster, a Kevin Gall chip or a Colin Pluck bullet header. Anything, anything. Hugo getting his first for the club would be great. Just give it to me.

Rituals done, check. Lucky knickers, check. Shirts, scarves and jester's hat, check. Eleven o'clock and we are off. One minute past eleven I return to the house for the tickets! They have been pinned to the kitchen notice board for a fortnight. I've looked at them every day, kissed them every other day and somehow I forget them. Easily done in the circumstances. We park on the Houndstone estate and join masses of people marching purposefully to the ground. New scarves are draped around many a neck, some of them are these mixed Yeovil green and Liverpool red monstrosities. I'm sorry, but how can anyone wear the other team's colours on a day like this? In fact, how can anyone leave the house wearing a red fleece or red hat, shoes or sweater? What are they thinking of? But there they are. Totally oblivious, I guess. Yeovil fans, many through-and-through, but wrong, wrong, wrong.

Outside the main buildings a sea of green and white stretches from one end to the other. With just under two hours to go, people are experiencing the atmosphere. Flags are waving, huge fingers are pointing, silver paper F.A.Cups are held aloft. A Rio carnival could not be more colourful or entertaining. Lin and I push our way towards the beer tent. Large bouncers bar the entrance, turning away thirsty punters. Fortunately, we have an appointment with Somerset Sound inside the marquee and are allowed to slip inside the otherwise-deserted bar. The BBC have invited me, as author of *Yeovil 'til I Die!* to say a few well-chosen words on the radio. They'll be lucky. Today I am a gibbering wreck, far too excited to string more than a couple of words together. Still, it gets us to the bar first at opening time and that's okay with me. John Jeanes is one of the first through the door, and we stand and drink cider together. All of a sudden, Andy with the headphones from Somerset Sound is introducing me. I don't know who to – after all, most Glovers' fans are now at the ground. I remember saying 'wonderful' and 'fantastic' about 50 times in two sentences. I added to that 'if', 'win' and 'Yeovil' and 'naked in Middle Street' and I was finished. That was quality, then.

The ground is electric. The Westland Stand is packed to capacity, a solid mass of chanting humanity, all with one cause. The Bartlett and Main are really up for it today. Singing, clapping, standing, sitting and still with an hour to go. The 'Kop' end, though, is not as red and white as I expected. A few big flags and banners, but not the massed ranks of shirts that the other three areas of the ground display. Too cold for them down south, obviously. It is very grey, and mist keeps rolling in across the pitch and then partially clearing again. A perfect day for a Cup upset. Bring on the Scousers!

Michael Owen's name is missing from the team-sheet. That is a great pity. It would have been something to have seen him on the hallowed Huish turf. No Stephen Gerrard either, a thigh strain keeping him out. But here they are, running out on to the pitch. International and national stars emerging from the tunnel. The welcome is tumultuous. The crowd goes wild. Liverpool trot out as well.

From the off, Yeovil kick towards their adoring fans. Nicky Crittenden whips in a sharp cross, which Jerzy Dudek, the Liverpool keeper, manages to hold but hurts himself in the process. Wave after wave of Yeovil attacks pummel the Reds. The passing is truly awesome. A series of one-touch passes are breathtaking. Gavin Williams shoots from the edge of the penalty box and Dudek makes a fantastic save to deny Yeovil a well-deserved goal. Liverpool hardly get out of their half, and do little to trouble Chris Weale. The only scary moment is when El-Hadji Diouf goes down in the penalty box. Mr Barry, the referee, awards him ten out of ten for diving and gives him a yellow card. Unfortunately, he misses the two bad tackles that cause Colin Pluck and then Paul Terry to have extensive treatment. Paul's injury is so bad that he has to be substituted by Andy Lindegaard. The boys are brilliant, every one of them.

I talk to James in Barnet on the mobile at half-time. He is watching on TV, and tells me that Alan Hansen says that he thought Liverpool were in green. The BBC panel of Gary Lineker, Peter Shmeichael, Mark Lawrenson and Alan

Hansen are amazed at the standard of play from the Town. We are not, of course. We all know the capabilities of our boys. I shall never forget this first-half performance. It was Premiership. It was better than that, it was Brazilian.

The second half opens with Liverpool still feeling the kick up the backside they must have had from Gerrard Houllier. They are much more organised and determined, and pin Yeovil back for long periods. The mist continues to roll across the ground, getting thicker by the minute.

Smicer, having hit the post, is replaced by Heskey and, all of sudden, Liverpool look much more dangerous. On 71 minutes the big man fires a shot past Chris Weale and they go one up. As always, Yeovil get stuck in. They play their way out of trouble and start to claw themselves back into the match. Then Harry Kewell, who had been having an extremely quiet game, decides that he will try to improve on the Diouf diving technique. Mr Barry is far more impressed by this one, and awards a penalty against Hugo Rodrigues. I am sure the television replay will show that there was only the slightest contact and no foul occurred. On 77 minutes, Murphy takes the penalty and makes it two.

A Yeovil crowd that has sung its heart out for the lads continues to roar them on. Chants of "Hugo for Portugal", "Wealy for England" and "Heskey for Weymouth" have us laughing, despite the scoreline. Back come the Yeovil boys, streaming up the pitch, giving everything they have got. Kirk Jackson, on for Lindegaard, forces another magnificent save from Dudek, Liverpool's player of the match.

Before we know it, the whistle for full time has blown, shirts have been exchanged, hands clap until they can clap no more, and we are all swallowed up in the mist as we go our separate ways. It's over. The weeks of expectation, the queues, the excitement, the sleepless nights. All over, seemingly in the blink of an eye. I feel emotional, proud of my team, grateful for having witnessed a brilliant performance, but a little disappointed that we couldn't have got a goal. AND LOOKING FORWARD TO GETTING THREE POINTS AGAINST ROCHDALE ON SATURDAY. Come on, you Yeo!!!

Well, of course, the television replay branded Kewell a cheat. No other word for it. Blatant cheating. Not professionalism, cheating. It is the worst of offences on the football field. Violent conduct can often be induced by the heat of the combat, but cheating? There is no excuse. The panel don't pull their punches, either. No place for that sort of thing in football. Even Liverpool through-and-through Mark Lawrenson says it was definitely a dive. The Monday morning papers are equally as scathing. No honour whatsoever in Liverpool's victory. Fans from all over swamp the *Ciderspace* forum with praise. Everton fans all agree that they particularly enjoyed the Yeovil chant of "Champions League?

You're having a laugh."

Concentrate now, Yeovil, this next match is a banana skin. You are in the Liverpool position tonight. Yes, it's Shaftesbury away. Shaftesbury are opening their new ground and have invited Yeovil to do the honours and play the first game. Rumours abound that Yeovil will unveil a surprise player this evening. A strong squad travels from Yeovil (well, we haven't got a weak squad we could send). Four-nil at half-time, then the mystery player turns up the tempo and Yeovil run in five more. Wearing Thomo's boots that are a size too big, he soon finds space and makes pin-point passes. He clinically slots home a penalty with all the nonchalance that a super star brings to these occasions. Some rather jaundiced fans on the terraces suggest he only got in the team because his son plays for Yeovil. It's true. He is Gary Johnson.

We've become trendsetters. Watching Chelsea v Liverpool on television, the crowd immediately begin to boo Diouf and Kewell. And, when a huge section of their 41,000 crowd began to chant 'Yeovil' and 'Champion's League? You're having a laugh', it made my night.

"Can I come to Carlisle with you?" I ask, after the congratulations have been offered to Gary. We are in his office. I thought by now he would have been moved to a whole new suite, with a huge desk and thick-pile carpet. Instead, he remains in his cubbyhole just down from the washing machines. There is a small desk, piled high with papers (probably requests to join the club from the disgruntled of Real Madrid). A TV and video perch precariously on a chair, and one of those many 'Manger of the Month' champagne bottles gathers dust on top of a filing cabinet. A large map of England has stickers showing all the exotic places that Yeovil Town travel to in the Third Division except, ominously, Carlisle. The map is too big for the wall, and something had to be chopped off. Gary had mentioned some time ago that the club was considering flying to Newcastle or Glasgow, and driving by bus back to Carlisle. There would have been several seats vacant on the plane and a few fans might have been able to get a lift. Things have changed now and it has been decided that a coach ride and overnight stay is preferable. Any chance, then? "I'll have to let you know after the Rochdale game, because one or two of our directors may wish to come along rather than drive all that way," says G.J. They won't want to go on a coach; they've got Mercs and Bentleys – plenty of comfort up the motorway. Leave a space for little old me.

To be honest, it's a relief to come back to normal and play a run-of-the-mill league game. What am I saying? There are no run-of-the-mill games. Every one this season is a first. This will be the first time we have ever played Rochdale at home. Perhaps I'm getting a little above myself. Am I looking too far ahead, wishing to be gone from the Third Division already? Drooling over that away fixture at Hartlepool in Division Two? I think a rousing chorus of the song is required. "Cos the sign of a true supporter, is the colour of their heart. Day and night I'm green and white. We are Yeovil Town. Oo Arrr." That's better.

We seemed to have turned into a town of inveterate queue-formers. It's just like the Second World War (so I'm told). See a queue and join it. You might end up with a loaf of bread or a bucket. In our case, you might get a half-season ticket (HST) or a Rochdale one. Fans who applied weeks ago for the HST, and have not had them through the post, are snaking around the temporary ticket office. On spec, fans are filing calmly for today's game. Lin and I wear a smug grin as we bypass all of that and head for our season-ticket turnstile in the Bartlett. Hang on, the queues here are ten times as long as anywhere else. Of course, now that almost everyone has a season ticket, the two turnstiles with the clever technology can't cope. In the end, and to prevent a delayed kick-off, the big gates are opened and we all swarm in whilst the stewards do their best to count the numbers. So we'll take the attendance figure of 5,800 with a pinch of salt, then.

They say that possession is ninth-tenths of the law but in football that doesn't always mean that the team will have a comfortable afternoon. Despite the vocal encouragement of the Westland End and the fair turn-out from Rochdale fans, neither team seem to be able to do anything very positive. Yeovil have total dominance of the ball but can't seem to get the flow going. Rochdale are sitting deep and breaking down moves on the edge of the penalty box. It's all a little flat. I want to stand up in my seat because I love Yeovil, but somehow I just can't manage it. There is always an expectation on the Yeovil team to play blinding, brilliant football, and today is no exception. Within ten minutes there is some moaner a couple of rows back who is on their backs. Why don't you just shut up and give them a break?

As luck would have it, Terry Skiverton and Gavin Williams conspire to drag us all out of our lethargy. From just outside his own box, Skivo smacks the most perfect of passes to Gav on the edge of theirs. He turns and hits the ball past the shortest keeper in the League and it nestles satisfactorily in the corner of the net. Yeovil continue with the vast amount of possession but nothing comes from it. In the second half, Rochdale decide that, as they have come such a long way, they may as well join in and have a kick. Their substitute, in his excitement at getting on the field, even goes as far as lobbing Chris Weale and seeing his effort come back off the bar. What should have been a comprehensive victory, with the supremacy that Yeovil have shown, turns into a nervous last few minutes. Fortunately, justice is seen to be done and three points are tucked in the bag.

One-nil, ten-nil, they all give three points. I wouldn't mind seeing a ten-nil occasionally, though.

This week, I've got a three-day trial down in my diary. When I arrive at the Crown Court I learn that it could well last six. Now, arithmetic possibly isn't my best subject, but even I can work out that if we start on Monday we won't be finished by Friday. So, if I get the okay from Gary to join the coach party for Carlisle, I can't go. I am due to give him a call at lunchtime. All morning I agonise over the problem. The jury is sworn in. What am I going to do? The prosecutor gives his opening speech. How am I going to get round this? And then, the Judge, complete with his curly wig, announces that he has to attend a meeting on Friday afternoon and the trial will have to stop at noon that day. Yippee. What a hero! I still don't know what time Gary is thinking of setting off for Carlisle, but the chances are that I can dash home from court, throw my suit in the corner, grab my hoops and be down at HP in time to take my seat. But Gary says phone back on Wednesday, and on Wednesday Owen's luck runs out. "Sorry, Brendon. The chairman has decided he wants to travel on the coach and, with us taking the whole squad, including the suspended players, we can't take you. With it being such a long journey, the lads need plenty of room to spread out."

"Sure, Gary, I understand. Another time, then. Good luck on Saturday." I'm stood in a car park in Taunton feeling miserable. When I think about it though, what if I had taken up that seat and one of the lads had not been able to spread out properly and then, on the field, just as he was about to score the winning goal, he got cramp? It would all be my fault. All the fans that made that monumental journey would know that it was me. I might get de-hooped by the Independents.

I've been looking at an alternative way of getting to Carlisle. Train, boat and plane, car, coach and bike have been looked at but, frankly, I think I've left it a bit too late. The plane fares started at a very reasonable sum a few weeks ago, but now they have gone sky high, as it were. I can't stand the thought of being squashed into the coach for the straight up-and-back journey of 600 miles. Lin had no intention of doing this game anyway, and I have now agreed that I will stay at home and put this one down to experience.

"Heavy snow is blocking the Pennine route and one lane is closed on the M6 at Penrith. Snow is also falling around Carlisle." So says the weather girl on the Steve Wright show as I drive home on Thursday. Sounds pretty nasty. I hope someone does an inspection of the pitch tomorrow before everyone sets off. I remember some people turning up at Hereford last year for the Trophy game and finding the place deserted. They were none too pleased. But to go all the way to the far edge of the known world and be turned away doesn't bear thinking about.

Gossip spreads following Gordon Strachan's announcement that he will be leaving Southampton at the end of the season. Gary Johnson is the man. The fact that there are about 50 men in front of him is neither here nor there as far as some people are concerned. Panic, suicidal tendencies, depression, have gripped the faint-hearted. Gary says he has not been approached and has an important job to do in Yeovil. I confess that I woke at around six o'clock on Saturday morning, thought about the Green and Whites just starting their epic journey north, and rolled over under the duvet. Have I become a fair-weather, part-time supporter? I should have been there, squeezed into that coach seat prepared to face seven or eight hours of misery in order to cheer on the lads for an hour and a half, and then another eight hours back again. I feel disgusted with myself. But frankly, with that freezing-cold weather outside, the warm bed I am in seems a much better prospect.

Carlisle have bounced along the bottom of the division all season, but they have put together a run of three wins out of the last four games. We, on the other hand, have been flying high all year, but have now lost three out of the last four. Where do we go from here? In order to pass the time before the Sky Sports programme begins, with the constant update of scores, Lin and I drive into Yeovil and pick up a pile of holiday brochures. It helps on a miserable January day to have that little ray of sunshine filter in from the pages of hotels and villas. From three o'clock to five I swing between the Cape of Good Hope and the Black Hole of Calcutta. Anticipation and enthusiasm give way after 21 minutes to frustration and annoyance. Scores pour in all afternoon – big scores.

1-6, 6-4, 4-4. Even Donny Rovers have put two away in seven minutes at woeful Southend. But nothing from Brunton Park. Nothing for Yeovil, that is. Carlisle are not having the same problem. Two-nil on 71 minutes. Silence again, big horrible silence. Ninetieth-minute goals are piling in, but not us. Stuffed by the lowliest of the low. We seem to be good at that.

My initial feelings are that we need a proven goal-scorer and we need him now. Edwards, Jackson and Stansfield, all fine, hard-working lads, have not proved that they have what it takes to bang goals in time after time. The step up from the Conference may be a step too far. Perhaps I'm being a bit hard on them, but I've got to take it out on someone. Kevin Gall, fine footballer that he is, does not seem to be getting in the right place at the right time. His tremendous runs take him away from the penalty box and into the corners. That is not the place for the team's striker to be. Others should be at that point, knocking over the quality ball for Gall to pounce on in the box. I suspect that, in the absence of the suspended Gavin Williams, we had no one who was able to run at the defence and get right into the shooting areas. I will have to look at *Ciderspace* and see what the poor souls who travelled there have to say. I may be completely wrong. We may have been the unluckiest team ever to hit the posts and cross-bar.

My first scan of the forum reveals that Carlisle just about pipped us in the first half but were all over us in the second. Just one of those days, I guess. With Lincoln City losing at home to Torquay, we remain in fifth place. Could be worse. My thoughts are with the faithful fans in cars, coaches, trains and planes. They must be feeling pretty sore at the moment. I reckon that a defeat can add about 300 miles and five hours to any journey.

Well, it seems that it was the forwards who failed to do the business, Gally missing two one-on-one's, Jake Edwards doing very little. I hadn't realised, but we were also without Nicky Crittenden. A slight hamstring injury caused him to miss out. No width by the sound of it. What's happening to Jacko? If Edwards was that ineffectual, Gary Johnson can't have much faith in poor old Kirk if he doesn't bring him on as a substitute. I know, there's nothing worse than someone who wasn't at the match giving all these opinions. Fair enough, I'll shut up. Well, I'll wait for Gary's post-match comments, and see how he views it. Fortunately, we have kept our fifth place in the tables, thanks to a Leyton Orient win over Mansfield. Talking of the 'O's, we meet them next week.

What I have gleaned from the *Ciderspace* fans is that a coachload of Celtic fans, who saw the Yeovil v Liverpool game on television, arrived in Carlisle to support the Glovers. Very vocal, good fun and added greatly to the whole experience. It's a strange world that we football fans inhabit. I wouldn't be surprised if we don't have a twinning ceremony between our two respective mayors. We could then do cultural exchanges. Could we borrow Henrik Larrson by any chance?

Just to add to the jitters, there is a rumour that Chris Weale is due to sign for West Ham on Monday morning. I hope not and I think not, but, if it was to be true, I hope we get a shed-load of money for him. Enter Steve Collis? Gary Johnson has said that he will be talking to the players individually regarding their performances lately. Somewhere I read that as: "Steaming into a few on Monday morning." He'd commented on the game and said: "We worked hard, but didn't show our quality. Their goals came at just the right time, and we didn't take our chances." I always have the feeling that Gary knows exactly what's going on and probably how to fix it if it isn't right. I never had such confidence in a manager before.

For once, a rumour has some validity. Chris Weale is off to West Ham. It was for two days initially to train with them, but it has now been extended so that he can play for West Ham Reserves against Arsenal Reserves on Wednesday night. With England's number one, David James, having just signed for Manchester City, West Ham are casting around. Gary Johnson says: "Obviously, with West Ham in the hunt for a new goalkeeper this is a great opportunity for Chris, and I would not dream of standing in his way." We'll see what comes of it. Apparently, Gary knew of the approach from the Hammers on Thursday but waited until Saturday evening to tell Chris, as he didn't want him to worry about picking up an injury against Carlisle. Alan Pardew, an ex-Glover of course, now Manager of West Ham, spoke about Wealey after the first couple of days. "This kid has got a fantastic chance of being a top goalkeeper; it may be it is too early for us to take him, but it might be that we take the gamble." Perhaps it's a little early to be waving Chris goodbye, but it sounds pretty likely. We will miss our local boy. Fantastic saves have become his speciality and, of course, we shall never forget that wonderful performance in the F.A. Trophy final at Villa Park when he denied Kirk Jackson. I feel very privileged to have witnessed this young keeper learning his trade at Huish Park. Not only that, but he is one of the nicest lads I have met. He always greets you with a smile and always has time for a few words. It would be nice to be able to say goodbye – if it is to be goodbye – at the next home game.

I think we might just get our wish to send Chris Weale off with a standing ovation. Although he kept a clean sheet against Arsenal, West Ham felt that Chris had not had the busiest of games and could not make their assessment. They will try again on Saturday. So come on, Chrissy, if you want to go, play a blinder. Other moves are afoot. Kirk Jackson who, in Gary's words, has "lost a bit of goal magic", has gone on loan to the Daggers. The plan is for Kirk to stay a month and get his touch back. And on the incoming side there is gossip about a 'Brazilian' trialling with the squad. Just the word 'Brazilian' sends shivers down my spine. Some bare-foot boy off the beach at Rio; samba; carnival; dusky maidens; gyrating hips. See what you've done now. I'm all a quiver.

Back to earth with news that Simon Weatherstone (no, he's not from Rio) has had a call late one night from Sir Gary. Knowing that Boston United were at last willing to part with him, S.W. raced down from Lincolnshire and signed on the dotted line. Described as a midfielder/striker. G.J. says: "He's been one of those that I have been after for a year and a half. He's a good footballer and I just want good footballers at this club. I see him as a striker primarily but, as I say, the lad is a good footballer and that is the main thing. Rumoured to have cost around £15,000, he is yet another former member of the England National Game XI. Is that seven we've got now?

I don't know if this rumour is true or not; if it is, thank you, Liverpool. It has

CUP FEVER: There was a carnival atmosphere the day Liverpool came to town in the F.A. Cup Third Round. Keeping calm were Steve Bown, Dan Ryan and Liam Ryan of Langport, Somerset.

RED MISSED: Yeovil's Gavin Williams bursts through Liverpool's Igor Biscan and Danny Murphy.

HEEL WORK: Nick Crittenden flicks the ball away from Liverpool skipper Sam Hyypia.

LE BOSS: Liverpool manager Gerard Houlier alights from the team coach.

HUGO FIRST: Rodrigues beats Emile Heskey to the ball.

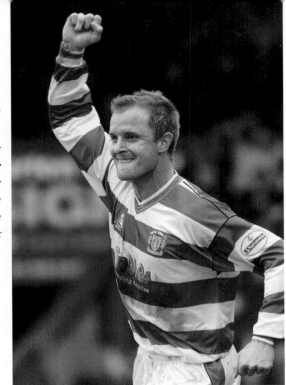

JAKE'S PROGRESS: Edwards celebrates after scoring Yeovil's opener in the home game against Macclesfield.

ANDY MAN: Lindegaard leaps for joy after scoring in the victory at York.

LOAN STAR:
Andy Bishop
celebrates with
Lee Johnson
after scoring
against
Oxford
United.

WELSH
WIZARD:
Gavin
Williams put
in yet
another man-
of-the-match
performance
against
Rochdale at
Huish Park.

*STRIKING
SMILES:
Kirk Jackson (left)
and Kevin Gall
after the former
had put Yeovil
ahead against
Scunthorpe.*

*POPULAR
PORTUGEEZER:
Dani Rodrigues
provided the goals that
kept the promotion
dream alive.*

LAST DAY TORMENT AT LINCOLN: Yeovil knew they had to win if they were to make the play-offs

Gavin Williams (above), Paul Terry (left) and Hugo Rodrigues (below) gave their all...

The result was a fantastic 3-2 victory, but events at Field Mill, Mansfield, meant it was all in vain.

THANKS FOR THE MEMORIES: Yeovil fans stay faithful to the last as they applaud their heroes at Lincoln.

AND THANKS TO YOU, TOO GJ: That's me with the great Gary Johnson.

been suggested that they have given us back the gate money that was due to them from the Third Round. £70,000 to them would just about pay a player's wages for a week, so perhaps they won't miss it.

In truth I had a quiet game against the Orient. I hardly made a peep in the first half. No "Stand Up if You Love Yeovil" got me to my feet. No "Hey, Gary Johnson, I want to know" to burst my lungs over. There was nothing to get excited about. It was pure agony. We all felt it, crowd and players. Having mis-hit another pass, out-of-touch Colin Pluck took out his frustration by kicking the advertisement hoarding on the wall. All that free-flowing football, the one-touch passing, the running into space, the great goals; all gone. Whether it was Leyton Orient's tactics of closing down quickly on the player with the ball, or the fact that they were big, strong and fast, I don't know. I'm no expert. What I could see, though, was that our first touch was usually poor, allowing the ball to travel just slightly out of control and therefore making it difficult to recover before the 'O' player was on it. An awkward debut for Simon Weatherstone. It's not easy to shine when the rest of the team are out of sorts. Perhaps he's left his talents in one of his unpacked suitcases. I hope so.

Two goals for the visitors, the first an unopposed header from a free-kick out on the right and the second an opportunist strike from the left of the penalty box, again from a crossed ball from the right. Huish Park fell virtually silent after the second. Total despair descends. I can see no way that Yeovil can claw back two goals. The only challenge on the Orient's goal comes from a few hopeful long-range shots that the keeper treats as catching practice. There is nothing going on in the forward line. It is totally blunt.

The only interest comes at half-time when Warren Pattmore walks on to the pitch and is invited to draw the 'lucky goal ticket'. What we couldn't do with a Wazza of ten years ago was the buzz amongst fans in the Bartlett Stand. A big, strong presence in the penalty box. Someone who could hold the ball up and distribute it to others. Someone who could score a hatful of goals.

The second half is little better. The ariel battle is won hands down by the opposition and, with little going right on the ground, Yeovil struggle once again. Only in the last 20 minutes, following a change of referee and the substitution of Nicky Crittenden for the injured Lee Elam, does anything change. 'Critts' begins to use the wing, something we hadn't tried all afternoon, and Yeovil begin to play a bit. It was Nicky Crittenden himself who scored, and, all of a sudden, it doesn't look so difficult. When Kevin Gall burst through on a one-on-one with the keeper I thought we had snatched a point but, with Gall and Yeovil's luck both being out, it hits the post and is hacked away. We didn't deserve that point. The 'O's saluted their happy fans, while few of the 6,200

Yeovil supporters stay to clap our boys off. It was turning into a cold evening and I guess we wanted to be away to lick our wounds.

I'm not having a panic attack. Here we are, first season in the League. It has been a miracle to have had such a great start to the season. The heady heights of fifth place. There are no complaints from me. Yet I feel a bit down about today's game; it's only natural. What does worry me a bit, though, is the similarity to the 2000/2001 season. Fantastic until we met Bolton in the Third Round of the F.A.Cup. After that, we fell apart. This time, ever since Liverpool's name was drawn out of the bag, we have struggled. Four defeats out of five. Is there something psychological going on? Understandable, I suppose. I don't know how I would handle the experience if I were a young player. Perhaps a few heads need to be cleared.

I need a dose of *Ciderspace*. A chance to put things into perspective by reading the views of my soul-mates with steadying words from Badger, HHH and Taff – pillars on to which I can cling when seeking comfort, support and reassurance; chance to laugh at the witty repartee from the likes of Snoz, Mad Trumpeter, Geordie Dazza, Hoagy, Mad Mal and many others. All as crazy as a box of frogs, of course, but then aren't we all? We are Yeovil Town. Today of all days my computer plays up. It tells me that *Ciderspace* is an error and I should consult my internet provider. I am cut off from the Yeovil world. I can't communicate with anyone. I'm on my own, stuck with my own slightly jaded thoughts on yesterday. No one to share them with. I go into the garden and build a nice big bonfire. You can't beat a bonfire for therapy. The joy of being a pyromaniac for a couple of hours. Feeding those crackling flames with not only tree branches but also secret fears and dislikes. Leyton Orient went right on the top of the heap. Nothing personal, lads, but you have just taken the full six points off us. That takes some forgiving and I'm not in the mood today.

Times like these are wobbly. Doubts and fears continue to surface. What if we don't win another game this season? Might we still get relegated back to the Conference? I know Carlisle and Darlington are still doing a pretty good job at going for the drop themselves, but are we mathematically safe? I'm only joking, of course. Give it a couple of weeks and this blip will be far behind us. As I say, wobbly times – reflected in the forum chat. Demands for that elusive forward to be signed, now, immediately – in fact, last week. Further demands to drop Kevin Gall. Bring in Adam Stansfield, Nicky Crittenden out on the wing, Lee Elam on the bench. Uncertainty as to the best combinations, experts to the left, right and in the goalmouth. What we do know for sure is that the mysterious Brazilian, whose name turns out to be Olivio, has gone. Did he get a 'butter' offer from somewhere else? Chris Weale has become a commuter. Two days a week he will train with West Ham while they continue to monitor him. This will go on until further notice. Must be good for Chris to mix with the First Division lads, gain some good coaching and hopefully bring it back to Huish Park for our games. It seems that Gary Johnson has been trying to find that elusive 20-goal-a-season front man, but perhaps the clubs in the market to sell think we should hand over a bit more of the 'Liverpool' cash. An offer to Rochdale for the services of Paul Connor may have been turned down for that very reason.

The Montacute Pantomimers have picked on me to assist them with this year's publicity. Just a question of making up a couple of posters and a little write-up in the village magazine. You know the sort of thing. After I had agreed, they then told me that I would also have to organise all of the advertising in the programme; that old embarrassing cap-in-hand routine to all of the local businesses. Oh, and could I also arrange photo-shoots and newspaper and radio coverage? Blimey, they'll want me to play the Dame next. Anyway, I put my thinking cap on and, because it's Jack & the Beanstalk this year, I thought it might be clever to do a link up with Y.T.F.C. Giant killers, Jolly Green Giant, that sort of thing. Yeovil kindly agreed to help out and so, on Friday afternoon, a strange sight appeared at HP. From out of the tunnel ran a girl pretending to be a bloke called Jack. He/she was followed by her father, who was dressed up to look like his mother, two guys in woolly tights disguised as a cow named Daisy, two enormous Giants, one jolly and one not, and, finally, 'Fat Harry' aka Adrian Hopper. To be honest, I thought Macclesfield had arrived a day too early.

Photos taken, the motley crew dashed for the warmth of the First Aid Room in order to change back into some semblance of normality. I lingered for a time to survey the ghost-like qualities of the empty football stadium. Row upon row of silent seats, acres of concrete terracing, a forlorn press box and deserted hospitality suites all waiting for the thousands of supporters who will pour in here tomorrow, wishing and praying for a good Yeovil performance. As I cast my eye around, I notice the latest G.J. idea for a Glovers' win. At the Westland End there stand not one but two sets of goal posts. At the other end just the one. Simple. When Yeovil play towards the home end in the first half we face double the opportunity of scoring. At half-time we get the stewards to carry the portable set up the other end and, hey presto, we have the advantage again. I think I'm getting a nasty case of Panto-itis. As soon as I've planted these funny-looking beans, I'm off.

I am surprised it has taken until the end of Chapter Six to be able to use the following phrases: fluorescent orange, swirling gale-force wind, eagle-eyed referee's assistant and that most unusual animal at HP 'home draw'. The first three conspired together to make the last one out of the Yeovil v Macclesfield

131

clash. It looked as if the Silkmen were in such a rush to visit Huish Park that they forgot their kit. Desperate attempts to borrow a spare Yeovil kit came to nothing and they eventually had to settle for stewards' jackets. Bright; we could have done away with the floodlights. Anyone who criticised our hoops earlier in the season should hang their heads in shame.

The icy blasts that blew between the stands made a monkey out of many a player, not least Colin Pluck. Because of a misjudgement of a bouncing ball he thought was destined for the terracing, Colin felt obliged to up-end the forward who had seen the wind hold the ball back and allowed him to race along the by-line towards the goal. One-nil from the penalty. When the boot was on the other foot, so to speak, Yeovil failed to harness the wind. No long-range shots were attempted when it seemed obvious that any goalkeeper would be in difficulty. Perhaps that was down to a lack of confidence. Too many players pushing the ball square to the next man, rather than having a go. We've seen it before when we've been in a bit of a trough.

I don't usually have the highest regard for the referee's assistants. Too often wrong with the offsides and rarely any use in helping the ref with who did what and to whom. I now take it all back. Thank you, lino on the Bartlett Stand side in the second half. With Jake Edwards equalising ten minutes after the penalty and then Macclesfield going two-one up before the break, the scene was set for a rip-roaring Yeovil all-out attack to capture the points in the second half. It didn't quite happen that way, of course. Poor old Plucky, who had a nightmare first half, was replaced by Rodrigues; later on, Chris Giles was sent on to give a bit of muscle in the box in place of our 100-metre sprint specialist, Kevin Gall. Neither of the big men could get on anything useful around the goal, but the diminutive dynamo that is Darren Way did. From a poor clearance by the keeper, Dazza blasted the ball goalwards only to see this large tangerine thing loom up and appear to head it off the line. I had partially leapt from my seat only to fall back again as the ball flew clear. The next instance I was up again as the ref had received the signal from 'our main man' that the ball had crossed the line. Thank you, lino, thank you, thank you.

And so it was that Yeovil Town recorded their first home draw of the season. Most, I think, would see it as points lost rather than a point gained. We are still not firing on anything like all cylinders. Two away games now follow – Northampton on Tuesday night and Kidderminster on Saturday. A good de-coke of the engine before then and who knows? Chances are that the team may appreciate playing away, with less pressure to perform. Let us hope so.

CHAPTER 7

THEY'RE PLAYING
OUR SONG

C rown Court trial permitting, I was planning to drive up to Northampton for the Tuesday night game, but fate had other ideas. Motoring home on Monday evening, I have a face-to-face encounter with a fully-grown female deer. Trouble is, its face was slammed up close to my windscreen as I hit it at about 50 miles and hour. It just leapt into the road, giving me no chance. The upshot is that the front of my car is stoved in and the headlamps smashed. I am all shook up, as I think what might have happened if another car had come round the corner as I skidded on to the wrong side of the road. It took 108 years to get in the League and I could have exited half-way through the very first season. I like deer – beautiful creatures – but bloody hell!

I can't drive to Northampton with the car in this condition, and I can't get on the Green and White coach because it leaves too early. I'm stuffed again. I seem to be making a habit of this. The only way I can get through 90 minutes of commentary on *Somerset Sound* is to flip the bottle top on a really strong ale and hope for the best. Just to hedge my bets, I also follow the internet channel that gives the minute-by-minute action. Well, it's not exactly action; it records each and every throw-in and free-kick and then, once every ten minutes, it tells you which team has the upper hand. It is totally tedious, to be honest. More ale, landlord.

Two more enforced changes in the line-up this evening. Colin Pluck and Terry Skiverton both carry injuries, so Andy Lindegaard and Abdelhalim El Kholti are drafted into defence. I must say that's probably not their best positions, but it seems that beggars can't be choosers. With Lee Elam and Nick Crittenden out as well, we aren't exactly spoilt for choice. Still, we are Yeovil Town. G.J. will make sure that our lads give a good account of themselves. This is certainly true of some 350 Glovers fans, who are giving it large on the radio. If there is one consistent in this merry-go-round of football, it is that Yeovil Town will be well supported wherever they go and the home crowd will know it. I am proud to be a Glovers fan. I like to think that when I am at away games (which is not quite as often as it should be) that I will give my 110 per cent, the same as the lads on the pitch.

It's not a good night. Two defensive errors; two goals – as simple as that, really. Effort in bucket loads from our boys but, once again, no luck up front. Even when the ball slips through the legs of the keeper, it hasn't got the decency to roll over the line. When a blip, wobble, slide, slip or sharp descent happen, all the luck deserts us quicker than sand in an hourglass. It happens at some stage to just about every football team in the land. If we won every game every season, it would be so boring. We would end up like Manchester United fans. No, the rollercoaster ride it has to be. Let's face it, we have been on the up for so long that this short fall seems like the descent into a dark, dark hole, but it is not. It is just a run of injuries and lack of confidence. We know that our players have skill, pace and stamina in abundance. That can't disappear overnight. As someone has just posted on *Ciderspace*, "Form is temporary, class is permanent". We'll be back.

A new boy joins shortly after the Northampton game. Andy Bishop has come on loan from Walsall. If we like him and he likes us, it could be permanent. Sounds like a dating agency. Fingers crossed, then.

I worry slightly that some of us are not staying the course. Picking up the *Western Gazette* tonight to thumb through the escort agencies (did I say escort agencies? I meant sports pages. On second thoughts, though, why would I be looking at the sports pages? With the drivel that certain football reporters churn out, I would be better consoling myself with some exotic escort. She might know if it is true that Chris Weale is just about to sign for Tottenham…) my eyes alighted on the small ad column and there, at the top, was the offer for sale of a Yeovil Town shirt, large, £30. Obviously some big guy can't take the tough time we are going through. It is a bit pricey, though, for a shirt that has seen half a season of sweat and tears. Perhaps he doesn't really want to sell it and, as soon as we have an upturn, he will want to wear it again. Hang on, further down the column someone – could it be the same guy – is selling a Burberry scarf. Perhaps what we are looking at is a disgruntled troublemaker. Thinking that our entry into the Football League would bring hordes of like-minded louts to HP, he bought a shirt and scarf at the beginning of the season. To his disappointment, he has learned that 99 per cent of the away fans we have seen and home fans when we have been away, are of a similar disposition to our old kin in the Conference – decent people who love their team and love their football, simple as that. I bet this guy is pining for Hereford as we speak. Let's hope he never comes back.

Thirty-three years we have known each other. It all started on 6 February 1971 in The Trafalgar Disco, King's Road, Chelsea at around 8.30pm. There she was, a sexy chick in hot pants and long leather boots, grooving to the music on a shiny metal dance floor. Coincidentally, I was there as well, three-piece suit, patent leather boots and shoulder-length hair. At 20 years old you could have been forgiven for thinking I had just played at Stamford Bridge and was now out on the razzle. Well, the rest is history and Lin and I have been together ever since. So you can see what an important anniversary this weekend is. Where to go, what to do, how to celebrate? I thought about a little hotel in the Malvern Hills. Romantic or what? That's just a short drive away from the Aggborough Stadium, isn't it? But before any of you accuse me of deceit, subterfuge or unchivalrous behaviour, I took a great big chunk out of the bullet and advised my loved one that I would be taking her away for a weekend of sheer decadent luxury that did not include a meat pie on the terraces at Kidderminster.

And so it was that we drove south rather than north on Friday 6 February. Two exotic nights in a four-poster bed with pool, jacuzzi, sauna and steam rooms, and all for the price of a handful of season tickets. We took no shirts of green and white, no lucky mugs, socks, knickers, jolly green giant dolls, pens or car stickers. In fact, none of those talisman that we could turn to first thing on Saturday morning to bring our boys good luck. They had to be on their own this time. We were out of reach for the weekend. We knew, of course, that they would be in good hands. Hundreds would be making the trip up the M5 to cheer them on, including the first-ever disabled supporters' coach, sponsored by the *On To Victory* fanzine. They didn't need us this time.

We strolled through the parks, watching the squirrels race up and down the pine trees. We immersed ourselves in the delights of Victorian paintings in a beautiful house overlooking the sea, and gazed from the windows of the yellow room and the boudoir as the watery winter sun lit up the foaming breakers that caressed the beach. We were once again young lovers with eyes only for each other. Well, until three o'clock anyway. We just happened to dine within the sight of a television with Sky Sports on it. No sound, just those all-important goal flashes to get the pulses racing. Our passions rose as the screen remained empty of that one scoreline we were searching for. By half-time, our meal having long been eaten, we were encouraged to leave the premises and so, with heads down into the brisk coastal breeze, we returned to our fantasy love nest and drank champagne. We missed that moment when Gavin Williams ran from the half-way line and blasted the ball from the edge of the box to make it 1-0. We missed the near miss by Kevin Gall and we knew nothing of the extraordinary events three minutes from time. We had no inkling that Chris Weale was about to pull off a great save from a dubiously-awarded penalty. Had we known we would have been screaming around the four-poster bed with apoplexy. As it was, we just chased each other round the bed for… well, you don't want to know.

Later, knowing the result, I swam lengths in my green swim shorts (I did have something lucky green, after all), singing, 'Yeovil 'til I die.' We steamed and jacuzzied. We were happy Glovers. Three juicy points. Back on the winning trail. Up one place to fifth, thanks to some other results going our way.

I have now given myself a dilemma. By virtually ignoring the Town, failing to comply with the usual coffee-drinking ceremony and eschewing previously followed rituals, we have come out with a win. What do I do next Saturday? Obviously, I shall not be ignoring them, because I shall be there to roar them on. No, the problem comes with all the pre-match stuff. To observe or not to observe. These rituals have stood us in good stead. The Conference was won on such conformity. I ditch it at my peril. Reading *Ciderspace*, I notice that others are wrestling with their own similar battles. Bucks Glover Lover informs the forum that it is his practice to wear his Yeovil shirt every match day, but, because of a washing machine fault, it was not available this Saturday. "What happens? We win. Bugger, that means I can't wear it again. Can somebody please reassure me that this was just a coincidence please?" Being one of a sympathetic and caring group of fans on the internet, Taff writes: "No, it wasn't a coincidence and it was your fault. You can never wear that shirt on a match day again. Hope that helps." But breast-beating has obviously been done by JB Westland Terrace who says, regarding fault, "No, it was mine. I've been neglecting my Y.T.F.C. tea mug lately. I gave it a good clean-up yesterday pre-match and we won. Shame on me. I have already written out 1,000 times 'I must take better care of my Yeovil Town mug/Holy Grail. Just off to find the birch branches now.'

Some of us even blame non-Yeovil items for loss of form. Lector writes: "I changed watches just as the bad run started. I left it at home yesterday and bought a new one at Cribbs. The rest is history." Perhaps, as therapy for my own fears and suspicions, I ought to start an Agony Uncle column in the match-day programme. Write to me, care of Fat Harry, and I will give you an explanation of your madness. One forum user with no such worries is Snoz. When challenged as to whether he was responsible for writing YEOVIL TOWN F.C. in the dirt on the back of a prison van seen on the M5, he quickly replied that he was "proud and unrepentant," and he justified it by saying: "To spread the word… is to spread the dream." Dream on, Snoz, dream on, *Ciderspace*, dream on, all Yeovil fans. We can do it.

In order to watch a couple of triallists, a 'behind closed doors' game has been arranged at Huish Park against Woking. I treat the 'behind closed doors' tag as a bit of challenge. Donning an all-black outfit, complete with balaclava, and carrying the compulsory box of chocolates, I slipped down below the snow line and hid in the pine trees. Noticing that the security guards were absent, I made a dash for the Main Stand. I thought if I could throw my grappling iron over the roof, I could shimmy up and get a bird's eye view. As it happened, one of the main gates was open, so I just wandered in and took a seat in the vice-presidents' enclosure. I found I was not alone and expected to be frog-marched out at any time, but no one turned a hair. The others looked like agents. Strange foreign accents drifted across from other seats, and I fantasised that Real Madrid or Barcelona had sent their men to view. It's an easy mistake to mix up Spanish and Welsh accents, don't you think? In reality, I think these guys were from Bangor Town. One in particular was obviously keen to promote one lad who turned out in our old pale-blue away strip. Well, I didn't recognise him, so he must have been one of the triallists. Trouble was, virtually every time he got the ball he lost it. He later suffered the ignominy of being substituted and disappeared down the tunnel. Sorry, Welsh agent, no chance of a £500,000 fee for introducing your lad. You might have better luck at Leeds United. For those wishing to keep a record of every Yeovil game, the result was a 3-3 draw. My major problem was the lack of a tea bar for a hot cuppa at half-time. I was frozen.

In a blaze of publicity, DJ G.J. and the squad launch the CD *Yeovil True* on an unsuspecting population. Pressmen fought with camera crews for the chance to hear the dulcet tones of the boys as they gave a live performance of what they hope will be a chart-topping song. Once again I just happened to 'pop' in at the right time and found all this excitement unfolding before my eyes. This time I got a cup of coffee and even a freebie bacon sandwich. They know how to look after an author at HP. All they have to do is sell 3,000 copies next week in W.H.Smith to ensure a position in the Top Twenty. So it is up to us lot then to propel them on to *Top of the Pops*. Pity the lads couldn't get their fake West Country accents around the word Yeovil, but never mind. Yeoville will do.

I have just watched the performance on the BBC's evening news. The lads looked good, as did Lisa-Marie and Bobby K, the two professionals in the outfit, but who was that balding old git who was wandering about in the background? Sorry, folks, I seem to get everywhere.

St Valentine's Day, Saturday 14 February. A day for lovers, romantics and those who enjoy a good massacre. Well, as far as the lovers and romantics side was concerned, I bought the regulation card, prepared breakfast in bed complete with croissants and the response was nothing, nothing at all. All Lin could say was, "I bought you a card, but I don't know where I put it." So much for that, then. I'll settle for the massacre this afternoon. Oxford United, third in the table and nine points ahead of us, are coming to HP. This has got to be the most important game of the season so far. Should we lose, I can see no way that we could regain 12 points to put us in the automatic promotion slot, and we could find ourselves out of the play-off positions as well. But, should we win, we will hold on to our fifth place and be only six points adrift of Oxford. We will be so in the hunt that adrenaline is coursing through me at the thought of it.

I am so up for this one I can't wait to get down to the ground. As we walk, hoops are coming from every junction. The weather is so mild that coats have been left off, allowing the green and white to sprout everywhere. It must be spring.

Oxford have brought a large number of supporters, just about filling the away end. It always looks so good when the ground is full on all sides. If there is virtually no one on the terraces, it looks like a gap in a row of teeth. There are few gaps in the Main Stand either, ensuring a large attendance. So it should. After all, if the fans can't turn out for a game like this, there is little point in being in the Third Division. This is what success is all about. Oxford United are a big club.

Once again, we have a makeshift defence. Abdooo is at right back and we had expected Colin Pluck to be taking up the left back position, but at the last minute there is a tannoy announcement that Paul Terry will be playing in his place. I don't know what happened there. Still, if Plucky has to pull out, I can't think of anyone I would rather take his place than Paul Terry. I always feel confident when he is on, or near, the ball. He radiates a certain calm – a 'don't worry I've got it covered' sort of air.

It is a chance for most of us to see Andy Bishop in action for the first time. I'm impressed just by his physical appearance as he limbers up before the game. Tall, just the right weight, and athletic – yes, he looks good. That's more than can be said for the Oxford crew. Tall yes, very, but some of them look decidedly porky. With a manager called Ian Atkins I would think that they should be following his diet a little more closely.

The game kicks off at a furious pace. Yeovil are doing all the running and, within the first minute, most of the crowd are on their feet hailing the first goal. Paul Terry, with a free header in the box, powers it but, unfortunately, it shoots across the face of the goal and out of harm's way. Still, a great start. At the other end, a free-kick is brilliantly saved by Chrissy Weale. It was another of his world-class, one-handed, top-corner-of-the-net jobs. Well, West Ham, if you haven't seen enough by now you never will. This is a keeper at his finest. The save obviously gives Yeovil great heart and they play some good team football. Everyone is involved; everyone playing an important role. I've never been a religious type, but on 29 minutes I was converted by the Bishop. In the right place at the right time, he smacks the ball in from close range after a good effort from Gavin Williams. The ground is humming, the roar is deafening and I have gone quite dizzy with the celebrations. All around me people are jumping, screaming (that's Lin), clapping, hooting, whooping and cheering. I have gone totally mental and now I feel that everything around me has gone into slow motion. What a drug this is – and they can't touch you for it.

This is the best football I have seen from the Town in a long time – free-flowing, and quick-passing. Oxford have no real answer. Big, ugly bruising tactics, even practised with the referee's approval, cannot overcome the Green and Whites. Half-time comes and most of the 7,400 crowd are wondering how the score line is only 1-0. The Bartlett Stand is wreathed in smiles. We all chatter like love birds on a perch (that's my Valentine's Day connection again) as we discuss the finer points of the first 45 minutes. Should Terry have scored? Should something better have come from El Kholti's dribbling run along the by-line? How long are we going to be watching the brilliant Chris Weale?

Yeovil serve up the same fare in the second half. The midfield pair of Way and Johnson have things pretty much under control, and this allows Williams to rove about in his usual style. Great through balls are giving Kevin Gall the chance to beat the offside trap. Several times he skips through and twice he slips the ball into the net, only for the lino to wave that wretched flag. Why doesn't he stuff it where the sun don't shine? Oxford are still employing the heavy tactics and a couple of names eventually go into the book. They play a high ball game, but fortunately Hugo Rodrigues is playing a blinder, and breaking down many of their attacks. But it is only 1-0, and, as the game goes on, I am getting more and more nervous. The Oxford fans, who have been very quiet for such a large number, begin to sense that they may still be in with a chance and begin to chant "Come on, you yellows." Any crowd that can't do better than "Come on, you yellows" over 90 minutes deserve to lose.

The minutes drag by like hours, and I'm in a hell of a state, but then Wealey does another of those superhuman stops and I know that the gods are with us. The final whistle blows – put me in the recovery position, someone. I honestly don't think I've felt such a need for those three points in a long time. I would have been devastated if Oxford had snatched a draw. There would have been no justice in this world. Yeovil, I love you. Each and every one of the players is a mega hero. I want to climb on the Bartlett Stand roof and bellow my praises. Instead we repair to the drinking tent and toast the boys in cider.

I'm home now, the nurse has just taken my temperature and I've stopped hyperventilating. I have time to reflect upon this new partnership of Gall and Bishop. I've got a feeling that this is the combination that we have been looking for all season. No disrespect to Jackson, Edwards or Stansfield, but Andy Bishop seems to have all the qualities that we need. Big and strong, able to hold the ball up well, quick to turn, bit of pace and gets in the penalty box at the right moment. He is also aware of what Gally is doing, and plays with him rather than in isolation. What more can you ask? I look forward to a hatful of goals between these two. This Third Division stuff is fantastic. Let's go for the big push. We are a million miles better than Oxford in skill terms, so we should be swapping places with them.

I know I've laughed about the boys' talents for singing, but I think I have to take it all back. I was seriously stunned when I heard on the local news that some 1,500 copies of *Yeovil True* had been snapped up on the first day. Unbelievable scenes are said to have occurred in Middle Street. Queues stretched as far as the eye could see as fans waited for hours to buy a signed copy. What was intended as a quick half-hour signing engagement for the lads turned into a three-hour marathon as the faithful kept coming. That *Top of the Pops* appearance might not be so fanciful after all. Will they want any groupies up at the studios?

Bad news for Jake Edwards has arrived this week. He is suffering from Gilmore's groin (why he can't just give it back to him, I don't know) and will have to undergo an operation on the abductor muscle in his leg. This is going to put him out of contention for at least four weeks. I'm just thinking ahead a little. What if Andy Bishop does the business and we sign him? Will Jake get a look in after that? After much to-ing and fro-ing, Chris Giles has now gone out on loan to Woking. He really needs a good spell of competitive football to put his career back on track. Whether that career will continue to be with Yeovil remains to be seen, but good luck to him anyway.

I have half an ear glued to the radio this evening. That conjures up a peculiar sight. Half an ear on the radio, half an ear on the fridge and the rest of me in the living room. What I was really doing was listening out for the Bristol Rovers v Huddersfield game. With Huddersfield breathing down our necks and having the advantage of a game in hand, I am taking the unusual course of cheering for the Gas. I end up pleasantly surprised that they manage to draw and restrict Huddersfield to the one point. That enables us to stay in fifth place. Our opponents on Saturday, Darlington, who beat the Rovers 3-0 at the Memorial

Stadium last week, have gone on a run of three consecutive wins. This is the first time in four seasons that they have managed to do this. Tonight, however, they have fallen 2-1 to Northampton on their own ground. Hopefully, this will have dampened down their revivalist ambitions and they will still be lingering around the drop, or worse, after our visit to the north-east.

It being pantomime time again (oh, yes it is!), Lin will not be able to accompany me to the delights of County Durham this weekend. Silly Billy will be giving both a matinee and an evening performance, thereby restricting her movements to the location of Montacute. Again, with no disrespect to the coach operators hired by the GWSC, I cannot face the loss of my bodily functions and endure the long haul to Darlington on their transport. With my own car still out of action (that bloody deer is now becoming expensive) I turn to the *Ciderspace* forum for help. I send out an urgent plea to anyone who may have a spare seat going north. Within an hour I am called up by Blew Stew, who offers me passage and the prospect of good company to boot. We leave at seven o'clock Saturday morning.

Love affairs can often blow hot and cold, and this seems to be the situation regarding Chris Weale and the Hammers. After his twice-weekly trysts in east London, it has been decided that the relationship should cool somewhat. The club announces that Chris will stay, at least until the end of the season. Gary Johnson says that the time has come for him to settle down and concentrate on the job in hand. The situation would only be reviewed if a big club came in with a realistic offer. You cannot toy with the lad, West Ham. Put up or shut up.

Montacute is deathly still in the early hours of Saturday morning as I sit on the steps of the King's Arms waiting for my lift. The only other person around is a member of the pub's staff, who himself is off to football. He, however, being a Scot, is off to Glasgow to watch his favourite, Rangers. Two very different journeys in prospect for us both. His, a 60-minute flight from Bristol, mine, a who-knows-how-long drive up England's motorways. We wish each other good luck and go our separate ways.

Our little band of four, being Stewart, Mark, Mally and myself, make very quick time, with Stew taking on a passing resemblance to one Michael Schumacher. By 10.45 we are ordering Olympic-size breakfasts at the Little Chef on the A1 at Doncaster. The only real concern during the early part of the journey was the choice of music being played by Stew. It turns out that he is a closet Petula Clarke fan and, by the time we have had the sixth rendition of *Downtown,* complete with his own variations, the will to live is beginning to seep away. Don't give up the day job, Stew.

Darlington Football Ground cannot be missed. Built by the side of the town's by-pass, it shouts at us as we approach. There can be no room for doubt as to who built this huge edifice – Reynolds Arena is spelt out in huge letters for all to see. How strange that the man who ploughed some £20million into building a Premiership ground is now denied access to the place. What complications arise between men with money, power and land rights. Will Darlo ever sort out these problems and move on?

Not as good a ground as Hull City's is my first thought. Impressive, of course. Any brand new ground with a seating capacity of 27,000 is going to be pretty grand, but somehow the design looks a bit bog-standard. All that criss-cross of tubular supports on the outside. I've seen it all before. What was rather amazing was the request for £5 to park the car in the 1,700 individually-marked spaces all around the stadium. Maintenance costs be must higher than I thought. Stew tried to explain that we had already bought our tickets for the match, but this cut no ice with the steward.

Where the ground did score maximum points was in the all-inclusive drinking facilities. A large bar catering for all allowed the several hundred Yeovil fans to mix freely with Darlo supporters. The atmosphere was very friendly and many a pint was consumed. What a far cry from the situation at home.

An unchanged Yeovil team run out into this superbowl to be greeted by a mere 4,500 crowd. That works out at about six seats for each spectator. Still, the turn-out from our fans is good and we cheer the lads for all we are worth. The Quakers start the match with more purpose and conviction than we do, and soon have us stretched with their quick-passing game. Isn't that what we normally do? What should have been a routine catch from a corner turns into a fumble and drop for Chris Weale, and the Darlington player has no trouble tapping it into the net.

All of a sudden I notice a cold wind whistling around where I am sitting behind our goal, and an involuntary shiver goes through me. To Yeovil's credit, heads do not drop, and they begin to get their game together. Paul Terry looks neat and assured at the back, and Lee Johnson is foraging forward with a purpose. In fact, more than a purpose. He lets fly from long range and beats the keeper in the top corner. We are punching the air and bouncing high up in the stand. Enter the star of the show – Dermot Gallagher, the man with the whistle. Obviously not content just to referee the game, he wants to be the centre of attraction. His first master stroke, in conjunction with his lackey assistant, is to allow a Darlo goal where a player in an obviously offside position actually jumped over the ball to allow the shot to beat Chris Weale. I know there has been a lot of controversy lately over FIFA's new interpretation of the offside rule, but come on. If a player was ever having any influence over the play it was this one. What were you thinking, Mr G?

Okay, it is 2-1, but Yeovil have had a great deal more of the possession and one glorious run by Gavin Williams results in his fine shot rebounding off a post. There is no reason to suppose that we can't still dig out a result. Oh yes, there is. I have failed to put the man in black into the equation. A good through ball allows a Darlington forward to run towards the edge of the penalty area. Paul Terry and Hugo are closing in. Paul Terry runs across the back of the player to get on the inside. I accept that there was some contact between them and the player fell like a sack of spuds into the box. Yes, a foul, maybe a yellow card, but the player was not denied a goal-scoring opportunity at that stage, and Paul Terry was not the last defender. So why a straight red card? Only Mr Gallagher can answer that. The Yeovil fans go mad. In fact, we go ballistic; all of us. One lad is so beside himself with rage he is eventually escorted from the stadium, having failed to heed warnings from the stewards to sit down and stop abusing the referee. Do you ever get the feeling that it is not going to be your day? This guy must have thought so. I heard that he turned up at Bristol Airport for the flight to Teeside only to declare that he couldn't overcome his fear of flying. He hailed a taxi to take him to Bristol Temple Meads where he paid £97 for the train journey. Another taxi had to be paid for to get him to the ground. And what did he get for his money? Half an hour of not the most scintillating football he is every likely to see, and a pillock of a referee.

Gallagher continues to dominate the proceedings when he books a Darlo player for diving in the penalty box when it was clearly a 50/50 ball. The consequences for this player only become apparent in the second half when, after an innocuous challenge, he is shown his second yellow card. At half-time I feel pretty miserable. I cannot see much chance of us rescuing anything from the mess that Gallagher has put us in. I am shivering with the cold and with rage. A hot steak pie helps with the former but there is no cure for the later.

The second half is difficult for Yeovil. With a large gap left by the absent Terry, it is a question of all hands to the pump to keep Darlo out. We make very few chances of our own and, as time wears on, both Bishop and Gall are withdrawn. Lindegaard and Stansfield try hard and get a little closer to that equaliser. Unfortunately, a good run down the wing and a hard low shot past the despairing Weale put Darlo strongly in the driving seat at 3-1. I would love to be able to click my fingers and be transported back to the warmth of my living room. I don't want to be here. This is a bad experience. One puffed-up, self-important, prima donna of a referee has ruined our day. At the death, El Kholti slams a ball low into the penalty box. It strikes Adam Lockwood and cannons towards the goal. It then strikes a defender and bobbles into the net wide of the keeper. Despite another shot from Lee Johnson striking the bar, that is as good as it gets. Beaten again. Perhaps it would have been that way whatever the referee did, but I honestly believe that if the second goal had been rightly flagged off-side and Terry had remained on the park, we would have gone on to win comfortably. It is all about quality. We demand quality from our players, and it is about time we had better quality from the officials.

On the journey back, Mark Kelly phones the Radio Bristol talk-in. Being exceptionally careful with his language he berates the referee but also gives a side-swipe at Kevin Gall who, in his opinion, should have swept in the rebound from the Gavin Williams' shot instead of wheeling away to celebrate before the ball had crossed the line. We all agree in the car. Having discussed in depth the pros and cons of the match and the club in general, we move on to more weighty topics – everything from the meaning of life and evolution to Mark Kelly's personal sightings of UFOs and ghosts.

At one point I am asked how I take a defeat by Yeovil. Am I one of these people who can shrug their shoulders, forget it and move on? The truth is, of course, that I am as miserable as sin and a poor result can influence my whole weekend. We all agree that this is how it affects us and so a sad little bunch of fans motor on through the night.

I arrive back home just as the triumphant cast of the pantomime are heading en bloc for the bar at the King's Arms. Triumphant, because they have now completed all of their performances and have survived without fluffing lines, collapsing scenery or falling off the stage, their adrenaline is up while mine is down. Many of the cast think I am stark starring bonkers for having travelled more than 600 miles in the day just to watch a game. I, in turn, think they are mad for wishing to put themselves on a stage in public and risk huge embarrassment. Fortunately, Silly Billy understands me and that is all that matters. We drink and curse Mr G. And the lad who was off to see the Glagow Rangers? He had a nightmare as well. He arrived at Bristol airport and realised he had left his match ticket at home and then, on returning to Glasgow airport for the return flight, found out that he had pushed the wrong button on the internet when booking and was told his ticket was not valid until next month. At great expense, he had to hire a car and drive all the way home. Still, Rangers won, so nothing to complain about.

It transpires that Gary Johnson was locked in the dressing room with his players for over an hour after the match. He had two areas of criticism when he eventually came out to meet the press. He complained that three or four of the players had not given 100 per cent during the match, and he would have to root them out and help them in the coming week. But having said that, he was still confident that we could reach the play-offs by winning half of our final 14 matches. The other blast he reserved for Mr Gallagher.

It is just as well we have a bit of light relief around Huish Park at the moment. Yes, it has happened. *Yeovil True* has smashed its way into the pop charts at number 36 this week. Apparently that is higher than either Pink or The Strokes. Well, I'm impressed. I can't say that I've heard anything by Pink or The Strokes, but I bet they are gutted to have sold fewer copies than a football team. Chart success brings with it mega publicity, and G.J. becomes a hit with interviews on Radio One and Radio Five. When asked if the Wurzels had influenced the song at all, Gary replied, "They have had an influence on our singing career, although judging by the way we played on Saturday, they have had a bit of an influence on our football too!" Even the lucky inhabitants of Australia have been given a taste of the rustic record. From Brisbane to Ballihooga, the BBC World Service has been making sure that they have not missed out. Good on ya, sport.

Have you ever wondered what the chairman of our football club does all day? What is it that compels Mr Fry to spend nearly every waking hour at Huish Park? How can there be enough pressing matters at a place where the major activity only takes place approximately once a fortnight? I haven't got a clue. So I have made arrangements to shadow him for the day and get some idea of what it is all about.

Nine o'clock, bright and early, I present myself at reception, only to be told that Mr Fry has not yet arrived. Not to worry, I'll go and have a chat with the lads in the commercial department. They seem to be up to their armpits in £1 coins, having been out on collection duty for the Gold Bond scheme the evening before. I have a coffee and chat about the *Yeovil True* CD. They have a stack of them on a desk waiting to be signed by the team. The players are not going to be happy when they see this lot. Their little old wrists will be aching by the time they have worked their way through them. How would I like to pull out the winning numbers for this week's draw? Why not? I might be lucky enough to pull out my own. Having been in the Gold Bond since its inception, it is about time I won a decent prize. Time ticks by and there is no sign of John Fry. Then a message arrives to say that he won't be in until about 12.30. Apparently he had asked someone to phone me yesterday to advise me of this. We'll call that an own goal for communication, then.

I am back at the appointed hour and there to greet me is the man himself. We are off at a pace – no time to be lost, things to do, people to see. He is in and out of the secretary's office, the press and publicity department and the inner sanctum, the finance office, checking to see that everyone is all right. No problems? Up the stairs to the first floor. He quickly explains plans to alter the upper foyer. "Wasted space up here," he declares. "We can move that wall, re-position the reception desk, put in a long trophy cabinet and alter the access." Hang on, John. I like the idea of the long trophy cabinet. This smacks of ambition. At the moment we have the Conference trophy sitting alone in a glass case, and that will shortly have to be returned, but I can visualise shelves full of shimmering silver cups, plates and shields. A full-time security guard sitting at one end, and a queue of visitors to the Yeovil Experience tour at the other. And why not?

John is using one of the hospitality boxes as his office and the desk is strewn with paperwork. He picks up a pile of letters from would-be work experience students, each anxious to spend a week or so at HP in the hope, probably, of bumping into Colin Pluck or Lee Johnson. Another pile of correspondence relates to charity applications, while a third contains new directives from the F.A., bound up in glossy booklets. There will be no time to answer the letters or read the directives this afternoon because he now has a pre-meeting meeting, and then the full meeting, regarding disabled supporters' access. We are joined by Irvin Morris, the honorary disabled liaison officer, and the club's finance controller. Irvin, at the club's behest, has drawn up a five-year plan to implement improvements for our disabled supporters. This is not an altogether altruistic gesture from the club, but needs to be done to comply with the final part of the Disabled Discrimination Act, 1996.

The full meeting is held in the marquee and is attended by, among others, representatives of the disabled from the Green and Whites and Independents supporters' clubs, the local authority, Westlands and officers of the club. Over a two-hour period, John Fry controls a lively debate, ensuring the agenda is adhered to, reining in speakers where necessary, and adding to a constructive discussion. As a mere spectator I was amazed at the task ahead. Access to the first floor of the Main Stand is seen as a priority by all parties and, to this end, plans had been drawn up to show a possible siting of a lift. I believe that the club is anxious to show that it is acting reasonably and, by providing a lift, will be visibly demonstrating commitment. But as the meeting developed it became clear that the lift would only be the start of it. Once the disabled supporter had been transported to the first floor, how would he or she then be able to watch a match? The discussions ranged over wheelchair platforms, removing rows of seats, provision of toilet facilities, problems of obtaining refreshments, and specially-trained stewards. What if the disabled supporters, who are presently accommodated in the Bartlett Stand, do not wish to transfer to the Main Stand? In order to comply with the Act, 75 per cent of disabled seating must be away from pitch side. Does that mean another lift would have to be fitted in the

Bartlett to take them to the higher tier seating? What about weather protection for those still sitting at pitch side? Wow, the problems kept coming. A meeting of all interested parties was arranged in order that the five-year plan could be discussed and taken forward.

Back in his temporary office, John Fry meets the catering management. A crisis had blown up regarding the provision of catering staff on match days. Some 130 people, sitting in both the restaurant and the hospitality boxes, expect a choice of good-quality hot food before and after each home game. Reliable chefs, it seems, are hard to come by and, with Saturday looming fast, it is important to rectify the situation. After all, it would be embarrassing to the club if visiting directors were not treated to the hospitality to which they were accustomed. Similarly, those in the boxes may not be that fussed over the football, but give them an unheated vol-au-vent and there could be a riot. No such problems with the bog standard tea bars. When the pies have gone, that's your lot.

Mr Fry took the time to take me around the first floor, pointing out where the lift would emerge in the VPs' lounge. I was shown how the bar will be moved to accommodate several more hospitality boxes, how the boardroom wall will be removed and replaced with a sliding partition, how the floodlights could be taken down to provide seating in the corners of the stands, and plans to provide concourse bars in both the Westland and Bartlett Stands. Any chance of a proper supporters' social club? His reply seemed to make that unlikely in the foreseeable future. And, finally, he just mentions that the grass may have to come off the pitch in the summer. What, again? What has happened? What is wrong? He wasn't too sure.

I was grateful to him for allowing me access behind the green door. He is enthusiastic about the progress of the club and wants to see it move on. It seems amazing that a ground that is only 14 years old needs so many alterations to bring it up to modern-day standards. Did they have no vision just over a decade ago? It seems that the only future contingency that they made back then was with regard to the desperately expensive super-duper crested carpet. John tells me that there is another roll waiting in the wings in a carpet factory in Kidderminster, just in case we want to build an extension.

"There may be a few more snow flurries overnight, with the temperature dropping in some rural parts to minus 11centigrade." So says the weatherman on Friday evening. This is not good news for Saturday afternoon. We have already had a couple of inches of snow on Thursday evening and very pretty it looked. My garden took on an alpine quality that we haven't seen for quite a few years, but it is no good for football. Sorry all you kids with trays sliding down the hills, but let's have a quick thaw. This, of course, is my heart ruling my head. If it were the other way round, I would be thinking "Hang on a minute, perhaps a postponement might not be the end of the world." After all, with the injuries that we are carrying at the moment and a hard away game at Huddersfield on Tuesday night, the rest might do us good. It might do Paul Terry good as well. His wife, Sarah, has just given birth to a baby boy, named Frankie. Perhaps a bit of paternity leave to coincide with the forthcoming suspension?

The alternative weekend sporting activity of bob-sleighing and slalom racing has been put on ice, because the game is on. Snow has been scraped off the pitch and stands in piles at the Westland End. The surface looks magnificent: I just hope the team are in as good a condition. A frozen group of Eskimos stand huddled together on the away end. They may have been Cambridge United supporters, but they were so quiet it was hard to tell. The contrast with the home end was enormous. As the chant of "Who are yer?" was bellowed out in greeting to the United keeper, I could tell that they were well and truly up for this one.

This was a game for the boys from the wilderness. It seemed only a short time ago that Abdou El Kholti and Adam Stansfield had little future at Huish Park. Abdou, especially, was almost out of here just before the Liverpool match, and Adam rarely got more than a few minutes as substitute. Today was their day. With both of them given starts due to injuries, they capitalised on the situation and dared anyone to take their place. Cambridge came to play football, and that is often the downfall of many a team at HP. Abdou was given the freedom to range down the wing at will, and his skilful ball control gave the whole team width across the park that has sometimes been lacking. Stansfield, with his good first touch and pace, caused United a headache from the word go.

Heavy pressure on the opposition goal creates a corner for Yeovil from which the hawk-eyed referee spots a foul. It seems like the usual pushing and shoving that takes place before every corner but he obviously sees something more sinister and points to the penalty spot. After last week's abysmal performance by Mr Gallagher I am more than happy to accept the scales of justice tipping in our favour. I wonder if the United fans saw it that way. Gavin Williams slots the ball past the keeper and it is 1-0. Only two minutes later, with Yeovil still pushing hard, Andy Bishop finds himself in the right place as the ball bounces around the box and stabs it in. All of a sudden the freezing cold temperatures seem to have melted away. I am flushed, hot with joy, relief, and happiness. Who knows? What a beautiful day. It becomes even better on 27 minutes when Adam Stansfield bursts into the penalty area with the ball tight at his feet. The keeper is rushing towards him and a defender is closing in from his right, but he keeps his head and strokes the ball into the far corner of the net. No great leather-bursting power, just pin-point accuracy. The roar is enormous. Everyone goes mental. Thousands of people are on their feet, hailing a master goalscorer. We haven't seen him score such a beauty since the F.A. Trophy final in 2002. This will do him the world of good, and Yeovil too.

Having rampaged up to 3-0, Yeovil then got caught with their guard down. A clever turn and cross was converted into a goal by the head of Danny Webb. Talk about a chip off the old block. He is the spit of his father, Dave, our old manager. Pug ugly!

The second half is less frenzied. Colin Pluck, back from injury, joins in the goal-scoring on one of his marauding forward runs to take us to 4-1, but after that Yeovil seem content to let Cambridge do most of the running around while they conserve their strength for the game against Huddersfield. Untied come close on two occasions with fine shots that strike the woodwork. But when it is your lucky day, everything pans out fine. Abdou is named man of the match and life is rosy.

We now have 56 points, and are up one place to sixth. Hull, Oxford and Mansfield all falter a little, and things are looking promising again. I reckon that March is going to be the make-or-break month, for not only ourselves but for all of the leading clubs. We all seem to be playing each other during the next four weeks and it will be interesting to see who can keep their nerve and consistency and who will bottle it. Please let that be someone other than Yeovil.

CHAPTER 8

NORTHERN WASTE

With the car still at the garage for repairs, I am grateful to accept another lift from Stew up to Huddersfield. There has got to be something seriously wrong with me to jump at te chance to drive to the back of beyond on a Tuesday evening when temperatures are hovering around zero. But here I am, in the car park of the McAlpine Stadium. We have been allocated a personal numbered parking space, only £4 this time, which, we are assured, is attended by car park staff throughout the match. Very nice. You wouldn't like to drive the car round to the front at the end and pick us up, would you?

I am becoming something of a student of modern-day stadia architecture. I could discuss the merits of cantilever, fully enclosed corners, double tiering, roofed floodlights, until the cows come home. I am thinking of producing a little trainspotter-type book of all the different grounds that there are. All us anoraks could then stand at the entrance to a new one and tick the 'been there, done it' box and feel a sense of achievement. I am waffling on in this way because I am not anxious to say anything about the real and ultimately disappointing purpose of our visit. On the journey up I find out that Stew not only has a Petula Clarke fetish but also a concurrent Carpenters affliction. Worse still, on the return journey we discover he is heavily into Meatloaf. You can see the sort of night I had.

Here are the bare facts. Three-hundred-and-fifty odd (some would say very odd) Yeovil supporters were present to witness a poor display by the Town. One glorious opportunity of taking the lead in the first half was wasted by Andy Bishop. I should imagine the lad panicked when presented with such a chance and he kicked it straight into the arms of a relieved keeper. From the subsequent kick up-field, Huddersfield lobbed it into the box, one of theirs was quicker than a couple of ours, and hey presto, from thinking a few seconds earlier that we would be one up, we are, of course, one down. I had a smashing meat-and-potato pie and a cup of tea at half-time. In fact, it was my second meat-and-potato pie. I felt I deserved it after singing my heart out with all the others. We were doing our bit in the face of 9,000 home fans. It is a pity others weren't.

As they say, hope springs eternal, and I take my seat for the second half with the vision of watching a rejuvenated Yeovil spring into action. It takes all of 60 seconds to disabuse me of that fanciful notion. Two down and going nowhere. When, on the hour, Huddersfield totally split the defence apart and their lad waltzes past Chris Weale, I don't know whether to laugh or cry. Perhaps another pie might have been the answer. But hang on, all of a sudden Yeovil have come to life. Passes are reaching hooped shirts, players are making good off-the-ball runs. Where have you been? Darren Way fizzes into a shooting position and lets one fly into the corner of the net. Twelve minutes left. We're gonna win four-three. Well perhaps not, but we give it a go. Kirk Jackson – yes, back from the depths and despair of Dagenham (having said his farewells last Friday after a 9-0 home defeat by Hereford), narrowly heads over the bar and a general sense of urgency is being shown. If we could just have those 60 minutes when we did nothing over again, who knows. The whistle blows, the team acknowledge our support, though Gary Johnson hasn't, and we are all heading back to the car for a short post-mortem before letting rip with the Meatloaf classics. Some people know how to live.

Yes, Huddersfield were good. They looked like a promotion-winning team, we didn't. I've got a nasty feeling that, come the weekend, we may well have fallen out of the magic seven. With the prospect of a grotty Saturday in Scunthorpe, I am feeling just a little bit jaded. Don't get me wrong, I'm not criticising the effort and endeavour that has always been there under Gary Johnson, I'm just a bit disappointed with the hot/cold displays that we are having. I'm tired out after the long trip and feel that I couldn't even fight my way out of a paper bag. Things will look brighter tomorrow.

Gary Johnson is asked to explain why he 'ignored' the travelling faithful after the game. He says that he needed just a few minutes on his own to compose his thoughts before he let rip into the team. He assures us that no slight was intended and he appreciates the support that the fans give on every occasion. I'm happy with that.

Saturday looms. I still do not have my car. They say it never rains but it pours. While I have been faffing about getting it sorted, Lin has had her car written off.

I think we'll both get bikes, paint them in green-and-white hoops, and call it a day. Because of the lack of transport, I receive an offer of a lift to Scunthorpe from Mark Kelly. Somehow I just can't face it. Just the word 'Scunthorpe' conjures up dullness, greyness, direness. I am sure we will win, but perhaps the lads will stand a better chance without me. After all, my track record is not very impressive at the moment. The only away win I have seen all season has been at Doncaster, and that seems a very long time ago. It might also turn out that Mark Kelly is a Bay City Rollers fan or something.

Just as I predicted, we have slipped out of contention. The table doesn't lie. We have been caught out. We were just not good enough. The team gave it their best shot, but the talent wasn't there. I doubt that there will be a late surge now to push us back up. We just have to take it on the chin and accept that we are only small fry in a very big pond. Still, to have reached number 34 in the charts was a surprise in the first place. Yeovil True has certainly made a little piece of football music history. Has any other Third Division club reached such giddy heights before?

Saturday it is, then. I'm trying, Yeovil. I have gone through just about every ritual in the book to ensure a victory today. I have been whistling *The Great Escape* and knocking out a few lines of *Yeovil True* – anything to keep upbeat and cheerful. I was mightily encouraged by Geoff Twentyman's prediction on the BBC news last night. He thought Scunthorpe were a good home team and would be too strong for Yeovil. As he gets about 90 per cent of his predictions wrong, I address a little Anglo-Saxon at the screen and look forward to a big win.

I get my car back this morning. I am pleased to trade in my anonymous hire car and drive off in mine with a Yeovil scarf proudly displayed in the back window. I have felt somehow naked these past couple of weeks, driving around with no visible signs of support for Yeovil on board. I want people to know who my team is. Lin and I spend the rest of the morning looking around second-hand cars to find a replacement for her. There is a lot of crap out there for a lot of money.

Oh, what joy, an afternoon in with Phil Tottle on the radio. The good news is that Scunthorpe have a few injury problems and a few suspensions. The bad news is that Yeovil have more than a few injury problems and a suspension of their own. Our once-strong squad seems to have shrivelled down to the point that anyone who can walk is playing. The loan spell for Andy Bishop has come to an end and Gary Johnson has decided to release him. He seemed to be having a problem with a foot injury and there is no point in carrying a half-fit player, especially when he is not yours. So that means we are another one short up front. Adam Stansfield pairs up with Gavin Williams. How many permutations of the front two have we tried this season? This has got to be the most difficult combination to get right. But looking back to last season, we only got the Jackson/Gall partnership going at about this time of the year, so perhaps there is still time for Gary to bring someone in who will just click with one of the others. Stephen Reed is drafted into the back, along with Andy Lindegaard to join Adam Lockwood, Abdou El Kholti and Hugo Rodrigues. No Plucky, Skivo, Critts, Terry and, of course, no O'Brien. Difficult times.

Scrappy play, poor ball control, wayward passing, off-target shooting. And that was just Scunthorpe. It sounds from the commentary as if we are worse. Still, I wasn't expecting a classic in the circumstances. What you do hope for, though, is a decent referee. Why do we keep bumping into the useless ones so regularly? Our chief chump is Mr Penn, who demonstrates his skills early on. Gavin Williams, having dashed into the penalty area, proceeds to fall over his own feet. No claim for a penalty, just jumps up and carries on. A deliberate dive, says Mr Penn, and writes Gav's name in his book (you can see where the phrase 'The Penn is mightier than the sword' comes from). And we've got another 80 minutes of this to come.

What a strange thing luck is. When a team is winning, luck seems to go hand-in-hand with the success. So many decisions swing in favour of that team when, on the law of averages, they shouldn't. But when you are struggling a bit, luck rears up and bites you hard. All the decisions seem from then on to run contrary to fairness and there is nothing that can be done – other than to win again, of course. On 24 minutes Hugo goes down with a head injury. Mr Penn allows the play to continue, which results in a free-kick for the Iron in a dangerous position. Hugo is led off the field with blood pouring from a broken nose and, while we are down to ten men and our luck having left the ground, Scunthorpe smack it in the net. How many times have we come back from being 1-0 down and won? Not many.

Things go from bad to worse as Hugo is substituted by Kirk Jackson. I wonder if Kirk has ever played in defence before? Still, it must be better than being with the poor old Daggers. Hang on, I may be wrong there, as Yeovil slip further behind just on the break. I won't bore you with the gruesome details of the rest of the match, suffice it to say that, on 60 minutes, we fall 3-0 down. Two of the goals are scored by an on-loan player from Glasgow Rangers. I wonder if he thought he was playing the 'old firm' and that's why he did so well? Kevin Gall comes on for Adam Stansfield, but nothing happens for the lad. As they say, he couldn't hit a cow's arse with a banjo at the moment. The only sound that brings a grin to my face is the Yeovil fans singing to the end. If there is one thing that is consistent at Yeovil, it is the great away support. I'm feeling sorry for those lads. With only one regular defender on the park it was always going to be a miracle for them to keep a clean sheet. Gary Johnson says afterwards: "We couldn't quite cope with the changes we had to make." When asked about Hugo, he says, "He wanted to come back on, but it was quite obvious his nose was broken and I wouldn't want to mess around with somebody's health like that. So I said 'no'." Asked about strengthening the squad with a loan player or two he says, "People are using loans like they are taking them off the trees. Scunthorpe had four loans today. I wouldn't have said having loans are a thing for the future. Maybe that is why they are where they are, because they have never had a settled side. I have to get people in that I want for the future. I don't really want to get people that are five-minute wonders. Having said that, we are very thin on the ground now, so I may have to get someone to add to our squad." No knee-jerk reactions there.

Despite our disappointing result, we still lie in seventh place. Good old Lincoln City managed to turn what looked like a win at Cheltenham into a defeat at the last moment. They still have a game in hand over us, but are two points away. We could be in for some nail-biting stuff, especially as we have both of the Rovers coming to visit Huish Park in the next ten days. For local pride we need to avoid a defeat against the Bristol variety and, for justice and decency, we must stuff the Doncaster variety. The Scottish Player will be with us on our sacred turf once again, and we cannot allow him to be crowing at the end. The message board has been full lately of how great he really was, how we miss him sorely and how we have yet to replace him. True, true, true, but I would still like to see him plucked good and proper.

I have been watching an object lesson in team support on TV this evening. The live match between Portsmouth and Arsenal in the quarter-final of the F.A. Cup was going, predictably, Arsenal's way. But at 5-0 down the Pompey fans put on the most amazing vocal display for their team. They chanted long and hard and won tremendous praise from Thiery Henry, who said he had never heard anything like it. It just shows the power of the supporters. I may not remember the score, but I think I will always remember that performance. Let's hope that we can give our boys a similar reception on Saturday. I could do without the scoreline, though.

Inevitably, there are a few wobbles on *Ciderspace* when the news comes through that Paul Sturrock, manager of Second Division leaders Plymouth Argyle, has accepted the vacant Southampton job. Sharp intake of breath, and then the question: 'Who may be lined up to take over from him?' The Board say they have no short-list at the moment and have advertised nationally. Their local paper, *The Herald*, suggests Trevor Francis, who is out of work at the moment, Sean O'Driscoll of Bournemouth, and then, of course, Gary. It would be very difficult to criticise him if the opportunity was to be presented to him and he said yes. I would be devastated, of course. He has been the best thing that has ever happened to Yeovil Town, and to replace him would be a tall order. I don't know that I trust the Board to get it right twice on the trot. I'm not going to think about this until such time as it is a done deal. After all, they may not even give him an interview. Then again, he might say no thanks – I've got a job to finish with the Best in the West.

A bit of exciting rumour rips around the website that Paul Connor, who we had chased a while back, was wobbling in his desire to sign for Swansea City. Swansea have apparently offered Rochdale £35,000 for his services and offered the player £2,000 per week. Despite all that, he has come down to Yeovil to talk to Gary. The whisper is that Yeovil are willing to break their transfer record and offer £30,000 with a further £10,000 appearance money. No hint, though, of how much they might offer Mr Connor himself. I've got a nasty feeling that we won't be offering anything like £2,000 per week. That is far in excess of anything that is paid to the rest of the lads (so I'm told). At six foot two inches he would be a useful addition up front, especially if he could stick one or two away. Well, to be honest 10 or 12 would be kindly looked upon. G.J. admits that he is in talks with several players at the moment saying: "I have got a few spinning plates. Some are wobbling, some are still spinning and some have crashed." At the moment, it seems that, if you can walk, you are in the team. It might be worth my while just hanging around the players' entrance this afternoon. After all, I've got my own shirt.

I didn't want him anyway. Too tall, too old at 25, and too out of form. Good luck, Swansea. Enjoy Mr Connor. Now the one we really want is Lawrie Dudfield, six foot one inch, only 23 and scores goals. He has been out on loan from Northampton to Southend, who themselves fancy their chances of signing him. In 2001, Hull City paid £250,000 to Leicester for him. What are our chances? I'm going up and down like a yo-yo at the moment. Every time I turn to *Ciderspace* my heart quickens at what I am about to read. Let's hope this one is the one for us. Gary Johnson, realising the mad frenzy that has taken hold of the Yeovil supporters over new faces, stirs it up a bit by reporting on Friday that he has THREE new signings for Saturday. Introducing Skivo, Plucky and Hugo. What, Hugo with his wonky nose? Careful, big man, remember your looks. Yes, thank God, they are all back and raring to get at Bristol Rovers. Even Nicky Crittenden was back in training until he got a gash on his shin requiring four stitches. One day we will look back on this period and laugh at how bloody unlucky we were.

You think it can't get worse, but it does. Chris Weale has broken his hand in training on Friday morning and will be in plaster for some weeks. Someone, or something, doesn't want us to get into Division Two.

It is Derby day. We have waited a long, long time for this one. The first ever game I saw as a ten-year-old involved Bristol Rovers (they were pretty crap then as well) and here they are playing a League game at the home of the Glovers for the first time. A full house is guaranteed and the atmosphere will be fantastic. Nature has done her bit to help make the day a special one. Gone are the freezing easterly winds and the snow. A beautiful blue sky has welcomed the day in with just the odd puffy white cloud. Let's hope the clouds are darker over the open terrace of the away end at three o'clock.

Geoff Twentyman has wound me up with his prediction of an away win for the Rovers. The man is mental. Given Rovers' current form, who on earth would announce on regional TV that they would win? Only someone with a bias that is always in favour of anything from the 'big' city. Stuff them, Yeovil, make me happy. I just switch on to *Ciderspace* to get the latest on our possible signing. Bugger me, if Dudfield hasn't gone and joined Southend after all. I reckon we had a lucky escape there. He obviously has no ambition. Why would you sign for struggling Southend when Yeovil could offer you the chance of Second Division football next season? Oh, hang on. Could it be anything to do with the wage packet on offer? Another plate has wobbled and crashed. Still, it sounds as if there are a couple more on the sticks. We move on.

As three o'clock draws near, those rain clouds begin to gather in an ominous way. Things are looking up. By about a quarter to three hailstones as big as marbles are hammering down on the players doing warm-ups and the 1,600 Gasheads, or Pirates as they are sometimes called, on the open end. All we've got to do now is win this game and a perfect afternoon will have been enjoyed.

The team looks a little more normal with Skivo and Plucky playing in a back three with Adam Lockwood. Abdou is just ahead, presumably with a brief to attack when possible. Up front, Kevin Gall, who so needs a goal against the Rovers (well, anybody really, but especially the Rovers), is partnered by Kirk Jackson, who told Woking this week that his future lies with Yeovil. Of course, the major change is Steve Collis between the sticks. He looks every inch the part in his all-gold kit. Good luck, Stevie.

8,726 settle down to watch local pride at stake. Both clubs need a win. The points are important at both ends of the League table, but it is top-dog status that is really the issue.

From the off, intentions are posted. Long high balls, hoof and run, niggly, dirty and lacking skill. Fortunately, that is the description of Bristol Rovers. Yeovil slip straight into a high gear and attack the home end. Abdou is becoming a real star these days and his dazzling runs and accurate centres are causing Rovers all sorts of trouble. On 16 minutes a Lee Johnson quick free-kick to Terry Skiverton sees the captain rush into the penalty box and smack a shot against the bar. From the rebound, Adam Lockwood forces it over the line. ONE NIL TO THE YEOVIL, ONE NIL TO THE YEOVIL. What a perfect start. Rovers become agitated and bad tackles start to fly in. One, from Graham Hyde, and his follow-up push earns him two yellow cards and it's goodbye time. Have you ever thought of climbing the north face of the Eiger? No, Bristol Rovers don't fancy it either. They sag and flop and El Kholti puts in the knife. A cracking angled volley takes a slight deflection and zips inside the far post. Huish Park goes wild. This is Yeovil at their smoothest. Fluid passing, with Lee Johnson orchestrating things from the midfield, Colin Pluck striking magnificent 60-yard passes out to the wings, Kirk Jackson winning just about every ball in the air and holding the line brilliantly. If only this had been the starting line-up against Scunny last week. Still, it is here now, so let us be thankful.

Shortly after the break, with the rain having stopped and sunshine filtering down on the anticipating crowd, Yeovil turn it on. Rovers hardly have a sniff, certainly no shots that you could call shots on goal. Steve Collis is looking confident in everything he has to do and there can be no worries about his ability to fill Chris Weale's boots for the time being.

Gavin Williams, with one of his mazy runs, rips into the penalty box and slams in number three. I'm up, we're all up. Bouncing, shouting, clapping and looking at the silent away end. Some of them have had enough and are slipping out of the exits. It is certainly Goodnight Irene for them. I almost had pity for them. Fancy having to watch this Rovers team week in and week out. Carlisle were poor when they visited Huish Park back at the beginning of the season, but I think that Bristol have taken the title of worst team I have seen. Just to reinforce this view, Paul Terry, with his first kick of the ball as substitute for Andy Lindegaard, puts in a pin-point centre, which Colin Pluck heads past the near suicidal keeper. Cue for mass exodus from the fans in blue and white.

A great afternoon, happiness restored. Vocal cords knackered. Up and down for the goals, up again for the call to "Stand up if you love Yeovil." Wonderful, wonderful. What more could you ask? Well, if I was being greedy it would have been for Kevin Gall to have scored at least one goal from the hatful of chances that he missed. Picky, picky, picky, that's me. We roar our approval of Gary and the lads as they come over to the Bartlett Stand at the final whistle. Everything is perfect, but there is just one more thing to be done before leaving HP. Just a few yards away from our seats is the press area, where I can see Mr Twentyman, headphones on and microphone to his mouth, tucked in with the other journalists. As I reach the steps nearest him, I bellow at him "What about your prediction now Twentyman?" He looks taken aback, and pulls an awkward face. I feel better for that. Little things, I know, but that man gets right up my nose.

Here we are on 59 points, seventh place, still in there. Lincoln, who are in eighth have beaten Mansfield, who are sixth. The Imps have a game in hand and are two points behind us. The Stags are on the same points with two games in hand. It makes Tuesday night's game with Doncaster quite important. I like understatements.

Understandably, Gary Johnson is a happy man this evening. More than satisfied with the afternoon's work, he just hopes that we can transfer some of this home form to the away trips. On the other hand, his opposite number, Phil Bater, is saying that he must consider his position as caretaker-manager. He points out that it is his job to motivate players and he obviously hasn't been able to do that. He confirms that Yeovil were better in every position. What the Rovers need is a real pirate. How about one from *Pirates of the Caribbean*? How about Jonny Depp? It just so happens that he is about 100 yards away from my house at the present moment shooting a film called *The Libertine*. Okay, so this is a tenuous connecting thread between football and film stars, but I felt I had to get it in. There have been bouncers the size of centre-halves manning the gates to Montacute House, and dozens of groupies hanging around the entrances just hoping for that glimpse of their hero. You wouldn't get me standing around outside anywhere just to be near some stars. Very foolish behaviour. Now, when am I going up to Huish Park next?

What you need after thumping a team is the opportunity to thump another team very quickly. The compilers of the fixture list have given us this chance by sending down Doncaster Rovers on Tuesday. Oh, how I would love us to repeat the 4-0 drubbing. I think, though, that my heart is ruling my head on this point. Let's face facts – Donny are rightfully at the top of the League and have been beaten only seven times this season (although once by us, of course). They must be doing something right to be in that position and will be coming to Huish Park full of confidence. They will also be full of the Scottish Person, and this could have a major influence on the whole match. It is sure to influence the fans. For most, it will be the first and possibly only time that they will be able to tell him what they thought of his decision to leave. Some will say it's water under the bridge and that he is just another opposition player, while others will be going mental at the very sight of him. I think I fall somewhere in the middle of these two reactions. I disapproved of the way in which he departed, but accept that he is a professional footballer who, in this modern game, bears no real allegiance to any club. Let's face it, he had no family ties or any connection with Yeovil and, in his eyes, no reason to be loyal. The only loyalty that can be relied upon at a football club is from the fans, and even that waxes and wanes depending upon the circumstances. We loved him when he was dashing down the wing and making monkeys of full backs. We loved his free-kicks hitting the back of the net. But he belittled OUR club, and for that he cannot yet be forgiven.

Who knows where our Yeovilcoaster will take us. We were at the bottom of the run at Scunthorpe, racing to the top against Bristol Rovers. Will we plateau out and enjoy a straight section or will we plummet back down again, screaming as we go? All will be revealed on Tuesday night.

My heart is racing nineteen to the dozen as Lin and I head for the bright lights of the ground. The adrenaline levels are as high as I can remember. I am just fizzing and popping with the anticipation of this game. Donny have quite a few coaches in the cage and several hundred fans on the terracing. We have a Westland Stand that is packed to capacity. This is going to be a highly charged evening. Two huge banners proclaim JUDAS McINDOE. I couldn't read the first part, but the second bit said 'we hate you so much'. I think we know where the home fans are coming from, then. The 'Macca' match is about to kick off. Booing accompanies every mention of his name and every move he makes. Some of the loudest chanting I have heard at HP tells him what the crowd thinks. It is a pity that chants in support of Yeovil are not quite as loud. It seems to give him a little too much importance. However, man of the match, Andy Lindegaard, saves us all the embarrassment of watching him score or play a blinder. With dedicated man-marking, Andy is able to restrict him to a couple of decent centres in an otherwise quiet performance. Despite that, Doncaster look potential champions. Having witnessed the worst team of the season on Saturday, tonight I think we are seeing the best. Strong and skilful in every department, they dominate large portions of the game. Yeovil hang in there as best they can, but always appear to be second best. With our ongoing problem of having no settled forward partnership, we never look like scoring – that is until Colin Pluck heads the ball in the net only for the very poor referee, Mr Fletcher, to rule it out.

By then Rovers had gone one up despite some great keeping by Steve Collis. The statistics of nine shots to one on target in Rovers' favour says it all, really. I could bleat on about the Gavin Williams offside that never was, or the bottling of sending-off decisions by the wimp in black, but it wouldn't make any difference. We were second in the race. If we should be lucky enough to still be in the play-offs at the end, and even luckier to win promotion, there will have to be some major additions to the squad. Perhaps some people still believe that we can win through with the same personnel that won the Conference, but I think not. Tonight could have gone any way. We could have played a blinder and everyone would have wondered why we weren't top of the League. We could have scraped a draw if the officials had been half-decent. But we lost. This was no disgrace. I think anyone watching the game tonight would say that they were glad to be there. 7,500 of us will probably settle for a defeat and be happy that we are in Division Three.

Lincoln stay in eight place one point behind us after coming back from 2-0 down to draw at home to Southend. They still have that one game advantage over us. Could it go down to the wire on 8 May, Lincoln away?

Yet another name clambers into the frame for star striker. This time we definitely have him, even if it is only on loan for a month from Bristol City. Lee Matthews is the boy. Yes, the Lee Matthews who was playing for Bristol Rovers last Saturday. To be honest, I didn't notice him on the park, but then I don't think I would have noticed David Beckham playing in that awful team. Some are describing him as 'big' – not as in tall, but as in porky. I am just hoping that, with the Yeovil training programme, he can reach our required fitness very quickly. His assets are his ability to use his size and hold the ball well in dangerous situations. That is certainly what we lack at the moment. Perhaps we shall see what he is made of at York on Saturday.

As one door opens another closes, and this time it has closed on Chris Giles. Chris has signed for in-form Aldershot of the Conference. He made his first-team debut in the 99/2000 season after rising from the youth team. I know that all Yeovil fans will wish him the very best for his future career and thank him for his part in lifting us into the Football League. Jamie Gosling has also gone to Aldershot, but this time only on a month's loan. He needs some competitive football if he is going to get back into the reckoning at Huish Park. And finally in the comings and goings this week, we have signed Ryan Northover from Woking. Ryan is a young goalkeeper who has presumably been brought in to give greater cover for Steve Collis than perhaps Jon Sheffield is able to offer. I just hope we don't see him in action too soon.

It is all in the planning, you know. The success of a long away trip is the thoughtful preparation. And so it was that I searched the internet for a suitable guesthouse for our visit to York. I was able to look at the bedrooms and other facilities, check availability, and make a reservation all from my armchair. A deposit was paid well in advance and all we had to do was turn up and enjoy a weekend in this interesting city. Apart from a severe weather warning, all was set fair for our trip up on the Friday. Lin wondered if we were doing the right thing, and thought perhaps it might be best to give up the deposit on the room and stay at home. I scoffed and said that a little wind and rain was not going to stop us going to Bootham Crescent and watching our boys come away with three valuable points. Now, I agree that the weather was pretty rough when we set out, with lashing rain accompanying us all the way up to Birmingham. But after that, it was just the strong winds that were a problem. Traffic reports told us of high-sided vehicles turning over here, there and everywhere. Then the motorways began to block up and so, with Lin navigating, we took off across country to beat the problem. Trouble was, everyone else was doing the same and we were soon down to a snail's pace through Nottingham. On the bright side, we did see parts of Britain that we had never seen before. Sherwood Forest looks particularly nice at this time of year! Oh, and it was a useful test drive for the new car that we have bought. We have named it Abdou, because it is Moroccan red.

Many hours late, we struggled into the Bootham Guest House, which was only a long throw-in from the football ground itself. After a shaky start, things were now going well. At breakfast on Saturday, we met two other Yeovil fans, Terry and Shelley, who had come up on the train. Perhaps we should have done that.

A delightful morning was spent enjoying the wonders of York. The Minster and the Shambles were all marvelled at, despite the rain and gale-force wind. I nearly got the part of Mary Poppins as I hung on to the big green-and-white umbrella that we took. We had a basin-full of culture by visiting a large restored Georgian house and then had a light lunch in anticipation of the game at three. Time to go back for a wash and brush-up in our room before strolling down to the ground. All was going well. That is, until the monsoon hit. We were forced to take cover in the York Arms in the city centre. As the tempest eased we made our way back down Bootham Crescent just in time to see the team coach turn into the road. We waved and shook the brolly and saw Paul Terry waving back through the steamed-up windows. Still an hour-and-a-half to go; nice to see the boys arrive in good time.

We stretched out on our bed and watched a bit of the Ireland v Italy rugby on the box and generally took things easy, until, shortly after two, I began to get into my usual pre-match twitchy state. Shouldn't we be getting ready to go? Yes, it is only 50 yards down the road, but we don't want to be late. It was then that Lin pressed the remote on the T.V. and a voice said: "There are two matches postponed this afternoon, one in Scotland and the other in Division Three, York v Yeovil." I nearly fell off the bed with surprise. It had to be a mistake. We'd had a drop of rain but not that much, surely.

I dragged on my hoops and went down to the ground to see what was going on. The pitch was a collection of various-sized lakes, and would have been ideal for a water polo team. Badger from *Ciderspace* was wandering around taking photos as evidence to show folk back home, I guess. I always knew he had special properties, but it was amazing how he was able to walk on water. In the social club I found the Yeovil fans. I felt for those that had just arrived on the coach and would shortly be climbing back on board for the long, long trip back home. It is bad enough going home when you've lost, but when you didn't even play, the journey seems to last for ever. The staff in the bar did their best to make us feel wanted and gave out some free food. But, hey, 280 miles for cold quiche? I met up with John and Janice, who had also booked into a nearby guesthouse. John was all for cancelling the booking and driving back home straight away, but Janice wanted to stay because it was a nice room and had a four-poster bed. John was eventually persuaded when we all agreed that a tour around the York Brewery would be a reasonable alternative to the football.

Three hours we stayed in the Brewery. Michael, the guy who runs the place, felt sorry for us in our green-and-white shirts with nothing to cheer at, and forced us to have drinks on the house. We must have sampled just about every brew that they made. By the time we staggered out of there and the subsequent pubs and curry house, we had almost forgotten why we were in York in the first place.

On the bright side is the fact that we did not lose any points. Had the pitch been playable, I think the wind would have given us great problems and would probably have assisted York. So better to play when the conditions favour Yeovil. The downside is that Lincoln have now played their catch-up game and have taken the full points, which puts them two points ahead of us and we are now out of the play-off places. We are replaced in seventh spot by Mansfield, our opponents on Saturday. I may have said this before, but this is now possibly the most important game of our season so far. Three points and we will still be well in the hunt. No points and we might find it more than a little difficult to climb back into those play-offs.

Monday brings a sad occasion. It is the funeral at Martock Church of Molly Burfield. Molly was the wife of Yeovil Town's president, Norman, for 63 years. Throughout his term as chairman at the old Huish ground, and since he has been president, Molly rarely missed a match. She had watched the Bristol Rovers game on the Saturday and passed away on the Sunday. Some would say that was the best way to go. I shall remember Molly, not so much for her connection with the club, but for warm summer days on Montacute rec. She and Norman were great supporters of cricket and would often drive over to see how the local team was doing. She will be missed by many.

Not having had my weekly fix of football I feel a great need to go and watch the reserves on Wednesday evening. There are a couple of other incentives. Firstly, we are playing the Gasheads again and, let's face it, it is always nice to beat them, at any level. Secondly, Yeovil will be playing three triallists who are being released by Premiership clubs. They are Nathan Talbott, a left-sided defender from Wolves, Jamie Gleeson, a midfielder from Southampton and Nick Matthews, another defender from Leicester. Lin and I were quite surprised at the size of the queue when we arrived and, because the game had started before we got in, I was not able to pick up a team-sheet. Had I done so, I would have learned that, in addition to the triallists, we had a new player signed on a short contract. Because I tried to concentrate on the three new lads, I didn't really notice our Number 10. He was Dani Rodrigues, another Portuguese, but no relation to Hugo. Originally bought by Glenn Hoddle for Southampton for a hefty fee, he suffered a bad injury and dropped out of the English game. He has recently been playing for Greek side Ionikis. Gary Johnson said: "Dani has signed on a short- term deal with a long-term deal in view. I know that sounds like a contradiction, but I want to give Dani the opportunity to get his fitness back to the level he had at Southampton. If I can get him back to anywhere near that level of fitness, we will have signed a very good player, but I must stress that he will need time to reach those levels and to settle in at Yeovil." At least he will have Hugo to chat to, which should help him feel at home. As for the triallists, Talbot looked more than a bit useful, fast and dangerous when attacking but solid in defence. Gleeson looked quite handy as well, showing a fair bit of skill in the middle of the park. Matthews was trying to impress a little too much. He ran about like a mad thing and threw himself headlong into just about every tackle. Could be a liability. We've got one of those already – Colin Pluck doesn't need a rival.

Yet another player on the move – this time it is Lee Elam going on loan to Chester until the end of the season. Is that the last we shall see of him, I wonder? He never quite made the grade at Yeovil – some promising touches, but never any major contributions. A more surprising move is Mark Kelly stepping down as Y.T.I.S.A. chairman. Mark started the Independents by hiring a mini-bus to drive a few friends to away games and found that it grew and grew. It now boasts around 500 members and regularly has coaches travelling away.

Saturday 27 March is here – the big, big, big one. A six-point game. Ever since my accident with the deer I have been very wary of those road signs that tell you that, for the next X miles, you can expect the little blighters to leap across the road. Mansfield, the Stags, now come into that category. I am very wary of them and want to see the back of them as soon as possible; with tail between legs, if that is possible for a stag.

The trouble with Yeovil is that our strikers don't strike. Once again, Kevin Gall and Kirk Jackson come away empty-handed. Chance after chance fell to them, with Gally going closest when he headed against the post with the whole goal gaping wide. There is certainly a jinx on him that needs to be laid to rest. Perhaps if he had been given what was an obvious penalty in the first half, it might have done the trick. Mansfield also missed a number of chances, including a rocketing shot that struck the underside of the bar, leaving Steve Collis stranded. For quite long periods Mansfield ruled the midfield and were able to set up useful attacking moves. But the deadlock was broken on 67 minutes when Terry Skiverton, threw himself headlong at a corner and blasted the ball into the net. It came at a personal cost to Skivo, as he appeared to be knocked unconscious, for the second time in the match, as he launched himself at the ball. Minutes later he was substituted, having done a great job. The referee, Mr Beeby, had not had a good afternoon up until the point when Yeovil took the lead. After that, he went downhill with a vengeance. I don't like to use the word 'bias' when talking about someone whose job it is to be totally impartial. We see incompetent referees on a regular basis, but usually they even out their incompetent decisions for both sides over the course of 90 minutes. But this time just about every decision was decided in favour of Mansfield. It was as if he was doing everything he could to get them back on level terms. And as sure as eggs are eggs, following a series of free kicks for tackles that were fair, Mansfield got into a scoring position. A good shot was well parried by Steve Collis but the resulting centre was then knocked in to make the ref a happy man. Some 6,000 people (there were not many from Mansfield) expressed their dislike of the way he handled the game. I'm sure I didn't moan about the officials half as much when we were in the Conference.

So that leaves us still one point adrift and a game ahead of Mansfield. On Tuesday night they play Torquay at home. If they should lose, then things will still be very interesting, especially as we have to go to the seaside to play Torquay on Saturday

It is always difficult to have to stand on the sidelines while others are deciding our fate. I know, as spectators, that that is all we ever do. But somehow, when Yeovil are playing and we are roaring them on, we can feel that we have a small hand in our club's destiny. Tonight the mid-week games are Macclesfield v Lincoln, Mansfield v Torquay, and Rochdale v Doncaster. The Rochdale match doesn't really worry us – Donny are too far ahead to matter – but the other results are very important. Can we rely on Macclesfield to take the points away from Lincoln, who are in sixth? What about a draw at Mansfield? A point apiece for the Stags and Torquay would be best for us, as they lie in seventh and fourth respectively.

At the end of the 90 minutes Mansfield are the happiest. A 2-1 win puts them up into sixth, while the losers, Torquay, may have had a knock to their confidence. Lincoln grab a point from a pulsating 0-0 draw and slip to seventh. That gives them a three-point advantage over us, but we now have a game in hand. I can still see us all at Sincil Bank, Lincoln, on 8 May, with it all to be decided. It could be a very testing day!

CHAPTER 9

A SPRING IN OUR STEP

There is a breaking story that Gary Johnson and John Fry have flown to the island of Mustique (or is that Mistake?) to talk terms with one Eric Cantona. There is even a photograph of Gary standing poolside with the man himself sporting the green-and-white hoops. A place in the line-up against Torquay, then?

Let me see. Could this have anything to do with the fact that it is 1 April today? I have a feeling that a certain Mr John Jeannes may be responsible for raising my blood pressure with this wicked tale. Nice one, John. Nice one, *Ciderspace*.

Spring has bounced into April with some fantastic weather. Glorious blue skies and warm sunshine have tempted me out into the garden, where I have mown the lawn and pulled up weeds. Well, I have to do something with all the spare time I seem to have at the moment. Work has almost dried up. Are all the criminals behaving themselves? I think that is highly unlikely, but sometimes the work comes in peaks and troughs. Cold winter nights tend to put the burglars off a bit and this filters down to my end of the business a couple of months later. Still, with the nights drawing out, things should pick up soon. Once again, I seem to be following Yeovil's pattern of success. We were both doing very nicely thank you earlier on in the season, but have both hit a rocky patch. I just hope that they are not involved in a relegation battle next year.

I was hoping that the fine weather would last for our trip to the seaside this weekend. Torquay in the sunshine is a much nicer prospect than Torquay in the rain. But rain it is. Some 1,600 of us, all lucky ticket-holders, make our way down to the English Riviera for this make-or-break clash with The Gulls. I think we all know in our hearts that this is the do-or-die moment of the season, when anything less than the full three points will not be good enough.

Lin and I choose to travel with the Independents on the double-decker coach. We now have a strict no-alcohol and no-smoking policy on board, and this is reinforced by a dire warning that we are likely to be stopped by the Devon police and, should they find any booze, the coach will be turned back. After that, the nearest we will get to the match will be watching the result on *Grandstand*. Leaving at 11am ensures that those who are desperate for a pint will have plenty of time to sit and sup in the pre-arranged pub stop on the edge of Torquay, watch the semi-final of the F.A.Cup (Arsenal v Man. Utd) and get to the ground in good time. Despite the plan, some on the coach cannot resist having a crafty fag and a sip of something medicinal. Well, I'm sure it wasn't Lucozade being passed around. Approaching Torquay, the promised police ambush takes place. The coach is directed off the dual carriageway on to a slip road, where large numbers of officers and vehicles are waiting. After what seems an interminable time, passengers are allowed off, and many rush to light up. Fortunately, the police do not come on to the upper deck. If they had, I am sure they would have found the bottle of Jack Daniels that was slipped out of the hatch and on to the roof. There is always someone who is prepared to jeopardise the enjoyment of the majority by taking a silly risk. I can live with the no-alcohol policy for the sake of a couple of hours. Why can't they?

The pre-arranged pub stop outside Torquay is cancelled by the police. We have had to pay a premium to Torquay for our tickets for the extra policing today, and we are certainly getting our money's worth. It seems they want all the coaches at the ground together, and all the fans in one area. Further advice is given not to go into the town centre because there may be some hostility from the natives, backed up by, it is rumoured, a group from Exeter. All that is left is Torquay's social club, or a couple of corner pubs full of natives. They are all stuffed to overflowing, so Lin and I give up and walk back to the ground. At least we get a decent place in the away end, unlike some who arrive later and find that they have to watch from a poor position on the side. By three o'clock the compact little ground is full. Torquay rarely find themselves in this position, normally attracting small crowds.

Our fans give everything for the lads. The singing is loud and defiant, and designed to roar the boys home to victory. One sour note, literally. Just as our boy trumpeter was opening his first number, a 'Burberry' moron pushes into him and knocks the instrument into his mouth, cutting his lip. We were several steps down from the incident, but I could see that the lad was shaken. After all, you don't expect that from your own supporters. The trouble with this handful of idiots is that they like to start singing the confrontational chants, having eyes only for the opposition fans. They dislike the trumpet boy starting songs that they don't want to sing. All I can say is, "more power to your trumpet, son." We don't need these few idiots who have more on their agenda than the football.

On a soft pitch in the rain, a hard-fought match takes place. Both sides give everything and, from a neutral's point of view, a fantastic games unfolds. From the start, Yeovil signal their intentions to come here and win. Corner after corner comes our way as Yeovil push and push for that first goal. Jake Edwards and Lee Matthews form a new strike partnership, and the two big men work well together. Neither is particularly pacy but, because they are equal, they can play off each other. A swirling wind is at Yeovil's backs and is being used to good effect against a nervous-looking Torquay keeper. The break comes when Abdou cracks the ball against a defender and it loops high and rebounds from the cross-bar. Darren Way is there to lash the ball into the open net. Our dream lives on, as we celebrate on the terraces. Better still, when Gavin Williams jinks into the box and slips over an inch-perfect cross, Jake Edwards taps in. We are 2-0 up in 27 minutes. This has got to be our day. I knew it would be as soon as I drew Wonder Weasel in the Grand National sweepstake on the way down. At the other end, all is safe and secure, with Steve Collis doing a great job in smothering a couple of good Torquay efforts. The boys are purring – the old Rolls Royce has been pulled out of the garage for this one. Then, as if the clouds weren't black enough as it was, another one looms up on the horizon. A free-kick, given against Terry Skiverton on the edge of the box just before half-time, is converted, and The Gulls are back in it. Not a good time to concede.

There is never a good time to concede a penalty either. Abdou El Kholti gets in a bit of a tangle with Torquay's star striker, Graham, and the referee is adamant that it is a penalty. Yeovil employ as many time-wasting tactics as possible, and Paul Terry gets booked for trying to dig up the penalty spot. Others argue, some encroach, but in the end it is all down to Steve Collis. Guessing correctly, he flings himself to the right and stops the ball, only for it to slither out of his grasp, allowing the penalty-taker to follow up and score. Yeovil never recover from this blow and spend the rest of the match fighting a rearguard action, as all the fluent play and fine shape disappear. Things get worse when Gavin Williams mis-times a tackle and picks up a second booking. Down to ten men, Yeovil hang on and take the one point from the draw, but we didn't so much gain a point as lose two.

The mood on the coach is subdued. We so needed to win, and we were looking so good, yet now the chance has gone. The play-offs are still a possibility, but that possibility is getting more remote by the day. Both Lincoln and Mansfield picked up points and this leaves us four points adrift of Mansfield, in seventh, on equal games. Lincoln are five points ahead, having played an extra game. Anything is possible, but my doubts are edging out my optimism. I'm not really complaining. Whatever happens from now to the end of the season we will be able to look back and take pride from this first-ever venture into the Football League. Heads up. We are Yeovil Town, Ooh Arr!

On *Ciderspace* there are the optimists and the pessimists. Good old optimists, still banging the drum for promotion. Win the next five games and we will still be in the play-offs – the glass-half-full brigade. The pessimists fear that all is lost and that we shall have to have a root and branch clear out before next season if we want to be in with a shout – the glass-half-empty supporters.

I just happened to be sitting in Gary Johnson's office, sharing a bag of doughnuts with him after a training session on Thursday. He had a raging toothache which, he said, had made him more than a little tetchy with the players. Every time he went to shout some instruction or other, the stabbing pain in his jaw turned it into a snarling bark. It seems he has tried every pain-killer known to man, but none has helped. "If I had a drugs test now, the F.A. would ban us from the league," he joked. We talk about the run in, and he agrees that we need the consistency of a couple of wins on the trot "Truth is," he says, "there are five or six players you could hang your hat on each game, but there are another five or six who you might as well toss a coin as to how they will play." That about sums it up. Ever since the name 'Liverpool' was mentioned, we have struggled to really play as a complete unit. Of course, we have had a list of injuries as long as your arm, but that is why you have a first-team squad. Some have just not performed.

"Guess what?" said Lin a few weeks ago. "We've had a wedding invitation for the Easter Saturday."

"That's nice dear. Are we away?"

Are we away? Of course not, it is Cheltenham at home. I keep cool, but my nerves are jangling. The prospective happy couple are Lin's work colleagues That is my angle, then. I don't know them that well, so they won't miss me, I claim and, without a fight, a row or even a knowing look, Lin agrees. She is a treasure. The plan is that Lin will attend the service and I will attend Huish Park. We will then meet up in the evening for the reception at The Old Barn. Perfect. That is how problems should be solved.

With Easter fast approaching, many matches begin to take on huge significance – not just our games, but those involving all of the teams around us. One day you want one team to win and then the next that same team needs to draw or lose to help us on our way. Recently it has been Mansfield that I have wanted on the banana skin, but allegiance has now switched to supporting them in their game against Oxford in the week. After appearing for so long to be a steady outfit that would possibly get into the automatic promotion places, Oxford have thrown a wobbly of late. Should Mansfield win, then Oxford would be five points ahead of us and have played a game more – an identical position to Lincoln.

Bless you, Mansfield, 3-1 winners. Now we lurch on to Good Friday's match – Oxford v Boston. As much as it goes against the grain ever to wish that Cheats United should even win a single point, this is the unpalatable situation that we have reached. Ideally, I am looking for a Boston win, but at a heavy cost in injury terms, so they have as few fit players as possible to face us on Easter Monday. I have no scruples. Half a dozen struck down with the plague would be acceptable. We need those three points at York Road. In the meantime it is COME ON, YOU PILGRIMS. Ugh, spit. I hope never to repeat that. It is almost as bad an experience as suggesting that Hereford deserve to be in the Football League.

There is only one way to pass the time before the results come in and that is out in the garden on the lawn with the spot weeder. Shooting dead those dandelions and other persistent pests is very therapeutic. With a little imagination those plants can take on the form of anything you like. I have just shot Graham of Torquay. That will teach him to dive in the penalty box and blame Abdou. And don't think you Cheltenham players can run and hide over there by the water butt. I've seen you, squirt, squirt. As you can tell, I may have taken a little too much of the sun this afternoon. We will know later when the straight jacket comes off.

Oxford 0 Boston 0. There we are then – not a Good Friday, but not a bad one, either. At least it keeps us in with a shout. But just as I take my eyes off Oxford, along come Northampton. Where have they arrived from? Most of the season they have been bumping along and now they are at our shoulder with the same points and games. Only a better goal difference gives us the edge.

Cheltenham Town at Huish Park. We are in the last chance saloon. No less than three points will do. Cheltenham, in seventeenth place, are the sort of team that we should routinely beat. It would help our cause if we won well. Our goal difference is inferior to all of the teams above us and, if this should go to the wire, those goals could be crucial. So there we are; no pressure.

Lin heads for the wedding, and I head for the delights of the football. Two hours later, I wish it had been the other way around. I shall probably need counselling for the horrors that I witnessed that afternoon. A crowd full of hope and expectancy went away broken and traumatised. This must have been the worst Yeovil performance under Gary Johnson's management. I don't intend to go through the match blow by blow, because that would be too painful for all of us. The boys have given me great pleasure over the past two seasons and I would not want to criticise them individually for one awful performance. I am sure they must be as gutted as the rest of us. It was like a contagious disease. One lost the ability to play football and the rest caught it within a few minutes. It was as if they were playing with a piece of slippery soap rather than a ball. First touches bounced away, passes skewed off at all angles, and the only consistent factor was that the ball would be played direct to anyone in yellow. It was a total shambles. The crowd caught the mood of the afternoon and, at times, the only voice I could hear was that of Gary Johnson as he shouted unheeded instructions at the team. The only chant that caused me to have a wry smile came after about 70 minutes of purgatory, when some on the Westland Terrace sang, "We're gonna score in a minute." At least we kept our sense of humour. The bare statistics are that the game ended in a 0-0 draw. Yeovil had one corner and one meaningful shot on target. Cheltenham did a little bit better. I fear we are dead and buried. Three points from the last 12 is not play-off material. Northampton, on the other hand, are now flying and have beaten Hull City 3-2 at the Kingston Stadium. They now leapfrog over us with 64 points to our 62.

I find that champagne and cider do not mix very well. I felt obliged to do more than a little research into that proposition at the wedding reception. How else could I blur the nightmare that I had seen? Fortunately, there was a guest at the reception who was able to take my mind off the present and return my thoughts to the 'good' old days at Huish. Jess Payne, Yeovil's centre half from 1979 to 1984, was more than happy to share his memories of those times. I felt a lot better after that. Everything needs to be put into perspective. During Jess's time at Yeovil, average crowds were around the 1,100 mark. The club was near bankrupt, scraping along the bottom of the Alliance League (the forerunner of the Conference) and the poor old ground was falling apart. I thank my lucky stars that we are now where we are. If we can grab the points at Boston, three from Bury, York, Southend, Hull and Lincoln, we might just...

Two little rays of light in this gloomy weekend. First, the Burberry boys have apologised to the mad trumpeter. Perhaps that is the first step in their growing-up process. Secondly, back by popular demand, is the one and only Mark Kelly. A change of heart means that he will remain as chairman of the Independents.

Easter Monday gives me a choice of a nine or ten hours' return drive in motorway madness Bank Holiday traffic to Boston, or a quick zip down to the coast at Burton Bradstock and a head-clearing walk along the cliffs. I know in my heart that I should be with the lads in their hour of need, but, after Saturday's display, I think that they will have to do it on their own. Fortunately, there are some 400 fans who have still got the stamina and are up for the fight. In a crowd of 2,800 and odd, that is pretty brilliant.

Down on the beach the sea was as flat as a millpond. We skimmed stones across the water and talked about all subjects other than football. It couldn't last, of course. By just after three o'clock we were back in the car, radio on, praying for something special. And there it was, 1-0 to the mighty Yeo – Simon Weatherstone from the edge of the penalty box after only four minutes. Pity they equalised on 14 and a greater pity when they scored again on 44. Once again, we had suffered an injury and were down to ten men. Things are looking up again when Adam Stansfield, who is playing ahead of Kevin Gall, side-foots in on 51. All still to play for. It must be our day when a referee actually awards us a penalty. Gavin, brought down in the box, steps up and puts it away! Hang on, it has to be taken again. Why? Because two Boston players have encroached into the box. So we get penalised. That's fair, then. You could have put money on it that Gav would miss the retake. Still 2-2, but chances galore. Into the last minute, and it seems that we will have to settle for a fourth draw on the run. They say that all things even themselves up in football. A good run can be followed by a bad one. Pathetic decisions by the ref swing the other way by the end of the season, but surely now is not the time to be evening up the number of draws that we usually have in a season. Four on the bounce, when what we need are wins, is cruel. Did I say four? Make that three. Cheats United have just won the bloody game with an offside goal. Thanks ref. Sheer genius. We slip further away from the play-off contenders. Northampton and Lincoln get a point each, leaving us five points away from the nearest spot. Oxford, still in freefall, lose and seem likely to be replaced by the Cobblers in the last position. I think that we shall end the season in ninth.

My mind slips back to that wonderful April day, a year ago. We were all packed into the away end at Belle Vue, Doncaster. The news came through before the kick-off that we had won the Conference. Our joy was uncontainable. We were the champions and we loved every minute. This afternoon Doncaster beat Cambridge United 2-0 and were promoted to the Second Division. What can I say but they have been brilliant and deserve their success? They have been consistent almost from start to finish. One notable wobble, of course, when we beat them up at their place, but apart from that, they have virtually run the show. It is sure to re-fuel the debate about the Scottish Player. He said that he was going to a bigger club with more ambition. Perhaps he was right after all, the little sod. It is time for us to sit back and try to enjoy the remaining games, hope that we can play the football that we have come to expect, and please, please, let Kevin Gall score a goal. Then we can all have a deserved rest and go hell for leather next season.

At a meeting with representatives of all the various supporters' groups, John Fry has asked for suggestions from fans as to how the club should deal with ticket allocation in the event of another big game in the near future. It is nice to know that at least they will listen. A little more news seemed to be on offer regarding drinking facilities for the fans. There is now talk of a single-storey building attached to the Bartlett Stand, complete with skittle alley. This sounds a bit more like a social club than I was hearing when I met Mr Fry in February. The only snag is capital funding. I wouldn't think about savouring that first pint just yet.

Yes, it's lucky bugger time again. As I haven't been able to arrange any more trips on the team coach, I suggest to Gary that perhaps I could shadow him for a day. After all, what does a manager do most of the week? He readily agrees and suggests Thursday before the Bury game. Thursday it is, then.

At 9.30am I find myself in Gary's office in the company of Steve Thompson and Tony Farmer, the physio. I realise that I am to be privy to the team selection process for Saturday's game. Gary asks Tony to run through the list of injured. It reads like an episode of *Casualty*. Dazza's ankle will keep him out until the following Saturday; Stephen Reed, stretchered off last night with a sprained ankle, is out for the rest of the season; Abdou's groin is not improving; Weale's hand is, well, still broken; Colin Pluck has a badly bruised right hip; Simon Weatherstone might be 60/40 to be available. Gary breaks in and asks what is the use of 60/40 availability? Will he be fit to play? Tony thinks he might if he has a pain-killing injection before the match. He'll take him out jogging in a minute and see how he is. Gary starts to write down who is likely to play. He acknowledges that we are down to the bones, with Gavin Williams suspended for this one. What about Lee Matthews? Doubtful, says Tony Farmer. I see my chance and immediately offer my services. They all laugh and move on. Talk about looking a gift horse in the mouth. I played for my primary school, I'll have you know. Steve Thompson suggests himself for a place on the bench. Gary grimaces and pretends to write him in. You are in good company then, Steve. Me and you out. So they agree, Collis in goal, Locky, Skivo, Hugo and Plucky at the back. Plucky will have to play, bruising or not. Johnno and Paul Terry in midfield with Critts on the left wing. Stansfield and Jake Edwards up front. What about on the right? There is deep discussion about whether to re-call Jamie Gosling from Aldershot. He is now in his second month on loan and can be pulled back immediately if required. They are not keen to do this if the lad is then made to sit on the bench. They are also conscious that Aldershot are likely to feature in the Conference play-offs, and to play would be good for Jamie. What about Kevin Gall down the right? I was thinking, "Yes, yes. After all, he usually ends up running down towards the right-hand flag." It is agreed. Gall to start, Lindegaard, Talbot, Jackson on the bench, and what about adding Dani Rodrigues? Gary says that he had a good game the night before last for the reserves. A typical Portuguese player, smooth and skilful, he seems to stroke the ball when passing. Yes, we will take a chance on him. Well, that is team selection settled, then. Pretty easy, really – especially when you have only got 14 players to choose from.

I ask Gary the big question. With only five games to go, is it realistic to think that we will get in the play-offs? He says that if we win the next two, Bury and away to York, we have every chance of being back up there. Others involved have difficult games, and who knows what might happen? A couple of good results from Hull, Southend and Lincoln, and we could be in. I give myself a mental slapping for having weakened and doubted my team. I am ashamed.

I go with Gary out on to the pitch and watch the lads go through a noisy, rigorous and very competitive training session. I ask Gary how the boys are dealing with this knife-edge situation. He likens them to gladiators in the arena. If they lose the next fight, they are dead. So they will be fighting for their lives on Saturday. Bring on the Bury lions, then.

Fortunately, the atmosphere is back. Where it went last week, I do not know, but it is business as usual from the Westland End, with more than a little help from us lot in the Bartlett. Bury have brought very few supporters with them, but that is to be expected. They are not in with a shout of the play-offs and have more than a little competition for fans' loyalty up in their part of the country. But the few who have made the journey dance wildly when the first Bury shot of the afternoon sails into the net. Up until that point, Yeovil had looked pretty good – bloody wonderful compared to Chelt... well, we won't dwell on that. Paul Terry smashes a decent header against the bar in the early minutes and I have an upbeat feeling about the proceedings. Until *that* goal, that is. Yeovil heads seem to drop and, despite having a brisk wind at their backs, they are unable to get the ball to heads or feet in the penalty box. I feel more than a bit glum at half-time, and cannot see how we are going to turn this around. Other results are going in our favour, and I feel even more depressed that we are not taking advantage of them. In our patch of the stand mutterings of "why doesn't he bring on Dani Rodrigues?" can be heard. An indication that Gary Johnson is listening comes when both Dani and Andy Lindegaard come out and do a bit of stretching and running on the pitch.

No changes, though, for the second half. Yeovil still can't get into the right gear. Stuttering and stumbling as they attack the Westland End into the wind, the prospects don't look good.

A little divine inspiration wouldn't go amiss. Then, like a shaft of light bursting through the clouds, Dani boy steps out of the shadows and into Huish history. Brought on to replace Adam Stansfield, he has an immediate impact. The team become a team and begin to pass it around with purpose. Kevin Gall finds space on the right wing and starts to menace the defence. Bury are beginning to look a little uneasy with their slender one-goal advantage. I shall always be able to say that I was there the day Dani scored his first, and wondrous, goal for the Glovers. Some 5,000 of us will genuinely be able to say that, but by the time the story is re-told the crowd might have been 10,000. It is a miracle moment. A long ball into the penalty box finds Dani with his back to the goal. He takes the ball on his chest and, with the agility of an Olympic gymnast, launches himself into an overhead scissors kick. He meets the ball as sweet as you like and it rips into the back of the net. Pandemonium breaks out. The stands go wild. Pensioners weep, babes in arms are thrown high in the air. Huish Park has gone mad. This is a once-in-a-season moment. Lin and I bounce dangerously, arms flying everywhere. Oh, what a passion from a boot and a ball. We may have settled back in our seats, but in our heads we are wheeling and turning. What a moment, what a strike. "Dani Rodrigues" is chanted from every corner. A hero is born.

Yeovil go for the jugular. Bury are rocked by that magic strike, and wobble and panic. It is all one-way traffic now. Gally is flying down the right, Critts down the left. Colin Pluck is spearing quality balls into the penalty box. Three minutes later, on 57, Lee Johnson puts a free-kick into the crowded penalty box. A foot comes out and, with the help of a deflection, the ball crosses the line before the despairing keeper scoops it back out. It is that man again. Dani has made it two. Once again, the crowd erupt and celebrate. From there on in, until that wonderful final whistle, the game see-saws back and forth. Bury decide not to take it lying down and make a hard fight of it. So excited did the Bury bench become that the manager is red-carded. The outpouring of relief at the end is enormous – players, manager, fans, as one in our joy.

Oxford lose, Northampton draw. We are in with a shout. Oxford 43 games, 67 points, Northampton 42 games, 66 points and Yeovil 42 games, 65 points. Northampton play Huddersfield at their place on Tuesday while we go to York for the re-arranged fixture. Who knows? We could be in seventh heaven by nine o'clock.

They had to do it sooner or later. Win the Conference, that is. Chester City have spent their way to the top at last. But congratulations anyway. At least they've stopped Hereford from crowing about being champions. They will be in the play-offs and must be favourites, if it is possible to be favourites in that lottery. My eye caught a little piece on *Ciderspace* which read: "Hereford will have an unusual claim to fame if they do come through the play-offs. They will be the first club to twice gain promotion to the Football League without winning anything at all." I couldn't have put it better.

The day has dawned: it is Tuesday, it is York City, it is no good. That awful phrase 'work commitments' has ruined any chance I had of getting up to Bootham Crescent for this evening's game. I thought, when I took the option to leave my full-time job and become my own master, that I wouldn't ever have to worry about work commitments. By scheduling any business around the fixture list I could be free to go anywhere, any time. It was that washout last month that mucked things up. I had agreed to do this job on Tuesday before I knew of the re-arrangement. So here I am, stuck with a huge game to be played in my absence. This is all a bit like Russian roulette now. The gun is loaded, the chamber is spinning, the trigger is pulled. Bang! Should we lose, we are as good as dead. If we win, play-off life continues. This is tough on mind and body.

I have been red-carded to the upstairs bedroom, following previous alleged bad behaviour when listening to Yeovil games on the radio. That is okay – I have got my scarf around my neck, and I am ready for the off. The crackling reception makes me think this game must be coming from the Arctic, rather than chilly Yorkshire. What I have heard, though, is that Dani Rodrigues is starting tonight, up front with Jake Edwards, while Kevin Gall is on the right wing again. Come on, then, let us get at them. York, who have been in freefall for some time, are in the second relegation spot. I think they have failed to win a match in 16 games and have only scored six goals in that time.

A good start from Yeovil produces a Gally shot that, with his typical luck, hits the inside of the post and runs along the line to the keeper. Seconds later, York get a free-kick, which deflects off one of our lads and Collis is given no chance. I can't believe it.

The rest of the first half is poor. Yeovil play scrappy stuff, with few meaningful passes and only one more shot on target. Shake 'em up in that dressing room, for God's sake, Gary. I've had a good old moan at Lin, blaming just about everything and everybody for our dismal performance. For crying out loud, Northampton are trying to help us with a 0-0 at home to Huddersfield at half-time. We have got to go on and help ourselves now.

So long do I moan that I miss the re-start. Climbing the stairs I hear the commentator say the Yeovil fans are cheering away at the far end. YES, YES, YES, it is Paul Terry with his first goal of the season. A right-foot volley. Bless you, Paul. And now it is Huddersfield who have gone one up at the Priestfield Stadium. Come on Yeo, you've got to do it now. York are flagging, heads are dropping. Hammer them, Yeovil.

Jacko is on for the ineffective Edwards, Skivo comes off injured and big Hugo is on. The play is still scrappy, York are coming back into it, until Andy Lindegaard chests the ball down and toe-pokes it home – 2-1 to the boys in green. What do we do now? Pull back and keep them out, catch them on the break? I don't know – there are still 20 minutes left. One minute to go and Dani is replaced by Nick Critts. THREE MINUTES OF EXTRA-TIME! Where the hell did the ref get that from? Blow that bloody whistle. More than three have gone. I fall to my knees and beat the floor. We've won, we've won. I'm shaking like a leaf, totally knackered, but I'm a super-happy Glover, even more so when Huddersfield take the points from the Cobblers. What a night. Everything has gone our way. We are in the magnificent top seven. Now the Green Army marches on Southend.

Oh, I don't know what to do. Shall I save the money and spend it on play-off tickets and a few drinks after the Millennium Stadium celebrations or blow it all on the club's 'Name the Main Stand' raffle? Of course, sitting in the Bartlett Stand, I don't really care what they name the Main Stand. The Owen Stand has a sort of ring to it, though it sounds as if we still have hire purchase payments to make on the thing. Truth is, whatever the stand is called, everyone will still call it the Main Stand. I applaud the club's attempt to get a little extra revenue from this stunt, but I really think it is time to name both the Main Stand and the Bartlett Stand after people who mean something to Yeovil Town F.C. Why the Bartlett Stand is still called that after all these years is beyond me. It is like calling your house after the builder – Wimpy Cottage or Bovis Villa. It is daft. I think the Main Stand should be the Alex Stock Stand and the Bartlett, the Bryan Moore Stand. I feel better for that.

Reading on *Ciderspace*, it seems that Lincoln City are not too keen on a huge number of us attending the last game of the season. Only a paltry 950 or so tickets are up for grabs. The dilemma is, do I rush straight down to the ground and buy a couple while they have a quantity for sale, or do I leave it until after the Southend and Hull games in order to see how vital the Lincoln game becomes? Decisions, decisions. Act positively is usually the best bet and so, bright and early on Friday morning, Lin and I are clutching two tickets for the Co-op Community Stand (do you think the Co-op won the raffle for that one?). We pop our heads around the door and watch the lads doing a little light training before they leave for Southend. I notice that Paul Terry is not with the rest of the squad, but is walking around the perimeter on his own. Not a good sign, but we do have the advantage of Darren Way back from injury.

Sipping an ice-cold beer and lounging on the garden swing seat at my parents' home in Southend brought back memories of living there as a teenager. How would it have been if Lin and I hadn't moved away? No doubt we would be looking forward to the match on Saturday against Yeovil – a chance to gain revenge for the 4-0 thrashing that had been handed out at Huish Park. We would be able to take comfort from the fact that Southend's form had taken a turn for the better following that match and, at home, no defeats had been suffered since January. After all, who are these cheeky upstarts from the West Country who think they have a chance in the play-offs? I expect our two sons would be talking like a couple of Cockneys and sporting the dark-blue shirts of Southend if we had not made that inspired decision to move back to the family roots in Somerset. Would I have written *Southend 'til I Die!* or *Behind the Blue Door* if I had stayed on the Thames Estuary? I think not. Let's face it, there would have been precious little to write about.

I feel such a buzz this morning. Only a few hours to go to the match. Once again, it is do or die. Every game is now piling on the tension. I can hardly hold the pint glass still in the Spread Eagle pub just outside the Roots Hall ground. Glovers fans are everywhere. Some have obviously visited the Golden Mile on the sea front and have come back laden with Mexican sombreros, big rubber rings, beach balls and other assorted seaside tat. Let's hope it is party time for them and us a little later on.

The old ground has changed a good deal since I was last here. The away end we are sitting in used to be the home-end terracing, so I am in the same place that I always occupied. It is a bit spooky, really. The vast open away terracing has now become two-tier seating for the home fans. The rest of the land has been developed and new houses loom over the ground. There must be 1,000 Yeovil fans in the ground and, because it is a hot day, all of our shirts are on display. We must look awesome from the other end.

Fortunately, it is not just the fans who look awesome. Yeovil, with Dani Rodrigues and Jake Edwards up front, Kevin Gall in his new role on the right wing and Hugo Rodrigues in for the injured Terry Skiverton, begin as they mean to continue. Dazza and Johnno grab the midfield and begin to spray great balls to the forwards. But it is a long throw by Adam Lockwood that unsettles the Southend goalkeeper. A poor punch out and Kevin Gall nods the ball across the box to Dani. He smacks the ball past keeper Flahavan and the hoops go wild.

Ten minutes later, on 31 minutes, another ball across the box from Lee

Johnson and our hero and saviour is there to do it again. We are playing like a team with a purpose. The passing is crisp, the tackling is ferocious but fair. The boys know what they want and are determined to get it. Steve Collis, although having a fairly quiet afternoon, deals brilliantly with a deflected shot and palms it around the post. Kevin Gall is teasing the life out of Southend out on the wing. He is putting in some fantastic crosses, one of which almost gives Dani his hat-trick.

The second half sees a performance from Yeovil that indicates that they have now learned a great deal from the Third Division. They keep it very tight and only attack Southend on the break. At the back, Adam Lockwood, Colin Pluck and Hugo Rodrigues are magnificent. Southend hardly have a sniff and, on the one occasion when their forward Bramble gets into a great shooting position, Andy Lindegaard is there to snuff it out. Town grow and grow in stature, and nothing is going to take the points away from them. Off the pitch, the Green Army are in fine voice and the good folk of Southend have to grin and bear it when the chant of "You are only a suburb of Canvey" echoes around the ground. This is a great day. A great, huge, enormous win that takes us within a cat's whisker of our dream coming true. Northampton keep the pressure up with a win at Swansea, but Oxford can only take one point from their game with Cambridge. Bring on the Hull Tigers!

While Chris Weale has necessarily taken a back seat of late, he is still voted Third Division goalkeeper of the season at the Professional Footballers' Association awards. This must be a great feeling for him. To be voted for by your fellow professionals has to be the highest accolade that can be given.

Here we are on the eve of possibly, no probably, no definitely, the most important match that any team of Yeovil Town players have ever been involved in, and I am in a state. Every time I think about the match tomorrow I break out in a sweat. One moment I think that we will lose, then win, maybe draw. I swing from ultra-confident to pessimistically downbeat. Fortunately, Lin and I have been away for most of the week visiting sights in the Derbyshire Peak District and this has temporarily distracted us, thus allowing the match to creep up gently. But now it is only hours away and I feel as sick as a pig. Adrenaline, excitement, anticipation, pride, passion, and desire are all bubbling away. I want these points so much. Hull City still need one point to be sure of automatic promotion, but I reckon that they will still go up in second place without it. Give it to us. Surrender now. Our need is greater than yours. How am I going to get through the night and tomorrow morning?

CHAPTER 10

DOWN TO THE WIRE

It is 3.11am on Saturday 1 May 2004. I am awake and seriously worried. I think it may be a combination of last night's beer and the excitement over the game today, but I fear I have had a mid-life crisis. I have woken up in a wet puddle in my bed. Does this mean incontinence pads for life? Look what you have done to me, Yeovil Town. When my thoughts clear a little, I realise that it's not me, it's the waterbed! We have sprung a leak. Abandon ship, women and children first. Luckily, it is only a very small leak and Lin can sleep on undisturbed on her side while I have to grab a pillow and head for the downstairs couch. My dreams are vivid but, fortunately, very happy. We reach the final at the Millennium Stadium and play Torquay. This time we do not let a 2-0 lead slip. I see some 30,000 hooped shirts celebrating while fireworks go off all over the place. A grey reality dawns at around eight o'clock, and I know we have it all still to do. COME ON, YOU GREENS.

The morning is interminable; seconds feel like hours, hours feel like, well, just about forever. At last, we are at our favourite place. Crowds are streaming towards our Mecca. Hull are there in large numbers, and it is their turn with the beach balls and seaside hats today. I reckon some of them must have overshot Yeovil and found themselves down at Weymuff for the night. Three o'clock arrives. I am puffing and blowing with nervous energy. I can't sit down and I can't stand still. I am a wreck. But wreck or not, I can give out a pretty loud rendition of *Yeovil True*. I'm ready – I just hope the boys are. Gally out on the wing, Dani and Jake in the centre. Hugo at the back and Andy Lindegaard making up the back four. I am more than a little worried that the officials are wearing yellow and black, virtually the same colours as Hull City. My fears are soon justified when the muppet in the middle turns down what seems a perfectly obvious handball in the City box. Naturally, to make up for this error, he awards Hull a penalty at the other end. A mistake at the back in thinking the ball was running out of touch allows a forward to slip along the by-line where, at the slightest touch from Adam Lockwood, he collapses as if he has been shot. Steve Collis makes a valiant dive, but the ball is nestling in the net.

Yeovil fight, and none more so than Colin Pluck. Despite picking up a bad shoulder injury early on, he refuses to bow out, and snarls and snaps at everything. He is obviously in pain and Terry Skiverton is warming up on the bench. A free-kick is given to Yeovil just outside the penalty box and Plucky lets fly. Only the thickness of the paint on the bar prevents the ball from ripping the net out. The whole goal structure shakes nearly as much as I do. That horrible feeling in my gut is telling me that we are going to have no luck this afternoon, and anything we do get out of this will have to be ground out. Hull are good – good at blocking players off, good at going down and quite good at football. They are a physical team that can muscle their way into positions, and our front line are not doing too well against this type of play. Dani is getting into the box, but the ball is not coming through. Following his fine free-kick, Colin Pluck roars into the box to try to reach the rebound and, once again, collapses in agony. This is the end for him and he trudges off to a great reception. This is what my Yeovil Town is all about – total effort and commitment. This is why I pour my passion and support into them.

Half-time news tells us Oxford are losing, Northampton are losing and Mansfield are drawing. It is still all up for grabs. Yeovil change their approach for the second half. Their play is much more measured, they are holding the ball better and keeping it on the ground. An anonymous Jake Edwards is replaced by Paul Terry, and he seems to bring more of an edge to the attack. A free-kick is awarded and, as usual, Hugo Rodrigues comes into the box. And then it happens. Hugo attacks the ball like I have never seen him do before and smashes it into the back of the net with his head. Wow, the noise is deafening. Every Yeovil supporter is celebrating the unbelievable. Hugo is ecstatic. HUGO, HUGO, HUGO is roared by every voice. Well done, big man. This could be just what we need to swing this game around. Yeovil have Hull on the wobble. Corner after corner is forced, but no more miracles come from the Portuguese giant. Lin says she will settle for a draw but, as always, I want everything. Attack, attack, attack, Yeovil, you have got them on the ropes. That is, until Darren Way, captain for the day, uncharacteristically seems to give up on a ball and the Hull forward picks it up and curls a fine shot past the diving Collis. It is like a knife in the belly. Hull supporters are now going wild, with their promotion party going into overdrive. Yeovil can find no way back, and end up as the bedraggled bridesmaid at Hull's wedding.

I am in pain – pain at losing (never much fun at the best of times), pain at having to watch the Tigers celebrate at the away end, and pain at having to watch my boys, my team, standing around waiting for the end of season awards to be announced. Talk about falling flat. It is very, very sad as Gavin Williams steps forward to scoop most of the Player of the Season trophies. I bet he would have traded all the silverware for Plucky's shot to have hit the net.

We say our farewells to our friends in block K. We are still not sure if we shall have another home game this season. Northampton have beaten Bury and push us out of the top seven, one point ahead with one to play. Everything rests on a result at Lincoln and a slip-up by the Cobblers.

What a strange feeling it is to leave Huish Park gutted and sad but still hear the jubilation of 1,500 fans going on back inside. Yeovil fans slip away like ghostly phantoms. You could hear a pin drop in the car park or down the road (if it wasn't for those chanting Tigers). A bad, bad blow this afternoon after the crest of the wave stuff that has brought us to this point.

An unhappy Gary Johnson faced the press after the game and said: "It isn't all doom and gloom and I'm not going to start slashing my wrists tonight, but we can't go to Lincoln and only play for 45 minutes with five or six players. Some of them have done well and enhanced their Yeovil careers, some haven't done enough and have ruined their Yeovil careers. We can't go playing Hull with a five-a-side team. We have got to have people doing it and I can tell the ones that are mentally strong. Yes, I should think there will be departures on Monday. I'm not going to enter into a war up there (Lincoln) with soldiers that are not brave and strong. I've got to go on with brave and strong soldiers and get something out of it."

Well, I think that's pretty clear – marching orders for a few coming up. Who, though? Thinking straight away about the forwards, I can see Edwards, Jackson and Stansfield moving on, but who else? Rumours begin to spread like weeds on *Ciderspace*. Darren Way about to sign for Doncaster Rovers. No, forget that, it is Super Gav.

An anniversary meal has been booked at the King's Arms in Montacute for this evening. You know the sort of thing – a single candle reflects in her eyes as she touches her partner's hand across the crisp white tablecloth. They sip red wine from fine glasses and mouth words of love. Well, we might have done if the place hadn't been full of champagne-drinking Hull City fans. Ambience? No chance. To be fair to them, they were very complimentary to Yeovil in their hour of triumph and naturally we to them.

I think one of the quickest ways to get stressed out is to watch any match that is connected with the play-offs. It doesn't matter if you haven't got an interest in any of the teams involved, somehow it is the biggest wind-up going. Shrewsbury v Barnet was one such nail-biting event. Come the penalty shoot-out, I was all over the place. I just didn't want any of them to miss and feel the whole weight of the world come down on their shoulders. One did, of course, and Shrewsbury bounce into the final at the Britannia Stadium, Stoke. One team that bounced, but this time like a lead balloon, was our old Welsh border friends from Hereford. Playing Aldershot, who finished some 21 points beneath them, they contrived to lose their shoot-out. It was wonderful to see Chris Giles and Jamie Gosling hammering in two of the coffin nails for the Shots. Cheer up, Hereford, there is always next season. Well, there might be if relegated Carlisle and York don't go and upset your plans.

I may be having a laugh at the Bulls, but I'm thinking how I'm going to feel if we actually get into that situation. The tension is going to be unbelievable, nothing like we will have ever known before. But before I get too carried away with these lofty thoughts we have got the matter of disposing of Lincoln City first and Mansfield doing us a favour with Northampton.

I have busied myself all week, anything to take my mind off the forthcoming wall-of-death experience on Saturday. I have even spent time in prison (again) to avoid the gossip on the streets. In just a few hours' time we will know our fate. It will be either a crazy carnival scene at Sincil Bank, or we will be retreating in an orderly fashion back on to the coaches. We can, of course, hold our heads high whatever happens. It has been a wonderful season, with some fantastic games and many, many memories. If we should slip and falter tomorrow, we all know that we will be back next season, stronger, and wiser.

Some good news has filtered through the tense atmosphere that surrounds me. Michael Rose, left-sided defender from Hereford, has seen the light and joined the Glovers on a two-year contract. Also good news for the stingy amongst us, Bradfords are going to sponsor the club for another year and, therefore, there will be no need to buy another shirt for next season. Problem is, the lettering is definitely peeling and fading fast on mine. I've got a birthday coming up soon. Perhaps I'll be lucky and get a new one.

I find getting up at six o'clock in the morning such a strange experience. The whole atmosphere of the house and the village streets seem so different. Everything is quiet before the day begins. That little lull before the storm. And it is a storm that we wish for today. Not rain and wind, but the rushing, attacking play of the Glovers as they wipe out Lincoln City. This is the day, the last match of the season, and we are still there clinging by our fingertips. Northampton travel to fifth-placed Mansfield needing a win to ensure that they are in the play-offs. A draw or a defeat, and a win for us will give us that last place. The alternative scenario is that if we should beat Lincoln, who lie in sixth, by five goals or more, then we would be equal on points and have a superior goal difference. Frankly, I'm not putting too much on that one. But you never know. So with points, scores and all permutations whirling around our heads, Lin and I board the seven o'clock coach from Huish Park.

It was a grey journey, with occasional rain and mostly heavy clouds – nothing like the last trip to Southend. I got to thinking that perhaps Yeovil Town play better in the warm sunshine and, if we ever move away from Huish Park, we should re-locate to some seaside town in Brazil. Well, you wouldn't want to end up in Milton Keynes, would you? We could all re-locate with them and enjoy the Samba lifestyle to the full. There are obvious flaws in my plan, though. Away matches would be a very long way to go to, and the F.A. would probably expel us from the League. But, with our boys, I'm sure we would soon make it to Division One of the Amazon League.

We park on common land next to the other seven coaches that have brought Yeovil fans to this eastern city. Cars are pouring in with flags and scarves shaking wildly from the windows. We have sold our full allocation of 1,100 tickets and we are ready to rock and roll. A short walk alongside the river and, there before us, rising in majestic state and dominating the whole city, is The Cathedral. Oh, and just to the right, by the allotments, is Sincil Bank. There is no time to offer up a prayer in this great church and, even if I did, I think that any favours granted would probably go to Lincoln people. After all, they did build the thing for that purpose. No, we are on our own. Destiny is partially in our own hands. I am confident the lads will do everything they possibly can.

Lincoln stewards insist on everyone sitting in the seat allocated on the ticket. Usually, we all gravitate to a seat that takes our fancy and the latecomers fill in all the gaps. But not today. It is like being at the theatre with people shuffling along rows past people already seated. It all begins to add to the tension. The team news adds to that pressure when we hear that both Colin Pluck and Dani Rodrigues have failed late fitness tests. This is a blow, especially up front. With Kevin Gall and Simon Weatherstone leading the line, I have put further from my mind thoughts of the five-goals-or-more option. No disrespect to either of the lads, but they are not exactly goal machines at the moment. Hugo starts in the back four, which I am happy about. Lincoln's game is hoof and hope, so Hugo will be essential this afternoon. By the way, how does a team that hoofs and hopes get into sixth place by the end of the season? Something wrong somewhere. Yeovil settle into a nice rhythm of attractive football, stroking the ball purposefully about the park. Lincoln's plan seems to be to kick it so high and hard that it punctures and stops Yeovil playing. In truth, there are not many scoring opportunities in the first half. Kevin Gall has a chance but misses the ball completely and falls in a heap. That's our Kev at the moment. Steve Collis makes a great save when a City player bursts through into the penalty area. We are all torn between what is happening out on the pitch and wondering what is happening at Mansfield. Just about every other person has a mobile phone in his hand waiting for a message. After about 20 minutes that message arrives: Northampton have taken the lead. A united groan shudders through the Yeovil fans. I feel terrible. I feel weary and old. Is it slipping away? Lincoln fans take great delight in chanting out the score, just in case we may have missed it. Thanks, lads.

There is no change by half-time and the carnival atmosphere that had preceded the kick-off has turned into almost a quiet acceptance of the situation. I said to Lin that I thought I was going to feel a lot more tense and uptight than I do. I feel almost calm. We have come a long way, through a long season. We have had our ups and downs and now we are about to close the book and plan for next year.

But if I am about to close the book, Gary Johnson is not. Two substitutes start the second half. Up front come Adam Stansfield and Jake Edwards and, within 60 seconds, Stansfield has put the ball in the net from short range and the Green Army are whooping it up with delight.

On 59 minutes, Adam Lockwood is brought down by a vicious tackle that only brings about a yellow card. The lad is being stretchered off when a roar rips out from the fans. Mansfield have equalised. We are all up, jumping, shouting, bouncing, dancing. We are in the play-offs. Hang on, Mansfield, hang on! Our voices grow as we blast out *On to Victory*. We are on top of the world. Even the sun is now shining brightly on us. Samba on Yeovil. And they do. Another great move on 71 minutes, Jake Edwards smashes the ball on the underside of the bar and, for once, it goes in. 1,100 green-and-white maniacs take off. Lin and I are holding each other and bouncing up and down. May this never end. I want this feeling forever. Then another roar, uncertain at first but then crashing like a wave on the rocks. Mansfield have taken the lead and we have 20 minutes to go. Ecstasy. We are all on our feet. The atmosphere is electric. I'm whirling my scarf above my head. I am going mad. It can't get better than this.

It doesn't. A guy next to me says that it is Northampton who have taken the lead. In front, a woman says that it is now 2-2. My brain is in turmoil. What is happening? What is going on? The Lincoln fans put us right. They are chanting at the top of their voices: "2-1 to the Northampton."

While all this is going on, Yeovil still attack for all they are worth, but get caught at the back by a quick break, and Collis stands no chance as his parried save is headed back in. I am still trying to take it all in when Lincoln repeat the move and sweep the ball into the net again. 2-2 and I am in despair – lurching from paradise to hell in one quick movement. Then, out of the blue, Yeovil get a free-kick just outside the penalty box. Gavin Williams strides up and, without any fuss or ceremony, smashes the ball low either through the wall or around it. I don't know which. All I can see is the ball hitting that net and all of us blasting off from our seats. Pandemonium breaks out. There is still time for Mansfield. Come on, you useless buggers, get a goal, now. The mobiles remain silent as the minutes tick away. Our season is slipping away like sand in an hourglass. Please, Mansfield, please. The guy next to me confirms that their game has ended and I just stare at him. Seconds later our own final whistle goes and, despite warning of dire consequences, hundreds of Lincoln supporters invade the pitch and begin to celebrate their play-off place. We stand proud and sing. Our players and manager come over to us and support each other as they salute us. Many of them are obviously choked and some are having difficulty holding back the tears. No need for tears, boys. You have done us so very, very proud. You have given everything for Yeovil Town today.

There is no anger or resentment on the coach, just a subdued acceptance that the last throw of the dice was in someone else's hand. Northampton have had a storming second half to the season, and have eventually justified the huge sums of money that they spent at the beginning. Good luck to them in the play-offs.

The brutal facts at the end are that both Yeovil and Lincoln achieved 74 points but Lincoln claim that final lucky seventh place by a goal difference of four. Ifs, buts and maybes flash up in my mind. If we had only held our 2-2 scoreline at Swansea. If we hadn't fallen to a last-minute offside goal at Boston. If we had only played to our average potential at home to Cheltenham. If Ashbee hadn't scored that fine goal for Hull City. If, if, if. But, as one fan on the coach said: "If we had lost to Lincoln and Northampton had lost to Mansfield, that would have been very hard to take. We did everything we could and then had to leave it to others."

Speculation has been rife over the internet as to who will be departing at the end of the season. Just about every member of the squad has been named by someone or other as a likely departure. For what it's worth, I don't think there will be a wholesale clear-out. I think we have the nucleus of a Championship side, and, with a few additions, we will be there. Gary Johnson says after the match: "This club is progressing every year. We have had our fair share of success and I have said to the boys that we will have more success – although they must make sure they are part of it. Some will be part of it, some won't be part of it... I've got a big Monday and Tuesday. But we have built a great foundation and a solid young group of what are now League players."

A long summer now stretches before us until we all assemble again in August. We have Euro 2004 to 'enjoy' (or not), the play *Becoming Giants* at the Octagon Theatre in July, and memories, beautiful memories, as we look back on our first and glorious season in Division Three.

My thanks to everyone at the club for that... directors, players, fellow fans, and, most of all, Steve Thompson and Gary Johnson, for being such decent, approachable guys. It has been a privilege to have shared some memorable moments with you Behind the Green Door.

POSTSCRIPT

A
t the end of the season the Club released seven players. They were:
Nathan Talbott, who was brought in by Gary Johnson as defensive
cover towards the end of the season.

Ryan Northover, a goalkeeper signed late in the season as cover for Steve
Collis following the injury to Chris Weale's hand.

Jamie Gosling, the man from Bath, who didn't figure too prominently in
League games.Having been out on loan to Aldershot he has chosen to sign for
them permanently.

Jake Edwards. I had high hopes in the beginning, when he scored a few goals
and looked promising. Then he seemed to fade.

Lee Elam, another player who failed to deliver. He started like Roy of the
Rovers, but soon lost his way, and has signed for Hornchurch.

Kirk Jackson, who almost won the Golden Boot during our Conference
championship season. But he failed to make the step up into Third Division
football. He has also joined Hornchurch, and I'm sure he willl score bags of
goals for them.

Nicky Crittenden, the big surprise on the released list. He was an important
part of the Conference team, but he picked up a couple of injuries that kept him
sidelined for long periods. Nick was one of my favourites and I shall always
remember his brilliant goal in the Cup at Blackpool, and the match winner this
season at Bristol Rovers. He has signed for Aldershot.

As I write there are question marks over several other players.

Roy O'Brien, Abdelhalim El Kholti and Adam Stansfield have all been invited
back for pre-season training in order that they can convince Gary Johnson that
they are worth a further contract. Our Portuguese pair of Hugo and Dani
Rodrigues have yet to decide on their futures with the club.

ANORAK'S CORNER

YEOVIL TOWN RESULTS 2003-2004

July 2003

						Att.	Yeovil Scorers
4th	Sporting Lokeren	Away	Frnd	D	0-0	242	
6th	RW Oberhausen	Away	Frnd	D	1-1	2500	Gall 15
7th	Royal Antwerp	Away	Frnd	L	1-2	1500	Crittenden 8
9th	Geminal Beerschot	Away	Frnd	L	1-4	600	Gall 52
14th	Chippenham Town	Away	Frnd	D	0-0	704	
16th	Chard Town	Away	Frnd	W	7-0	750	Own Goal 5, Pluck 22, El Kholti 42, Thompson 67, Gall 70, Jeannin 90, 90
19th	Brentford	Home	Frnd	W	2-0	1936	Gall 50, H. Rodrigues 80
22nd	Preston North End	Home	Frnd	D	4-4	2185	Gall 5, 43, 44, Edwards 84
24th	Dorchester Town	Away	Frnd	W	5-2	755	Lindegaard 48, 85, Jackson 60, 80, El Kholti 78
29th	Wolverhampton Wanderers	Away	Frnd	W	2-1	5884	Own Goal 42, Gall 62

August 2003

1st	Brighton and Hove Albion	Home	Frnd	W	2-1	2310	Own Goal 1, Stansfield 89
4th	Tiverton Town	Away	Frnd	W	2-0	721	Lindegaard 31, 40
9th	Rochdale	Away	DIV3	W	3-1	4611	Gall 26, 67, Johnson 55
12th	Luton Town	Away	CC1	L	1-4	4337	Own Goal 47
16th	Carlisle United	Home	DIV3	W	3-0	6347	Gall 4, 18, Jackson 79
23rd	Leyton Orient	Away	DIV3	L	0-2	4431	
25th	Northampton Town	Home	DIV3	L	0-2	6105	
30th	Macclesfield Town	Away	DIV3	L	1-4	2221	Lockwood 63

September 2003

						Att.	Yeovil Scorers
6th	Swansea City	Home	DIV3	W	2-0	6655	Stansfield 39, Jackson 55
13th	York City	Home	DIV3	W	3-0	5653	Jackson 21, Pluck 34, Stansfield 90
16th	Doncaster Rovers	Away	DIV3	W	1-0	4716	Williams 35
20th	Mansfield Town	Away	DIV3	W	1-0	5270	Jackson 42
27th	Torquay United	Home	DIV3	L	0-2	7718	
30th	Boston United	Home	DIV3	W	2-0	5093	Williams 21, Lockwood 38

October 2003

						Att.	Yeovil Scorers
4th	Cheltenham Town	Away	DIV3	L	1-3	4960	Gall 40
7th	Bristol City	Home	SPC1	L	2-3	716	Gall 36, Edwards 60
11th	Oxford United	Away	DIV3	L	0-1	6301	
14th	AFC Bournemouth	Home	LDV1	W	2-0	5035	Edwards 74, Williams 86
18th	Darlington	Home	DIV3	W	1-0	4892	Williams 5
21st	Huddersfield Town	Home	DIV3	W	2-1	5274	Skiverton 4, Johnson 51
25th	Cambridge United	Away	DIV3	W	4-1	4072	Edwards 16, 59, Gall 61, Way 87

November 2003

						Att.	Yeovil Scorers
1st	Bury	Away	DIV3	L	1-2	3086	Edwards 31
4th	Colchester United	Home	LDV2	D	2-2	3052	Edwards 11, Gall 66
8th	Wrexham	Home	FAC1	W	4-1	5049	Gall 39, Williams 46, Pluck 59, Edwards 66
15th	Southen United	Home	DIV3	W	4-0	5248	Elam 33, Way 40, Johnson 43, 56
22nd	Hull City	Away	DIV3	D	0-0	14367	
29th	Lincoln City	Home	DIV3	W	3-1	4867	Pluck 54, Stansfield 85, Gosling 90

December 2003

						Att.	Yeovil Scorers
6th	Barnet	Home	FAC2	W	5-1	5973	Pluck 9, Williams 18, 27, Crittenden 74, Edwards 78
13th	Bristol Rovers	Away	DIV3	W	1-0	9812	Crittenden 43
20th	Scunthorpe United	Home	DIV3	W	2-1	5714	Lindegaard 71, Jackson 82
26th	Kidderminster Harriers	Home	DIV3	L	1-2	5640	Gall 58
28th	Swansea City	Away	DIV3	L	2-3	9800	Williams 73, Gall 89

January 2004

						Att.	Yeovil Scorers
4th	Liverpool	Home	FAC3	L	0-2	9348	
6th	Shaftesbury Town	Away	Frnd	W	9-0	937	Stansfield 12, 39, 81, S Smith 32, Edwards 43, 63, Welch 59, Johnson 80, Giles 84
10th	Rochdale	Home	DIV3	W	1-0	5806	Williams 13
17th	Carlisle United	Away	DIV3	L	0-2	5455	
24th	Leyton Orient	Home	DIV3	L	1-2	6299	Crittenden 76
31st	Macclesfield Town	Home	DIV3	D	2-2	5257	Edwards 30, Way 60

February 2004

3rd	Northampton Town	Away	DIV3	L	0-2	4363	
7th	Kidderminster Harriers	Away	DIV3	W	1-0	3255	Williams 64
14th	Oxford United	Home	DIV3	W	1-0	7404	Bishop 29
21st	Darlington	Away	DIV3	L	2-3	4500	Johnson 22, Lockwood 90
28th	Cambridge United	Home	DIV3	W	4-1	5694	Williams 18, Bishop 19, Stansfield 27, Pluck 48

March 2004

2nd	Huddersfield Town	Away	DIV3	L	1-3	9395	Way 78
6th	Scunthorpe United	Away	DIV3	L	0-3	3355	
13th	Bristol Rovers	Home	DIV3	W	4-0	8726	Lockwood 16, El Kholti 43, Williams 49, Pluck 72
16th	Doncaster Rovers	Home	DIV3	L	0-1	7587	
27th	Mansfield Town	Home	DIV3	D	1-1	6002	Skiverton 61

April 2004

3rd	Torquay United	Away	DIV3	D	2-2	6156	Way 17, Edwards 27
10th	Cheltenham Town	Home	DIV3	D	0-0	6613	
12th	Boston United	Away	DIV3	L	2-3	2848	Weatherstone 4, Stansfield 51
17th	Bury	Home	DIV3	W	2-1	5172	D Rodrigues 55, 59
20th	York City	Away	DIV3	W	2-1	2802	Terry 46, Lindegaard 70
24th	Southend United	Away	DIV3	W	2-0	5676	D. Rodrigues 21, 32

May 2004

						Att.	Yeovil Scorers
1st	Hull City	Home	DIV3	L	1-2	8760	H. Rodrigues 64
8th	Lincoln City	Away	DIV3	W	3-2	8154	Stansfield 47, Edwards 71, Williams 89

NATIONWIDE LEAGUE DIVISION THREE FINAL TABLE

		Home					Away					
Team	P	W	D	L	F	A	W	D	L	F	A	Rts
Doncaster Rovers	46	17	4	2	47	13	10	7	6	32	24	92
Hull City	46	16	4	3	50	21	9	9	5	32	23	88
Torquay United	46	15	6	2	44	18	8	6	9	24	26	81
Huddersfield Town	46	16	4	3	42	18	7	8	8	26	34	81
Mansfield Town	46	13	5	5	44	25	9	4	10	32	37	75
Northampton Town	46	13	4	6	30	23	9	5	9	28	28	75
Lincoln City	46	9	11	3	36	23	10	6	7	32	24	74
Yeovil Town	**46**	**14**	**3**	**6**	**40**	**19**	**9**	**2**	**12**	**30**	**38**	**74**
Oxford United	46	14	8	1	34	13	4	9	10	21	31	71
Swansea City	46	9	8	6	36	26	6	6	11	22	35	59
Boston United	46	11	7	5	35	21	5	4	14	15	33	59
Bury	46	10	7	6	29	26	5	4	14	25	38	56
Cambridge United	46	6	7	10	26	32	8	7	8	29	35	56
Cheltenham Town	46	11	4	8	37	28	3	10	10	20	33	56
Bristol Rovers	46	9	7	7	29	26	5	6	12	21	35	55
Kidderminster Harriers	46	9	5	9	28	29	5	8	10	17	30	55
Southend United	46	8	4	11	27	29	6	8	9	24	34	54
Darlington	46	10	4	9	30	28	4	7	12	23	33	53
Leyton Orient	46	8	9	6	28	27	5	5	13	20	38	53
Macclesfield Town	46	8	9	6	28	25	5	4	14	26	44	52
Rochdale	46	7	8	8	28	26	5	6	12	21	32	50
Scunthorpe United	46	7	10	6	36	27	4	6	13	33	45	49
Carlisle United	46	8	5	10	23	27	4	4	15	23	42	45
York City	46	7	6	10	22	29	3	8	12	13	37	44